The Challenging of America: 1920–1945

Michael L. Kurtz
Southeastern Louisiana University

The Forum Press, Inc.
Arlington Heights, Illinois 60004

Library of Congress Cataloging-in-Publication Data

Kurtz, Michael L., 1941–
    The challenging of America, 1920–1945.

    Bibliography: p.
    Includes index.
    1. United States—History—1919–1933. 2. United
States—History—1933–1945. I. Title.
E784.K87   1986   973.91   85-20643
ISBN 0-88273-107-6

Cover photo: See page 96.

Manufactured in the United States of America
90 89 88 87 86 EB 1 2 3 4 5 6

Contents

Preface   vii

1   The Age of Normalcy   1

2   Republican Diplomacy   17

3   The Roaring Twenties   31

4   The Great Depression   51

5   The First New Deal   69

6   The Second New Deal   87

7   American Life and Society: 1930–1945   108

8   From Isolation to Intervention   125

9   World War II   143

10   The Home Front   164

Suggested Readings   187

Appendix   193

Index   195

Preface

The theme of this book is the manner in which America met the challenges facing it in the years from 1920 to 1945. This quarter century witnessed many events that had a profound impact on the course of American history. In the 1920s, the United States experienced many changes in everyday life and in the transformation from a rural, primarily agricultural society to one predominantly urban and industrial. The Republican presidents of the decade pursued laissez-faire economic policies that contributed to an era of unprecedented prosperity for most Americans, but at the end of the decade, that era came to an abrupt end, and the American people struggled to overcome the severe economic and social dislocations created by the Great Depression. The election of Franklin Roosevelt in 1932 marked the beginning of a new era in American history, an era in which the federal government would assume greater responsibility for the welfare of its citizens. With an engaging and domineering personality, Roosevelt brought the New Deal into virtually every aspect of American life, made the presidency the center of national attention, and shifted the focus of politics from the state capitals to Washington. As the 1940s began, the United States slowly became embroiled in the war raging in Europe, and as a result of the Japanese attack on Pearl Harbor, actively intervened on the Allied side. While it was successfully resisting German and Japanese aggression, America faced what appeared to be a growing threat to world peace posed by its wartime ally, the Soviet Union. As this volume closes, America confronted one of its greatest challenges, the Cold War in the nuclear age.

1

The Age of Normalcy

In 1920 the American people handed Warren Harding and the Republican party a resounding mandate to make good on promises of economic prosperity and domestic tranquility. Harding and his successor, Calvin Coolidge, responded with policies decidedly favorable to the interests of big business: high tariffs, low taxes, balanced budgets, and laissez-faire economics. As economic and political conservatives, the Republicans also rolled back many of the progressive reforms enacted under Theodore Roosevelt and Woodrow Wilson. These policies resulted in a decade of unprecedented economic expansion and industrial growth. By the end of Coolidge's presidency, most Americans enjoyed a standard of living so high that the United States became the model for the rest of the world.

Beneath the surface of national well-being, undercurrents of corruption and poverty manifested themselves. The Harding administration experienced many scandals reminiscent of the Grant era. Large segments of the population did not share the general prosperity, and farmers suffered a continuing depression that brought ruin to many. Organized labor found the full resources of government employed against its persistent struggle for higher wages and improved working conditions. Blacks everywhere remained the victims of a deep-rooted racial prejudice which excluded them from the American dream. A wild speculative boom, unrestrained by government regulation, threatened economic and financial disaster.

1

The Election of 1920

As the year 1920 began, Americans desired a change. Throughout 1919, they had experienced turmoil and unrest. The Spanish flu, the greatest epidemic in American history, killed several hundred thousand people. Attorney General A. Mitchell Palmer's "Red Scare" campaign led to the arrest of thousands of aliens, anarchists, and others suspected of subverting the government. A series of bombings rocked the nation. The transition from a wartime to a peacetime economy featured strikes by organized labor, massive layoffs in industry, and rapidly increasing prices. America's wartime Allies seemed torn by dissent, and political revolution swept across Eastern Europe. These and other tumultuous events led most Americans to yearn for a return to what seemed a more peaceful, moral, and predictable age. As the incumbent president, Woodrow Wilson bore the burden of popular discontent. Wilson had promised a "war to end all wars" and a war to "make the world safe for democracy." But now that the war had ended, his call for United States participation in the League of Nations, an international organization whose purposes few people comprehended, had divided the nation politically.

For Woodrow Wilson, the presidential election of 1920 represented more than a political contest; it would become a mandate on American entrance into his cherished League of Nations. By joining the League, he saw America bringing about a postwar world of peace and democracy. Characteristically, he envisioned the issue in moralistic terms and saw himself as the only possible instrument for carrying out the goals he had set. Thus, despite his failing health, Wilson decided to run for an unprecedented third term in the White House. Calling the election a "great and solemn referendum" on the League, he tried to make it the main campaign issue. When on March 19, 1920, the Senate rejected ratification of the peace treaty, the president came to the conclusion that the Democratic party must renominate him as its candidate.

Wilson's determination to seek reelection reflected his increasing inability to grasp the realities of American politics. The American people saw postwar Europe rent by dissension among the Allies, leading to a resumption of international tensions. Most people did not want the United States to become involved in world affairs, and Wilson's clarion call for such involvement only served to enhance the popular appeal of the opposition. By the time the Democratic National Convention opened in June, the popular mood had taken a decidedly conservative bent, and the leaders of the party realized that their only hope for success lay in nominating someone who offered a fresh approach and a clear alternative to the progressive, internationalist policies Wilson espoused. Although determined not to renominate Wilson, the convention delegates could not agree on an acceptable replacement. For ballot after ballot, they split their votes among the three leading candidates: Attorney General A. Mitchell Palmer; Secretary of the Treasury William G. McAdoo; and Governor James M. Cox of Ohio. After the thirty-seventh ballot, Palmer withdrew, but the convention still failed to break the deadlock. At the end of the forty-third ballot, the party bosses met to end the impasse. After much deliberation, they agreed to endorse Cox because as Wilson's son-in-law, McAdoo was too closely identified with the unpopular administration and because Cox came from Ohio, the home state of the Republican nominee, Warren Harding. The weary delegates complied, and they nominated Cox on the forty-fourth ballot, and selected the Assistant Secretary of the Navy, Franklin D. Roosevelt of New York, as Cox's running mate. The convention closed with the Democratic party badly split. Disgruntled supporters of Palmer and McAdoo refused to endorse Cox, and many loyal Wilsonians agreed with the president's description of Cox's candidacy as a "joke."

At their convention, held before the Democrats', the Republicans averted factional divisions and agreed to unite behind their nominee. Five contenders vied for the Republican nomination: General Leonard Wood, a member of the Theodore Roosevelt–Bull Moose wing of the party; Governor Frank O. Lowden of Illinois; and Senators Hiram W. Johnson of California, Robert M. La Follette of Wisconsin, and Warren G. Harding of Ohio. After four ballots, none commanded a majority of the delegate votes, and it appeared that the convention was hopelessly deadlocked. On the evening of June 11, 1920, the party bosses, led by Senator Henry Cabot Lodge of Massachusetts and Will H. Hays, the party chairman, met in a "smoke-filled room" in Chicago's Blackstone Hotel to select a nominee. One by one, they eliminated the contenders. Wood, Johnson, and La Follette had antagonized the party's dominant conservative wing because of their support of Wilson's progressive programs. Lowden had support only from the Midwest. Only Harding had demonstrated his loyalty to the national party, had backing among delegates from all regions, and had shown a willingness to comply with the wishes of the party leadership. Knowing that virtually any Republican could win the election, the bosses therefore picked the least capable and most docile of the candidates. They then applied their muscle to the delegates, who caved in and nominated Harding on the tenth ballot.

Such is the traditional interpretation of the Republican National Convention of 1920. Recent studies have shown that this interpretation contains more legend than fact. Far from being a meek and docile tool of the party bosses, Harding actively sought the nomination long before the convention opened. His close friend and campaign manager, Harry M. Daugherty, could hardly be considered a pawn manipulated by Henry Cabot Lodge and Will Hays. The delegates did not simply surrender to the bosses, for it took six more ballots before they nominated Harding, while the Democratic delegates gave the nomination to Cox on the ballot immediately following their bosses' "smoke-filled room" meeting. That the Republican delegates did not simply rubberstamp the bosses' wishes is further evidenced by their rejection of the bosses' choice for the vice-presidential nominee, Senator Irvine L. Lenroot of Wisconsin, in favor of Governor Calvin Coolidge of Massachusetts. Finally, as president, Harding was not a figurehead dominated by the party leadership. His reliance on the notorious "Ohio gang" clearly suggests his independence from the national party leaders.

In the campaign, the Republicans exploited popular discontent with the Wilson administration. Handicapped with an unpopular president and wracked by a divided party, the Democrats failed to wage an effective campaign. The election results showed Harding capturing one of the largest percentages of the popular vote in American history and the Republicans winning large majorities in both houses of Congress. If the election truly represented a "great and solemn referendum," as Woodrow Wilson maintained, the American people handed him, his administration, and his party a devastating vote of no confidence.

Warren G. Harding

In many respects, the man who became president in 1921 epitomized the ideals and aspirations of the American people. Born in 1865 in the small rural community of Blooming Grove, Ohio, Warren Gamaliel Harding grew up in a family atmosphere that stressed the traditional values of hard work, individual initiative, and material success. As a young man, Harding moved to Marion, a small, middle-class Ohio town, and after a brief fling at selling, turned to journalism for a career. Like many of his contemporaries, Harding was a man on the make, and he did all the right and acceptable things to ensure his favorable reception by the leading citizens of Marion. He joined civic and professional clubs, became an active member of his church, and married into money. His father-in-law, the wealthiest man in town, provided the financial backing for Harding to become the owner and editor of the Marion *Star* newspaper. Carefully avoiding sensationalist yellow journalism in this conservative community, Harding promoted the benefits of free enterprise and endorsed the policies of the McKinley-Taft wing of the Republican party. In his early thirties, Harding won the backing of the local business community for a political career, and he gradually rose to a position of prominence in the Ohio Republican party. After serving two terms in the state senate, he won election as lieutenant-governor in 1906. He lost the gubernatorial election in 1910, but four years later, gained a seat in the United States Senate. In Washington, Harding attracted the attention of the party leaders. His stirring keynote address at the Republican convention of 1916, his faithful support of party stands on issues, and his congenial personality and handsome appearance earned him a reputation as a solid, trustworthy team-player.

Most historians have emphasized Harding's lack of intellectual accomplishment, his overall mediocrity, and his mainstream America political ideology. Others have depicted him as an incompetent oaf, henpecked by his domineering wife and led astray by the unscrupulous Harry Daugherty. Harding's extra-marital sexual liaisons and his drinking and gambling revels with a group of shady characters lends some credence to this portrait. As president, Harding indeed exhibited a singular lack of the qualities necessary to effective leadership. He enjoyed nothing better than spending the day with his cronies at the infamous little green house on K street, savoring the pleasures of the prostitutes provided by Harry Daugherty and Jesse Smith and imbibing the illegal liquor supplied by his bootlegger, Mort Mortimer. Upon assuming the office of president, Harding proclaimed, "Gee, what a job!" Aware of his own limitations, he made little effort to study the pressing issues of the era, and he made no attempt to exercise control over his appointees. For such able cabinet members as Secretary of the Treasury Andrew Mellon and Secretary of State Charles Evans Hughes, this approach proved reasonable. But rewarding many hometown cronies with important government positions led to disaster, for some of these appointees engaged in dishonest and illegal activities on a scale so broad that the Harding administration became one of the most scandal-ridden in American history.

The Scandals

Three major scandals afflicted the Harding administration. One involved the newly established Veterans Bureau. Created by Congress in August

1921, the bureau was one of Harding's proudest achievements. Under the able administration of Charles R. Forbes, the Veterans Bureau built dozens of hospitals providing free medical services to World War I veterans. Forbes managed the bureau ably, but he used his position to profit from the enormous amount of business it conducted. For example, he bought such supplies as bedsheets and bandages at exorbitant prices, then sold them to wholesalers at ridiculously low prices in return for substantial "kickbacks." In less than two years, Forbes had stolen or squandered an estimated $200 million of the taxpayers' money, the largest such theft in American history. Informed of Forbes's complicity in early 1923, Harding was genuinely shocked and forced him to resign, but he made no attempt either to recover the stolen funds or to have Forbes prosecuted. It was not until after Harding's death that a public disclosure of the scandal pressured the Justice Department to prosecute Forbes, and he eventually received a two-year jail sentence and a $10,000 fine.

A second scandal implicated Secretary of the Interior Albert B. Fall. In 1921, Fall talked Harding into transferring control over the United States Navy's strategic petroleum reserves at Elk Hills, California, and Teapot Dome, Wyoming, from the Navy to the Interior Department. The following year, Fall leased the Elk Hills reserve to an oil company owned by Edward L. Doheny and the Teapot Dome facility to one owned by Harry F. Sinclair. An investigation of the leases by the Senate's Public Lands Committee revealed that Doheny had loaned Fall $100,000 and that Sinclair had given him $300,000. Despite substantial evidence against them, all three were acquitted of conspiracy to defraud the government. Sinclair did receive minor sentences for jury tampering and for contempt of Congress, and Fall got one year in jail and a $100,000 fine for accepting bribes.

The third scandal involved Attorney General Daugherty, who allowed his close friend, Jesse Smith, to secure favors from the Justice Department for bootleggers, income tax evaders, and other disreputable characters. Daugherty and Smith also conspired with Thomas W. Miller, the Alien Property Custodian, in turning over control of the American Metal Company to a German corporation in return for a bribe of over $250,000. Of the three men, only Miller went to jail. Smith committed suicide, and Daugherty won acquittal of receiving illegal income. Not personally involved in any of the scandals, Harding appeared shocked when he learned of them, but he did not vigorously pursue a thorough investigation. On June 20, 1923, Harding left Washington for a vacation in the West. In Alaska he became violently ill and was rushed to a hospital in San Francisco, where he died on August 2 of a blood clot in the brain. Although allegations persist to this day that Harding was poisoned, the available evidence does not substantiate them.

Warren Harding: An Assessment

In a recent poll of historians, Warren Harding ranked last among American presidents and was considered a "failure." Most scholars have agreed with this evaluation. In most historical studies, the Harding administration is portrayed as lacking form and substance, failing to accomplish anything of lasting significance, promoting the interests of big business at the expense of the common man, and engaging in widespread fraud and corruption. In the first volume of his history of the New Deal, Arthur Schlesinger, Jr., faults Harding for his failure to employ the resources of the federal government to assist the poor. In their history of the United States, Samuel Eliot Morison, Henry Steele Comager, and William E. Leuchtenburg assert that with the exceptions of the Washington Arms conference and the establishment of the Bureau of the Budget, Harding's presidency proved devoid of positive accomplishment and heavily contaminated by scandal.

Recent revisionist works by such historians as Andrew Sinclair and Robert K. Murray have provided a more balanced account, covering both the successes and failures of the Harding administration. In the field of civil liberties, Harding's record stands in stark contrast to that of Woodrow Wilson. Harding ended the "Red Scare," pardoned Eugene V. Debs and numerous other Americans unjustly imprisoned for violating the Espionage and Sedition Acts of 1917 and 1918, and in 1921, Harding became the first president to publicly support civil rights for black Americans. He delivered an impassioned plea for racial equality in Birmingham, Alabama, at a time when few whites exhibited any concern for the plight of America's blacks.

The Harding economic record also cannot be dismissed simply as one catering solely to the interests of big business. He secured one of the largest debt reductions in American history, cut federal income taxes, balanced the federal budget, and substantially reduced the rates of unemployment and inflation in just two and a half years. The criticism of Harding for not establishing federal welfare and social programs to assist the needy appears unjustified, for such concepts were not advocated even by the most liberal political leaders of the time. His lack of concern for the poor must be tempered by the fact that he did obtain federal assistance for displaced persons and by his program of massive federal medical help for veterans. Harding also won one of the most significant landmark measures in the history of labor relations. He personally persuaded the heads of the leading steel industries to institute the eight-hour work day, a policy that became the standard practice in most American industries by the end of the decade.

Throughout his presidency, Warren Harding remained enormously popular with the American people. Through his domestic program of laissez-faire economics and his foreign policy of diplomacy and disarmament, he made good on his campaign promises of prosperity at home and a more stable world abroad. No one would rank Harding as a great or even an average president, but his rating as the worst president in American history seems unjustified. Any objective analysis of his accomplishments would give him credit for the things he did do.

Calvin Coolidge

George M. Cohan certainly did not have Calvin Coolidge in mind when he wrote "Yankee Doodle Dandy," yet in many respects, Coolidge embodied the attributes the stirring patriotic tune promotes. Literally born on the Fourth of July, in 1872, in a small Vermont village appropriately named Plymouth, the man who succeeded Harding as president fulfilled in his life the old-fashioned Yankee ideals of honesty, frugality, hard work, and a deep committment to serving one's fellow citizens. As a child, Coolidge struggled long and successfully to overcome frail health and a tendency toward extreme shyness. Never complaining, he clung to his personal goal of becoming a lawyer. After graduating from Amherst College, he opened a law practice in Northhampton, Massachusetts, where he built a reputation as a competent attorney. At the age of thirty-three, having established his practice, Coolidge married. Quiet, taciturn, with a heavy Yankee twang, Coolidge became a natural candidate for the sarcasm of such contemporaries as H. L. Mencken and Will Rogers, who remarked of Coolidge as president: "He said he wouldn't do anything, and he fulfilled the promise." Most historians have depicted him as a weak and ineffective man, whose reluctance to engage in public discourse and to take decisive action demonstrated his neglect of the country's problems.

As president, Coolidge practiced Thomas Jefferson's famous adage: "That government is best which governs least." Coolidge became president during a period of unparalleled economic growth, and he desired nothing more than to maintain the status quo. He deliberately kept a low profile, sleeping eleven hours a day and spending much time in his rocking chair on the White House balcony. At a presidential press conference, he once answered three questions with "no's," and he insisted that the reporters not quote him. William Allen White's sarcastic depiction of him as a "Puritan in Babylon" became the model for future historical portrayals. Hardly a bold leader, Coolidge nevertheless became one of the most popular and beloved presidents in American history. When the occasion demanded, he could communicate very effectively. As a lawyer, he proved so adept in the courtroom that he won a coveted seat on the Massachusetts General Court. In two decades of running for public office, he never lost an election, serving in both houses of the Massachusetts state legislature and as lieutenant governor and governor. In 1919 he won nationwide acclaim for his handling of the Boston police strike. After policemen struck for higher wages, Coolidge fired them and employed the state National Guard to enforce law and order. His response to labor leader Samuel Gompers's plea to rehire the striking policemen captured the public imagination: "There is no right to strike against the public safety by anybody, anywhere, anytime."

A Free Market Economy

In his most famous remark, Calvin Coolidge summarized the general economic philosophy of the Republican administrations of the 1920s: "The business of America is business." By that he meant that the federal government should promote a benevolent capitalism from which the entire nation would benefit. As the United States moved farther in the direction of a nation increasingly reliant on industry and constantly spurred to further growth by the advances of modern technology, economic progress would follow through government policies providing a favorable atmosphere for business. Just as in the nineteenth century, when American businessmen had used a combination of individual initiative, Yankee ingenuity and a beneficent government to transform the United States into the greatest industrial nation on earth, so, too, in the 1920s should the country's destiny be guided by the leaders and owners of business. Such a policy, Coolidge believed, would result in general economic prosperity and a better way of life for all Americans.

To implement this theory, both Coolidge and Harding relied on their Secretary of the Treasury, Andrew W. Mellon. The head of the immensely wealthy and influential Mellon family of Pittsburgh, he epitomized the successful business leader of the twenties. The Mellons had made their fortune during the halcyon days of unrestrained capitalism in the nineteenth century, and he wanted the government to pursue those policies which had proved so effective during the Gilded Age: laissez-faire economic policies characterized by high tariffs and low taxes. A high tariff protecting American industry and agriculture against foreign competition formed a cornerstone of the Republican economic policies of the 1920s. Many Democrats also joined the chorus clamoring for protection. Farmers and labor unions, for example, desired high tariffs more than did industrialists, and the proponents of free trade, mainly Wilsonian Democrats, found their support dwindling, as protection became one of the most popular programs of the decade.

After passing an emergency tariff bill in May 1921, Congress began work on a complete overhaul of the Underwood-Simmons tariff of 1913, which had reduced rates to an average of 26 percent of the value of the imported goods. In July 1921, the chairman of the Ways and Means Committee pushed a bill through the House of Representatives that provided for moderate increases in tariff rates. But when the bill got to the Senate, the Finance Committee, under its chairman, Porter J. McCumber, held prolonged hearings, during which lobbyists for innumerable special interest groups successfully persuaded the committee to add their products to the growing list of protected items. So extensive were the changes made by the Senate in the original House bill that it took Congress over a year to iron out the differences. The Fordney-McCumber tariff, which finally became law in September 1922, resembled the notorious Payne-Aldrich tariff of 1909. It contained a long list of high tariff rates catering to special interests. To appease the powerful farm bloc, Congress set extremely high rates on all agricultural products. The bill did lower rates on most manufactured items, but it increased them on chemicals, dyes, textiles, and certain products of European and Japanese monopolies. The law also established a Tariff Commission with the authority to raise or lower rates by as much as 50 percent. Since European countries retaliated by imposing higher tariffs on American exports, Fordney-McCumber led to a sharp decline in foreign trade. Many American businesses also relocated in Europe, where they could produce and sell their goods free from the high prices caused by the tariff. Historians generally have viewed the Fordney-McCumber tariff as an unproductive and reactionary attempt to revert to discriminatory nineteenth-century economic practices and as a symbol of the isolation of the 1920s. The law, however, did little more than reflect prevailing popular attitudes, and it enjoyed widespread support among the American people.

The second part of Mellon's economic program, a tax cut, did not receive the same bipartisan support as had the tariff. Most Democrats and many progressive Republicans believed that a tax cut would simply add to the already excessive incomes of the wealthy, and Mellon encountered difficulty in steering his tax program through Congress. The Revenue Act of 1921 did revoke the excess profits tax, which had been enacted in 1918 to raise money for the war effort, but it retained the high 50 percent surtax on incomes, increased corporation income taxes, and maintained the prevailing high level of estate taxes. During Coolidge's presidency, the enactment of the Revenue Acts of 1924 and 1926 brought about drastic reductions in all categories of federal taxes. Mellon's theory that substantial reductions in federal income taxes would prove beneficial to the national economy resembled that of the supply-side economists of the administration of President Ronald Reagan. By reducing taxes, Mellon argued, the government would leave more income in the hands of the people, who would invest this money, thus providing the capital necessary for the expansion of industries and for a corresponding increase in employment. The result of this would be additional revenue for the government, since a much larger proportion of the population would have permanent jobs. Mellon's program worked, at least temporarily. Private capital investment, employment, and industrial productivity reached record heights during the latter half of the 1920s. The extra revenue generated for the treasury enabled Mellon not only to balance the budget, but to accumulate annual surpluses, thereby reducing the national debt, a feat that would make him seem an economic wizard today. Mellon's fiscal accomplishments, however, were not accompanied by corresponding measures in other aspects of federal economic policy, and the lack of government control over the economy would soon prove disastrous.

General Economic Trends

When Harding took office in March 1921, the economy was in bad shape. Postwar disruptions led to a 50 percent decline in foreign trade and in national industrial production, and a growth in unemployment to nearly five million. Within a year, these trends were reversed, and except for a brief recession in 1927, the upward momentum of the economy continued until late 1929. No single factor caused this boom, but most economic historians credit the free market policies of the Harding and Coolidge administrations with contributing to its endurance. In general, most Americans shared in the prosperity of the twenties. After adjusting for increases in the cost of living, average family income rose by over 10 percent, enabling people to buy automobiles, refrigerators, radios, and numerous other products. Industrial workers received a 25 percent increase in income during the decade, and they responded with an enormous increase in productivity. Corporate profits, stockholder dividends, and industrial production increased substantially. The statistics of the national economy of the 1920s painted a bright picture. Americans had more money to spend than ever before, and the things they spent it on gave them a more comfortable standard of living than their ancestors ever dreamed possible.

During the twenties, American industry entered the modern technological age, featuring such innovations as modern management practices, conglomerates, and sophisticated marketing techniques. Industrial management was revolutionized by the application of the theories of Frederick W. Taylor, who had made exhaustive studies of factory management and production in the 1890s. By eliminating wasteful and repetitious practices, industries could vastly increase productivity. In the twenties Taylor's studies led to the development of the new field of industrial engineering and to the division of corporate management and labor into highly specialized units. Complementing this new policy was the innovative marketing and public relations work of Edward Bernays, who did studies of public opinion and introduced modern methods of mass advertising to sell the products of industry to the consumer. In 1908 Henry Ford pioneered the moving assembly line, in which the time required to manufacture an automobile was reduced from six to two hours. By 1925 the moving assembly line had become an integral part of most large industries and contributed to the enormous rise in production in the decade.

Modern technology led to the rise of many new industries in the 1920s. The automobile industry, for example, mushroomed from a small business catering mainly to the luxury of the upper classes into America's largest industry, providing transportation for the masses. Fewer than seven million cars travelled the nation's streets in 1919. A decade later, that figure swelled to twenty-three million. Ford, General Motors, Chrysler, and other companies mass-produced automobiles costing an average of $300 each, well within the means of most families. Similarly, home appliances, telephones, radios, cigarettes, and a variety of other products gave rise to new industries and to the expansion of older ones. Although this industrial expansion would eventually result in an excess of supply over demand, for much of the decade it was one of the leading elements in the national prosperity.

During the nineteenth century, ownership and control of most industries remained in the hands of such titans of high finance as John D. Rockefeller, Andrew Carnegie, and Cornelius Vanderbilt. In the 1920s corporate ownership became far more diversified, as the climb in national wealth enabled a significant number of Americans to invest in stocks. By 1929, some twenty million people owned stock, and most large corporations were no longer controlled by individuals. The new stockholders did not concern themselves with the daily operations of the businesses, and actual management fell increasingly under professionally trained individuals. In certain areas of business activity, the historical pattern of monopoly control by giant corporations continued: the big three (Ford, General Motors, and Chrysler) in automobiles; the Samuel Insull utilities empire; and the American Telephone and Telegraph Company domination over telephone communications. In most instances, however, competition greatly increased, as numerous new companies entered fields formerly monopolized by giant trusts. The old Standard Oil monopoly in oil, for example, gave way to a highly competitive industry in which no single company controlled more than 10 percent of the nation's petroleum production and refining capacity.

Organized Labor in Retreat

America's working men and women shared significantly in the boom times of the 1920s. They enjoyed substantial increases in wages, considerable improvements in working conditions, and virtual full employment. Organized labor, however, experienced a steep decline in membership and strength, and several unions found themselves weakened by industrial strife. A combination of factors contributed to the decline of organized labor in the decade: a generally conservative, pro-business attitude by the public; anti-union practices of the federal and state governments; and vast improvements in the workplace atmosphere for most American workers. Many industries voluntarily inaugurated labor policies which effectively reduced the need for unionization. In addition to high wages, labor received from management such benefits as the eight-hour work day; profit sharing plans; paid vacations; health and life insurance programs; and company pensions. Many companies instituted collective bargaining arrangements which permitted employees to voice their grievances without the fear of retaliation. Other policies like company grievance committees and company unions served as substitutes for formal unions. Because of the favorable conditions in which most Americans worked, the number of strikes in the 1920s averaged only one-third of those in the 1910s, and the number of labor union members fell from nine million in 1920 to five million in 1930.

For coal miners and textile workers, the 1920s brought hard times. Both groups fell victim to one of the most significant economic developments of the decade. The new technology created many new jobs, but it destroyed many old ones. Coal, for example, had long been the nation's leading source of energy, but it was rapidly being replaced by oil, gas, and electricity, and its share of total energy production in the twenties declined 25 percent. Led by its aggressive president, John L. Lewis, the United Mine Workers of America (UMW) staged the most prolonged coal strike in history in 1922. A bloody conflict between UMW members and company strikebreakers in Herrin, Illinois, resulted in the deaths of twenty-one persons. The strike ended with the UMW winning most of its demands, but by 1930, the closure of mines across the country led to high unemployment and drastic reductions in wages in the industry. Textile workers suffered a similar fate. After New England textile owners cut industry wages by 20 percent in 1921, a series of strikes plagued the industry. To combat the unions, many textile manufacturers relocated their plants in the South, where they reaped the benefits of cheap, nonunion labor and an abundant supply of energy.

The conservative policies of the federal and state governments also proved detrimental to organized labor. In 1921, President Harding sent two thousand troops to break up a UMW unionization movement in West Virginia, and in 1922, an injunction obtained by Attorney General Daugherty crushed a nationwide railroad strike. In many states, governors employed the National Guard to block membership drives and organization efforts by unions. Unions also found the United States Supreme Court hostile to their goals. In 1923, in the case of *Bailey* v. *Drexel Furniture Company*, the court ruled that Congress could not impose a prohibitive tax on products manufactured by child labor. In the same year, in *Adkins* v. *Children's Hospital*, the court struck down a District of Columbia law mandating minimum wages for women. The court also ruled that the Clayton Act did not exempt unions from prosecution for violating antitrust laws, a decision used to cripple the power of many union locals. Throughout the decade, lower federal and state courts upheld the practices used by employers to destroy unions.

Progressivism in Decline

The 1920s witnessed the decline of the progressive movement that had dominated American politics for the previous two decades. The two great progressive presidents were dead (Theodore Roosevelt died in 1919, Woodrow Wilson in 1924). The policies of the Republican administrations offered little opportunity for reform, and many progressives deserted the political arena for such social and moralistic crusades as prohibition and antievolution. Although in decline, progressivism did not expire, and some of the issues it espoused in the 1920s laid the foundation for the New Deal.

One such issue was the public power controversy, in which progressives advocated government ownership, operation, and regulation of certain public power projects and public utilities. Under the Water Power Act of 1920, a Federal Power Commission, comprising the Secretaries of War, Agriculture, and Interior, was established and given the authority to license, regulate, and audit all hydroelectric power projects on public land. The Boulder Dam Project Act of 1928 provided for the construction of a huge dam harnessing the power of the Colorado River and bringing water and electricity to several western states. Many state governments also established agencies with regulatory control over public carriers and utilities.

Another, much more controversial issue concerned the fate of two federally owned nitrate plants and a large dam on the Tennessee River at Muscle Shoals, Alabama. One of the leading progressives in Congress, Senator George W. Norris of Nebraska, convinced the Senate Agriculture Committee to reject an offer by Henry Ford to lease the Muscle Shoals facilities for an annual fee of $1.5 million. Instead, Morris persuaded Congress to pass a bill calling for federal control of the plants and dam. President Coolidge vetoed the bill, and a second Muscle Shoals bill received a veto in 1931. Despite these defeats, Morris's proposals became the basis for the much more ambitious Tennessee Valley Authority program of the New Deal. Progressivism, then, did not expire during the 1920s. It went into hibernation and would be fully awakened by the coming of the Great Depression.

The Election of 1924

In the 1924 presidential election the American people handed Calvin Coolidge an overwhelming victory. Coolidge probably would have won in any event, but the division within the Democratic party made his campaign even easier. Sharply divided into factions clashing over such volatile issues as prohibition, the League of Nations, and the Ku Klux Klan, the Democratic party could not form a united front at its convention. For two and a half weeks and one hundred three ballots, the Democrats failed to nominate a candidate to oppose Coolidge, who, of course, was nominated on the first ballot at the Republican convention. The Democrats finally nominated John W. Davis, a relatively obscure corporation lawyer on the one hundred fourth ballot and emerged from their convention badly divided. Discontented with the two major parties, a group of progressives held their own convention and nominated Wisconsin Senator Robert M. La Follette as the Progressive party candidate. La Follette waged a vigorous campaign, condemning both parties for their neglect of progressive reforms. Although La Follette captured one of the highest percentages of the popular vote in third-party history (16.6 percent and thirteen electoral votes), Coolidge won in a landslide, and the Republicans retained solid majorities in both houses of Congress. The 1924 election was a popular vindication of the conservative domestic program and foreign policy of the Republican party.

2

Republican Diplomacy

America's experience in World War I shaped its approach to foreign policy in the 1920s. That war generated much disillusionment in the United States, and the American people responded to it with a deep commitment not to become actively involved in foreign affairs again. This popular aversion to world politics was reflected in the refusal of the United States to join the League of Nations and in the Washington disarmament treaties of 1922. In contrast to the post–World War II era, when the United States assumed leadership of the free nations of the industrial world, the post–World War I era saw America refusing to act as the world's policeman.

The 1920s, however, did not produce a return to the traditional policy of isolation. On the contrary, American foreign policy was never more active than in the postwar decade. Diplomatically, under the brilliant leadership of Secretary of State Charles Evans Hughes, the United States persuaded the other leading powers to disarm, and succeeded in securing a treaty outlawing war as an instrument of national policy. Economically, America employed formidable financial resources to resolve the thorny reparations problem, and used the American dollar, never stronger or more plentiful, as one of the main weapons in its diplomatic arsenal.

Japanese-American Rivalry

Since the 1850s, American foreign policy had been directed as much toward the Far East as toward Europe. The opening of trade with Japan, the protectorate over the Philippine Islands, and the active involvement in China reflected this country's interest in the Orient in the nineteenth century. In the early twentieth century, Secretary of State John Hays's Open Door policy and President Theodore Roosevelt's mediation of the Russo-Japanese conflict of 1905 provided two further examples of American diplomatic concern with the Far East. Private American interests, including businesses eager to exploit the riches of the Orient and missionaries bent on converting the Asiatic masses to Christianity, heavily influenced government policy in the region.

After a great victory over Russia in 1905, Japan encroached on American interests in the Far East. As the only Asiatic nation with the manpower and resources to challenge the western powers for hegemony in the area, Japan envisioned itself as the defender of oriental culture against Western imperialism. The conflicting interests of the United States and Japan had been temporarily settled by the Taft-Katsura agreement of 1905 and the Root-Takahira agreement of 1908, in which the two countries spelled out their respective spheres of influence: Japan in Korea; the United States in the Philippines; and both in China. Neither country regarded these agreements as permanent, and when World War I broke out, Japan extended its domain in China, especially in the province of Manchuria. President Wilson and Secretaries of State William Jennings Bryan and Robert Lansing viewed the Japanese actions with alarm. After strenuous negotiations, Lansing secured a 1917 agreement whereby the United States recognized special Japanese interests in Manchuria and Japan accepted the principle of the Open Door policy (equal access by all nations) in the rest of China. At the Paris Peace Conference of 1919, Wilson attempted to force Japan to relinquish control over the Marshall, Mariana, and Caroline island chains, the former German colonies which Japan had conquered early in the war. Wilson also tried to persuade the Japanese to evacuate the Chinese province of Shantung. Feeling, with some justification, that Wilson regarded them as a second-rate power, the Japanese decided to build up their military and naval strength in the Pacific to a position of equality with the western powers.

These tensions were aggravated by a growing naval rivalry among the United States, Great Britain, and Japan. For several centuries, the British navy had dominated the seas, but during the war, the American navy had developed as a leading rival. To regain their former status, the British announced a massive five-year shipbuilding program, an action which the Americans responded to with the revelation of their own program. Jealous of the British and American control of the seas and alarmed by the expanding American military and naval presence in Hawaii and the

Philippines, Japan formulated a naval program that would give it the largest naval force in the Pacific.

The Washington Disarmament Conference

Such are the kinds of international jealousies and rivalries which lead to war. It was precisely this type of naval arms race between Germany and Great Britain which produced the alliances contributing to the outbreak of World War I. Although they had strongly endorsed America's war effort, the American people had become quickly and deeply disillusioned with the war's results. The petty personal and national disputes which permeated the discussions at the peace conference, the mutual distrust among the Allies, the military intervention in Russia, and the naval competition generated a popular movement for disarmament. In June 1921, Congress overwhelmingly adopted a resolution by Senator William E. Borah of Idaho calling on the United States to initiate disarmament talks with Great Britain and Japan. President Harding and Secretary of State Charles Evans Hughes endorsed the resolution and invited Japan, Italy, France, and Great Britain to attend a disarmament conference in Washington in November 1921.

Neither the British nor the Japanese favored disarmament. The British government yearned to return to the days when His Majesty's Fleet ruled the oceans. But after calculating the costs of their five-year shipbuilding program, the British discovered that it would bankrupt their treasury, already badly depleted by the enormous expenses of the war. The Japanese Diet (Parliament) considered disarmament an insult to their national integrity, but it succumbed to the pressure of world opinion, which favored the conference. Both countries, therefore, along with France and Italy, agreed to attend the conference in Washington.

On November 12, 1921, Secretary of State Hughes opened the conference with a stirring and convincing plea for disarmament. Aware that world opinion strongly supported him, Hughes stunned the delegates with a series of specific proposals for reducing the world's armaments. After reassuring the conference that disarmament threatened no one and indeed made world peace more likely than a continuation of the arms race, Hughes advocated a ten-year ban on all naval construction and a limitation on naval tonnage for the United States and Great Britain to 500,000 each, for Japan to 300,000, and for France and Italy to 150,000 each.

Hughes's proposal generated worldwide excitement. Because at that time the United States possessed the world's largest navy, the plan called for America to scrap more ships than any other country. Such an offer of national self-sacrifice in the cause of world peace was unique in history, and people all over the globe enthusiastically welcomed the proposal. The British, French, and Italian delegates quickly endorsed the plan, but the Japanese refused to scuttle any part of their cherished navy. Undeterred, Hughes persisted in his attempts to win Japanese compliance. After two months, the Japanese delegates relented and agreed to the plan. Formally signed in February 1922, the Five Power Naval Treaty stopped the costly and dangerous naval arms race and preserved the balance of power in Europe and the Far East. The first disarmament treaty in world history, it was a dramatic testimonial to the remarkable diplomatic capability of Charles Evans Hughes.

Most historical studies omit mention of the most formidable tool in Hughes's diplomatic pouch. At the Washington conference, the secretary of state possessed more than a gift for statesmanship; he also had access to secret information about the true intentions of the Japanese government. During World War I, a group of State Department cryptologists under the direction of Herbert O. Yardley had broken the Japanese diplomatic code, and the Japanese had not yet learned of this when the Washington conference convened. Japan's delegates had been instructed to resist the American proposals at first, but eventually to yield if Hughes persisted in his demands. The decoded messages between Tokyo and Washington provided Hughes with the information he needed to win all his points. When he adamantly refused to compromise with the Japanese, diplomatic experts all over the world predicted that the conference would end in failure. But Charles Evans Hughes knew better. The Japanese did submit, and the conference ended a brilliant success. To the astonishment of the world, Hughes had successfully negotiated the difficult disarmament problem, and he appeared at the time to be the most effective diplomat since Metternich and Talleyrand. That he used the secret information to America's advantage should not detract from his considerable achievement in statesmanship.

Since naval disarmament represented only the first step on the road to lasting peace in the Far East, Hughes used the Washington conference to deal with other sources of friction in the region. The Anglo-Japanese alliance of 1900 had long been regarded as a potential source of trouble. Originally conceived to prevent Russian expansion into China, the alliance obligated both Japan and Great Britain to provide each other with diplomatic and economic assistance in the event of war. Under this alliance, it was entirely possible that a minor dispute in a remote section of the Orient could erupt into a world conflict. A similar alliance between Germany and the Austro-Hungarian empire led to the outbreak of World War I after the assassination of the Archduke Franz Ferdinand. Hughes therefore proposed that the alliance be replaced with an agreement among the United States, Great Britain, France, and Japan, in which they concurred in the maintenance of the status quo in the Far East and in the negotiation of any future disputes. The other three countries eagerly accepted Hughes's proposal, and the Four Power Treaty was signed in early 1922.

A third Washington conference treaty dealt with the Chinese question. Under heavy pressure from Hughes, Japan joined the United States, Great Britain, China, France, Italy, Belgium, the Netherlands, and Portugal in signing the Nine Power Treaty of 1922. All countries agreed to respect China's sovereignty and independence, its right of self-government, and equal access to it by all nations. Because of Japan's proximity to China and because of its continuing rivalry with the Soviet Union, the treaty recognized Japan's special interest in China. It did, however, require the Japanese to evacuate the Shantung province and to sell the Shantung railroad to the Chinese government. In effect, the Nine Power Treaty gave legal sanction to the Open Door policy, under which all nations shared in exploiting China's economic resources while simultaneously guaranteeing its political independence.

After the Japanese attack on Pearl Harbor, critics denounced the Washington conference treaties because the United States yielded naval supremacy in the Pacific to Japan and because the treaties lacked any machinery for enforcement. In reality, the treaties simply ratified what a war-weary public demanded—an end to the arms race and a peaceful, negotiated settlement of the differences among the powers. The United States could have secured naval supremacy in the Pacific only at a frightening cost, not just to the national treasury, but also to world peace. The American people were not ready to support the massive military and naval buildup necessary to achieve America's goals in Asia, and the Navy did not even attain the level of tonnage allowed by the treaty until 1939. The treaties, of course, lacked enforcement provisions, and all treaties ultimately rely on the good faith and willingness of the signatory nations to observe their provisions. The Washington conference treaties achieved success for over a decade. For a brief period, they halted the volatile naval arms race, guaranteed China's national integrity, and established the diplomatic setting for America, Britain, and Japan to settle their differences. The revival of Japanese expansionism and militarism in the 1930s destroyed the spirit of the treaties. Nevertheless, they marked a diplomatic success of major significance both for the statesmanship of Charles Evans Hughes and for the ideal of peace among nations.

The Japanese Crisis of 1924

For a couple of years, the spirit of the Washington conference produced a genuine atmosphere of cordiality in relations between the United States and Japan. But in 1924, congressional hearings on an immigration bill polluted that atmosphere into one of hostility. In 1908, a gentlemen's agreement negotiated by President Theodore Roosevelt with the Japanese government had set the policy for Japanese immigration into America. In general, the agreement stipulated that with the exception of peasants and industrial laborers, all categories of Japanese citizens could migrate to the United States. Although fewer than 100,000 Japanese had emigrated to America between 1900 and 1920, their presence aroused considerable hostility. An industrious and diligent people, the Japanese immigrants developed a thriving, prosperous community in California, where the vast majority lived. Many Americans viewed the Japanese as depriving whites of land and jobs. When the House Immigration Committee held hearings, numerous groups testified in favor of severe restrictions on Japanese immigration. The American Federation of Labor, for example, feared job competition. One official of the American Legion called the Japanese "uncivilized, yellow-skinned, slanty-eyed pagans," and the Ku Klux Klan, then at the height of its power, added the Japanese to its growing list of enemies threatening the foundations of American civilization.

Succumbing to this pressure, the House committee ignored Secretary Hughes's plea for a tactful bill and instead recommended one that restricted annual Japanese immigration to less than two hundred fifty, and it deliberately worded the bill in language which insulted Japan's government and culture. In March 1924, Hughes asked the Japanese ambassador, Masanao Hanihara, to write down his government's position on the immigration question. In the letter, Hanihara warned of "grave consequences" if Congress enacted the bill. Displaying an uncharacteristic lack of tact, Hughes "leaked" the Hanihara letter to the press. The "grave consequences" threat aroused American ire, and a storm of anti-Japanese sentiment roared across the country. The public outcry led to the passage of the immigration bill, which President Coolidge signed into law in April 1924. The immigration controversy was not limited to the Japanese issues. The new law severely restricted immigration from every country on earth. But the Japanese, a people whose national pride was just beginning to assert itself, felt especially insulted by it. As a consequence, Japanese-American relations deteriorated, and hostility between the American and Japanese people intensified.

Reparations

The end of World War I saw the United States emerge as the world's leading economic power, a position it would strengthen throughout the 1920s. In 1914, the United States owed European countries a total of $200 million. By 1920, that situation had dramatically reversed. In that year, European indebtedness to the United States reached the staggering sum of $13 billion, $3 billion in private debt and $10 billion in government debt, most of it accumulated during the war and in the immediate postwar period. This revolutionary shift in the balance of economic power in the world accelerated in the twenties, as European nations paid portions of their wartime debts to the United States and America's favorable balance of trade brought in additional revenue.

In the 1920s, American foreign policy assumed the role of what has been termed "dollar diplomacy," since one aspect of that policy fostered the expansion of American business interests all over the world. The Nine Power Treaty of 1922, for example, secured equal American access to the lucrative Chinese market. Soon after the treaty's ratification, American businesses pumped several hundred million dollars into China, mainly through expanded trade concessions and the construction of new plants. In 1925, Hughes obtained the right of American oil companies to share with their European counterparts in the exploitation of Middle Eastern oil lands. This agreement produced a number of new international oil conglomerates, among them the Royal Dutch Shell empire, based in the Netherlands, and the Arabian American Oil Company (ARAMCO), based in the United States. So rapid was the expansion of American overseas investment in the 1920s that by the end of the decade, it had reached the sum of $15 billion.

The most troublesome international economic issue of the 1920s was war debts and reparations. During and after the war, the United States loaned over $10 billion to the Allied governments. In 1922, Congress established a World War Foreign Debt Commission to supervise the collection of this debt, but the commission failed to fulfill its purpose. Although Great Britain agreed to pay its debt, France, Italy, and other Allied nations refused, claiming that the United States was morally obligated to cancel the debts. Outraged, the State Department prohibited any further private or government loans to countries which refused to pay their debts to the United States. This pressure forced all the Allied governments to agree to pay, but they made this payment conditional on Germany paying war reparations to themselves.

Faced with enormous debts because of the war, the victorious Allies looked to defeated Germany as a source of revenue, and one of the provisions of the Treaty of Versailles demanded that Germany pay the entire cost of wartime damage suffered by the Allies, an amount calculated by the Allied Reparation Commission in 1921 as $33 billion. Although they had forced the French to pay a huge reparation after the Franco-Prussian War of 1871, the Germans refused to pay. With some justification, they did not accept responsibility for all war damages, much of which had been inflicted by the Allies. When the Allies insisted on payment, Germany defaulted in 1922, and France retaliated by occupying the Ruhr, Germany's leading center of industrial production. With its main source of industry under French occupation and with its international credit ruined, Germany went bankrupt in 1923. In that year, the German people experienced a spectacular inflationary surge, in which it took a lifetime of savings to buy a loaf of bread. By the beginning of 1924, the European war debts problem resembled a maze with no exit. The United States demanded that the Allies pay their war debts. The Allies would pay only after Germany paid them. The German government pleaded the inability to pay.

The problem had two possible solutions: the Allies could resume the war, conquer Germany, and confiscate German property; or a reasonable and economically feasible program of reparations payments could be devised. All Allied governments rejected the first alternative. Full-scale military occupation of Germany could be effected only with American cooperation, and the Americans refused to consider such a drastic solution. Furthermore, the very idea of a resumption of the war horrified the American, British, and French peoples. The war had cost too much in human lives to justify any action that might lead to its resumption.

To resolve this dilemma, Charles Evans Hughes performed yet another of his diplomatic miracles. Through patient negotiation, he convinced the British and French to accept a more sensible reparations plan, drawn up by a committee of the Reparations Commission, on which two American financial experts, Charles G. Dawes and Owen D. Young, served unofficially. In April 1924, the committee adopted a plan that Hughes pressured the British and French into accepting. Commonly called the Dawes Plan, it set up a system of flexible reparations payments by Germany, the annual amount to be determined by prevailing economic conditions. In addition, the plan provided for a private American loan of $200 million in gold to enable Germany to establish a sound national currency. In 1929, a revised reparations program, the Young Plan, called for gradual German reparation payments over a sixty-year period of $2 billion.

Both the Dawes and Young Plans depended on a sound, stable German economy for their success. To ensure the stability of the German mark, American bankers loaned $2.5 billion to the German government between 1924 and 1929. The Germans gave the Allies a total of $2 billion in reparations, and the Allies paid $2.5 billion to the United States. One of the more amazing results of the reparations riddle was that defeated Germany took in more money than she paid out, while the victorious Allies suffered a net loss. The Great Depression of the 1930s brought about a collapse of the system, and the United States has written off as uncollectible the more than $40 billion in principal and interest still owed her by her Allies in the war.

The Quest for Permanent Peace

Although they vigorously supported the war, the American people became disillusioned with its outcome. The victory over Germany had not made the world any safer for democracy, and the international tensions of the postwar era appeared as fraught with danger as did those which started the war in the first place. Consequently, various proposals for ensuring world peace received much popular support in the United States. For the most part, these peace initiatives ignored the realities of world politics and focused on idealistic and impracticable schemes for international brotherhood.

One such initiative was the campaign for the United States to join the World Court. Officially entitled the Permanent Court of International Justice, the court functioned as an adjudicator of disputes between nations. Most of these disputes entailed minor issues, and the court lacked the machinery necessary to enforce important policy decisions. The court was not a part of the League of Nations, and its member nations did not have to assist in the enforcement of its decisions. Since membership in the World Court did not require serious international obligations, President Harding, strongly backed by Secretary of State Hughes, advocated United States membership, as later did Presidents Coolidge and Hoover. In 1924, the House of Representatives approved the suggestion, but the Senate amended the court's charter by limiting its authority to render certain decisions. The other nations that belonged to the court refused to accept the Senate reservations, and despite repeated efforts by the three presidents, the United States never did join the World Court.

The United States carefully avoided formal contact with the League of Nations, but Hughes did send many "unofficial" delegates to meetings of League agencies. These American representatives assisted the League in establishing guidelines for the suppression of illegal international trafficking in arms, opium, and female slaves. American observers also participated in such humanitarian endeavors sponsored by the League as the International Health Organization and the International Labor Organization. However, the United States did not participate in any of the League's most important activities.

The American desire to secure permanent world peace reached its peak in the peace crusade of the 1920s. In 1921, Salmon O. Levinson, a wealthy Chicago businessman, started a movement to convince the world's nations to outlaw war. After several years of promoting his cause, Levinson won the endorsement of the prestigious Carnegie Endowment for International Peace. Levinson visited Aristide Briand, the French Foreign Minister, and persuaded him to endorse the concept of an international treaty outlawing war as an instrument of national policy. In April 1927, Briand wrote an open letter to the American people requesting their support for the idea. The public responded with enthusiasm. The American secretary of state, Frank B. Kellogg, who had succeeded Hughes in 1925, bowed to public opinion and informed Briand that the United States would sign the treaty. In August 1928, all the leading nations of the world except the Soviet Union formally signed the Pact of Paris, commonly called the Kellogg-Briand Pact, prohibiting aggressive war as a solution to international disputes.

Clearly, the Kellogg-Briand Pact reflected a large measure of idealism. It expressed popular aversion to war and promoted lofty principles of peace and negotiation as alternatives to armed conflict. The pact, of course, proved utterly ineffective in preventing the aggressive actions of Germany and Japan in the 1930s. It was also contradictory, since the only means of enforcing its provisions lay in the signatory nations going to war against those who violated its provisions. Nevertheless, the Kellogg-Briand Pact did express the deeply held sentiments of a war-weary public.

Latin American Diplomacy

When Warren Harding took office in 1921, the relations of the United States with its Latin American neighbors had fallen to their lowest level in history. American troops dictated policy in Nicaragua, and American naval commanders controlled the governments of the Dominican Republic and Haiti. The interventionist policies of the Wilson administration had so alienated the government of Mexico that all normal channels of communications between that country and the United States had been closed. The prevailing attitude of American officials toward Central and South America were aptly summed up by Franklin Roosevelt, the Democratic nominee for vice-president, during the 1920 campaign when he boasted that the United States "controlled" twelve Latin American countries and therefore should join the League of Nations.

Under the supervision of Charles Evans Hughes, ably assisted by Sumner Welles, his chief assistant for Latin American affairs, the United States inaugurated a new policy which greatly improved its relations with Latin America. The new plan emphasized the American dollar rather than military intervention to secure United States interests in the Western Hemisphere. The policy of nonintervention promoted goodwill for America throughout Central and South America, and it laid the groundwork for the Good Neighbor policy of the 1930s.

The new policy's first test came in the Dominican Republic in 1922. Hughes assisted the Dominican people to set up the mechanism for free elections and for the establishment of an independent government. By 1924, the program proved so successful that American troops were withdrawn, leaving the new government to manage its own affairs. In Haiti, the new policy could not be implemented. Although Hughes tried to restore self-government there, the American special commissioner warned that anarchy would result if American troops were withdrawn from the country. Reluctantly, Hughes gave in, and the military and naval commanders continued to rule the country.

In the Central American republic of Nicaragua, the Hughes policy failed at first. A liberal, Carlos Solorzano, won the presidency in 1924, and United States Marines stationed in the country were removed the following year. Led by Emiliano Chamorro, a conservative faction overthrew the Solorzano regime. Because Solorzano had been elected in a free and fair election, the United States refused to recognize the new government. Because of this nonrecognition, another conservative, Adolfo Díaz, became president. As a longtime supporter of the United States, Díaz received immediate recognition from Secretary of State Frank Kellogg. In early 1927, the liberals, led by Juan Sacasa, organized a revolt against Díaz, who pleaded for American intervention to suppress the uprising. President Coolidge complied by sending 5,000 Marines to Nicaragua to defend the Díaz regime. Because this blatant display of force aroused opposition both in the United States and in Central America, Coolidge sent the veteran diplomat, Henry L. Stimson, to negotiate a peaceful settlement. In return for a promise of free elections guaranteed by the American forces, the liberals agreed to end the revolt. In 1928, the elections were held, and the liberals captured the presidency. After remaining in Nicaragua several years to stabilize the new regime, the Marines were gradually withdrawn in the early 1930s.

Although the Republican policy won new respect for the United States throughout Latin America, relations with Mexico had become so strained during the Wilson administration that there seemed little chance of improving them. Wilson's policy of direct intervention in Mexican affairs had led to the success of the anti-American Revolutionary party, which promised to expel all American interests from the country and to expropriate all American-owned oil land in Mexico. For three years, Charles Evans Hughes had negotiated with the government of President Alvaro Obregón, and in 1923, had persuaded Obregón to sign an agreement recognizing the validity of American ownership of Mexican oil lands. In return, the United States recognized the Obregón government. The following year, however, the radical Elias Calles won the presidency and threatened to abrogate the Hughes-Obregón agreement. Calles further antagonized public opinion in the United States through his systematic persecution of the Roman Catholic Church. Under strong public pressure to intervene in Mexico and personally horrified by the actions of the Mexican government, President Coolidge nevertheless adhered to the policy of nonintervention. In 1927, he named Dwight Morrow, a prominent financier, as American ambassador to Mexico. Through patient diplomacy, Morrow won Calles's confidence and inaugurated a new era of friendship between the two countries.

A final feature of the new American policy toward Latin America came at the Pan American Conference held in Havana in 1928. There the United States unofficially agreed to repudiate the Roosevelt Corollary to the Monroe Doctrine, in which Theodore Roosevelt had proclaimed the right of the United States to intervene in Latin American affairs if such intervention became necessary to enforce the Monroe Doctrine. In reality, the Roosevelt Corollary served as a convenient justification for armed intervention. Charles Evans Hughes, who headed the American delegation to the conference, stated that the United States fully endorsed the right of self-government for Latin American countries and that the Monroe Doctrine did not sanction agressive intervention by the United States. Hughes did not give an unequivocal promise of nonintervention, but the new policy he upheld earned goodwill for the United States throughout the Western Hemisphere.

The Diplomacy of the Twenties: An Assessment

In general, historians have treated the foreign policy of the United States in the 1920s with the same critical attitude as they have displayed toward domestic policy. Samuel Eliot Morison, for example, severely criticized the Washington conference treaties for their reduction of American naval strength in the Far East, a reduction that had disastrous consequences in the early stages of World War II. Many historians, such as Samuel Flagg Bemis and Thomas A. Bailey, condemned the Kellogg-Briand pact as symbolizing an idealistic, utopian vision of the world community without imposing any of the attendant responsibilities nations must assume in world affairs. In more recent years, members of the "New Left" revisionist school of American historiography, such as William Appleman Williams, have interpreted the foreign policy of the 1920s as a concentrated effort by the United States government to dominate the world in the interests of big business and American imperialism.

A more balanced interpretation may be found in the studies of Robert H. Ferrell, Ethan Ellis, Richard W. Leopold, and other diplomatic historians. These writers view the decade as a struggle by Charles Evans Hughes, Henry L. Stimson, and Frank B. Kellogg to find a new role for America in an increasingly complex and uncertain postwar world. They depict Hughes as one of the ablest secretaries of state in American history, and they commend Harding, Coolidge, and Hoover for their selection of men like Hughes, Stimson, Sumner Welles, and Dwight Morrow to give American diplomacy a new direction.

The Republican presidents of the 1920s were neither naive idealists nor greedy imperialists. They and their secretaries of state were realistic men who sought to employ the economic strength of the United States to bring about a more stable, peaceful, and prosperous world. Isolation did not characterize their foreign policy, for they remained acutely aware of the critical role America would have to play in world affairs. At the same time, they remained sensitive to public opinion in the United States. Embittered and disillusioned by their experiences in World War I, the American people were in no mood to endorse far-reaching programs similar to the post–World War II Marshall Plan and NATO. In addition, America's principal allies, Great Britain and France, discouraged any attempts to remake the world order.

Charles Evans Hughes and his successors knew that the Washington conference treaties and the Kellogg-Briand pact hardly guaranteed a world free from war. The treaties did earn the United States the respect of the world for its support of the principles of disarmament and peace. The settlement of the reparations problem brought the European nations closer together and helped stabilize the European economy. The Latin American policy of nonintervention laid the foundations for the Good Neighbor policy and generated mutual trust in the Western Hemisphere. If events in the next decade ultimately destroyed the diplomatic accomplishments of the 1920s, those accomplishments nevertheless did help to secure a world free, however briefly, from instability and war.

3

The Roaring Twenties

Few decades have witnessed as many profound changes in American society and culture as the 1920s. Economic prosperity enabled people to purchase a variety of material items previously unavailable and to enjoy a standard of living that made the goal of the good life come true for millions. The radio revolutionized communications, as the automobile did for transportation. These and other innovations contributed to the development of a way of life which signalled a radical departure from the past and which fostered social attitudes challenging those traditionally upheld. New views on marriage, sexual morality, and social mores brought about a style of living which reminded many of the hedonistic excesses of ancient Rome. Rising hemlines, "speakeasies," silent movies, dance halls, and other popular attractions symbolized an era that seemed to mock the cherished values of the past. Writers, artists, film producers, and architects reflected the new ideals in works rebelling against the standards raised by their nineteenth-century counterparts.

Many Americans refused to accept these changes. For a considerable number of people, the social, cultural, and ethical values of the twenties threatened the ideals that had made America great. So they took up the challenge and attempted to restore the values of their ancestors. A wave of religious fundamentalism, carried to millions by fiery evangelists, reinvigorated a moral faith whose foundations seemed on the verge of cracking. A nativist movement, which reached its most vicious form in the revival of the Ku Klux Klan, preyed on popular prejudices against foreigners, Catholics, Jews, and blacks. Crusades against the drinking of alcoholic beverages and the teaching of biological evolution fostered intellectual debate and a general disregard for the law. Whatever the issue, the 1920s generated such a seemingly endless series of change and reaction that the decade never appeared dull and indeed fully deserved the appellation "roaring twenties."

A Society in Flux

During the 1920s American society changed dramatically. The 16 percent increase in the nation's population, the lowest rate for any ten-year period in American history, appeared to signal a slowdown from the hectic pace of the past, but just the opposite proved true. Severe restrictions on immigration were responsible for much of the decrease in the rate of population growth, and changing attitudes about the family caused much of the rest. Traditionally, Americans espoused large families because of the need for as many family members as possible to work and to assist in the task of surviving. In the twenties, general prosperity reduced this historical reliance on large families. As divorce and family planning became commonly accepted features of life, the historical veneration of family solidarity waned. Young adults left home to seek opportunity elsewhere, and social mobility characterized millions of families.

One of the most striking social changes of the 1920s lay in the extraordinary rise of the middle class to predominance in the American social scale. Until World War I, American society resembled a pyramid with a tiny apex, a narrow middle, and a wide base; very few rich, a small middle class, and a huge lower class. By 1930, that society resembled an ice cream cone, with the cherry on top representing the rich, the ice cream the middle class, and the cone the lower class. The enormous scientific and industrial needs of the war and the technological revolution of the twenties created a seemingly insatiable demand for engineers, accountants, managers, lawyers, stock brokers, bookkeepers, clerks, teachers, and a host of other white-collar professions. By the millions, people left the farm or the sweatshop for the office, and because of the skills necessary to perform these jobs, people went to school as never before, and the educational level of the American people increased substantially during the decade.

As the middle class grew, so did the urban areas, because the vast majority worked in offices located in large cities. In the 1920s, over five million people moved from the countryside to the city. Combined with a steady birth rate and a declining death rate, the cities' population increased by fifteen million between 1920 and 1930. Places like Atlanta, Houston, Miami, and Los Angeles mushroomed from small cities to large metropolitan areas. Because of its central location, Atlanta became a leading center of air and rail transportation. Miami experienced a real estate boom, its favorable climate attracting thousands. Houston became the headquarters of the oil industry, Los Angeles of motion picture studios and production, and Detroit of automobiles. Dozens of other metropolitan areas underwent similar expansion in the 1920s, luring millions of new residents with the attractions of rapid transit systems, growing white- and blue-collar employment opportunities, and the cosmopolitan atmosphere of big city life.

Nothing symbolized these changes or indeed made them possible as much as the automobile. In 1920 the family vehicle remained a luxury item enjoyed by the few able to afford one. By the end of the decade, the automobile had become an integral feature of the life of the average American family. The technological advances pioneered by Henry Ford enabled companies to mass-produce cars at an affordable price, and all over the country automobile dealerships promoted the desirability of owning a "tin lizzie." By the tens of millions, Americans fell in love with the automobile, and in the short space of one decade, it effected an economic and social revolution. The automobile gave people the chance to enjoy the pleasures of weekend drives to the country and seashore. It transformed a relatively static society into a highly mobile one. It linked remote, isolated rural areas with urban metropolises. It revolutionized family lifestyles and dating practices, spawned the rise of suburbia, and ended the isolation of rural America. It gave the American people a marvelous new means of having fun and made the car note as inevitable a part of the family budget as the utility bill.

More than a mere means of transportation, the automobile served as a highly visible status symbol, a certain sign that a family had attained the American dream. It gave common people a sense of kinship with the wealthy, for their Model T's, Dodges, and Chevrolets offered the same opportunities for travel and hell-raising as the Duesenbergs, Pierce-Arrows, and Stutz-Bearcats of the rich. The significance of the automobile in American society and the impact it had on everyday life can scarcely be exaggerated. In their classic sociological study of middle-class America in the 1920s, Robert and Helen Lynd encountered a factory worker's wife who proudly exclaimed that she would rather go without food than forgo the family car. She was not alone in her adulation of the automobile. So common and integral a part of today's society that it is taken for granted, in the twenties the automobile provided a new and fabulous addition to life. More important, it quickly became an essential part of life, as millions of Americans relied on their automobiles to get to work, buy groceries, and transport their children to school.

The automobile changed the physical appearance of America. Although there were some three million miles of roads in the United States in 1920, these had been constructed primarily to accommodate horse-drawn transportation. The influx of over three million new cars a year in the decade generated an enormous demand for state and national highways with the capacity for handling the tremendous new volume of traffic. Because a significant proportion of vehicular traffic fell in the interstate category, the federal government assumed the responsibility for accommodating it. The Federal Highway Act of 1921 charged the federal government with the construction of interstate highways, and by 1930, over ten thousand miles had been built. The automobile gave rise to a whole new social phenomenon based exclusively on transportation. Service stations, roadside cafes, and motels became the most visible signs of the increasing mobility of Americans. Problems arose from the mass use of the automobile. The nation's highways became congested. Air pollution increased markedly, as automobile exhaust systems belched millions of tons of gaseous and solid pollutants into the atmosphere. The annual death toll from traffic accidents climbed into the thousands, and state and local governments enacted complex laws governing driving habits. The highway patrolman and state trooper joined the growing ranks of law enforcement officials, and the defacement of the landscape by billboards and junkyards provoked cries of protest. Whatever the problems it raised, in the 1920s the automobile established itself as a permanent and integral feature of American society.

The Revolution in Morals

By 1921 more than a half dozen states had enacted laws prohibiting women from wearing dresses and skirts whose hemlines rose more than three inches above the ground. In several states policemen arrested women who smoked cigarettes in public or who wore bathing suits that exposed their legs, and the women were charged with various violations of local ordinances on

Fundamentalists and flappers. Kansas showgirls receive a Gideon Bible, 1927. *Library of Congress*

public decency. Such actions came from pressure placed on local officials by an indignant public outraged at the wave of immorality that seemed to be flooding the country. By today's standards, the 1920s appear a quite conservative and puritanical decade, but to many who lived at the time, those years embodied a radical departure from the rigid Victorian strictures of the past. During the twenties, traditional values declined, and society placed much greater emphasis on secular and materialistic ones. Many Americans of deep religious conviction considered the new mores as posing a serious threat to the moral fibers of civilization itself.

Nowhere was the new morality more evident than in the changing status of American women. In the 1920s, women emerged from the Victorian straightjacket in which they had been bound for over a century. The traditional image of the staid, demure female whose only desire in life lay in serving her husband while bearing his children gave way to that of the emancipated woman eager to compete with men for jobs, money, and social status. The ratification of the Nineteenth Amendment to the Constitution, which gave women the right to vote, served as the catalyst which unleashed the feminist reaction against the social, economic, and political restraints that had relegated women to the status of second-class citizens for much of American history.

Some of the leading feminists of the 1920s advocated radical solutions to the problems of women. Charlotte Perkins Gilman, for example, urged women to avoid sexual intercourse because the act made women submissive to men. In 1924 Dorothy Canfield Fisher wrote a novel, *The Home Maker*, in which the heroine deserted her homemaking duties for a successful career as a business executive while her husband quit work to manage the house and raise the children. Gilman and Fisher won little sympathy for their extremist views, but Margaret Sanger was more successful. The first public advocate of family planning and birth control, Sanger opened clinics, published manuals, and gave public lectures. The object of much criticism by organized religion, she persisted in her work and became one of the pioneers of scientific methods of planning family size.

The extent of the feminist revolution of the 1920s cannot be accurately measured. From the way they dressed to the way they conducted themselves in public, American women drastically and permanently altered the character of traditional male-female relationships. The floor-length dresses of the 1910s were replaced by an array of feminine attire characterized by above-the-knee hemlines and plunging necklines. Hairstyles changed from the quietly feminine bouffant to the controversial "bob," a closely cropped hairdo that from the rear resembled a man's. To emphasize their new, undisguised sexuality, women applied heavy layers of rouge, lipstick, and makeup, and scented their bodies with a variety of aromas. More significantly, women refused to remain confined to the house and demonstrated their new freedom by engaging in activities previously reserved for men. They shocked their elders by drinking, dancing, and smoking in public, and by visiting nightclubs, "speakeasies," and other establishments formerly prohibited to "respectable" ladies. Perhaps most shocking of all, courtship and dating practices, heretofore marked by horse and buggy rides in the park, were symbolized by back-seat-of-the-car liaisons in "lovers' lanes." The new woman of the 1920s was bolder, more aggressive, and prouder of her feminity than ever before.

These and other manifestations of female emancipation had an inevitable impact on traditional family life. Because of the wartime demand for industrial labor, hundreds of thousands of women left their homes and went to work in factories, and by 1920 over two million women held jobs. The 1920s accelerated this trend; by 1930 over ten million American women worked. Although the great majority of these held teaching, nursing, and clerical occupations, and rarely won the opportunity for equal pay and promotion with their male counterparts, the working woman had become a permanent aspect of American society. As regular members of the work force, women experienced a sense of freedom denied those who remained home all day. The cosmopolitan atmosphere of big-city life, the regular professional and social contacts with a variety of men and women, and the relaxation of dress codes and social mores all contributed to a decline in family life. Divorce became a socially acceptable way of terminating a marriage, and state legislatures made it easy for women to obtain divorces by rewriting laws governing alimony, child support, and community property. Extramarital liaisons became more common, and children no longer received the constant attention of their mothers outside the classroom.

These changes brought about profound shifts in the traditional lifestyle of the American people, especially women, but they have been often exaggerated. The highly publicized "flapper" no more represented the

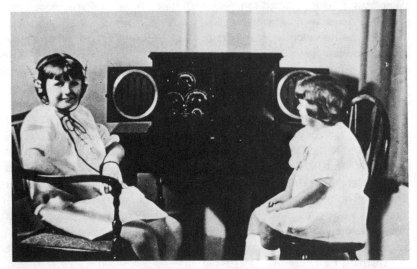

Listening to the radio, 1923. *Library of Congress*

average woman of the 1920s than the *Playboy* centerfold represents the average woman of today. The majority of women continued to regard marriage as their natural, desireable, and permanent station in life. Women remained victimized by legal, social, and economic policies which discriminated against them and effectively denied them equality of opportunity in employment and in many other facets of life. By today's standards, the social mores of the 1920s appear quite innocent, but to many who experienced them, the decade seemed to bring about revolutionary changes in cultural attitudes and moral values which threatened the basic spiritual character of American civilization.

The Fundamentalist Backlash

At the end of World War I, many Americans developed hostile attitudes towards the foreign influences they believed posed a threat to the nation's principles and ideals. Most people regarded the United States as a superior civilization whose integrity must not be eroded by foreign cultures. Most Americans also believed in the superiority of Anglo-Saxon culture and of the white race, a belief that had been nutured by writers and social scientists since the late nineteenth century. In the immediate postwar era, several influential persons cultivated these nativist and racist sentiments. President Woodrow Wilson returned to the United States from the Paris peace conference irritated by the machinations of the Allied powers at the conference. Wilson's ambassador to Great Britain, Walter Hines Page, urged his countrymen to view the culture and history of England as the only ones worth emulating. In a series of articles in the widely read *Saturday Evening Post,* the popular novelist Kenneth Roberts condemned the "good-for-nothing mongrels" of Asia and Latin America and advocated a total ban on Japanese immigration into the United States.

The intensification of these popular attitudes coincided with the immigration into the United States of over one million people between early 1920 and mid-1921. Mainly war refugees from Eastern Europe, these newcomers strained the resources of the Immigration and Naturalization Bureau. The influx promised to be only the beginning of a tidal wave of immigration, as millions of Poles, Jews, and Russians displaced by the war made preparations for emmigration to America. Alarmed by the growing flood of immigrants and pressured by the increase in nativist sentiment in America, Congress in 1921 passed an emergency bill which restricted annual immigration to a mere trickle. In 1924 the National Origins Act permanently fixed the annual immigration quota at 140,000, a marked decline from the prewar average of 700,000. The act also stipulated that the number of immigrants from each country would be limited to 2 percent of the national origins of the foreign-born population of the United States in 1890. Since the majority of Eastern Europeans had come to America after 1890, the act effectively ended further immigration by these peoples. Further limitations on immigration passed in 1929 and 1931 restricted the annual average during the 1930s to just seven thousand. These measures clearly reflected popular hostility towards Southern and Eastern Europeans, most of whom were Roman Catholics or Jews. America, the great "melting pot," would suffer no further dilution until the 1960s.

The celebrated Sacco-Vanzetti case showed the extent of xenophobia prevailing in the United States. In May 1920 two Italian aliens, Nicola Sacco and Bartolomeo Vanzetti, were arrested for the armed robbery of a South Braintree, Massachusetts, shoe factory and for the murder of a guard and paymaster. The arrest caused a national sensation. As aliens and anarchists, Sacco and Vanzetti received open condemnation in the press before their trial began. At the trial, their alien status and Italian nationality drew as much attention as the physical evidence. The presiding judge, Webster Thayer, displayed blatant prejudice against the defendants, and went so far as to refer to them as "damn Dagoes." The jury found the men guilty and recommended the death penalty, to which Judge Thayer willingly assented. The case became a *cause célèbre* with many of the nation's leading intellectuals. Such well-known writers as Edna St. Vincent Millay and John Dos Passos wrote stirring accounts of the "travesty of justice" perpetrated at the trial. The noted jurist, Felix Frankfurter, wrote a scathing critique of the numerous legal errors committed by the prosecution. For six years, appeals to the Massachusetts courts and governor, to the United States Supreme Court, and even to the President of the United States, delayed the final outcome, but the appeals were of no avail, and in August 1927, Sacco and Vanzetti were executed. Many historians have portrayed the men as innocent victims of mass hysteria against foreigners, as sacrificial lambs on the altar of popular prejudice. For one thing, though eyewitness accounts of the crime leave no question that more than two men were involved, only Sacco and Vanzetti were made the scapegoats. A recent careful analysis of the evidence by historian Francis Russell, however, provided overwhelming proof of Sacco's guilt and considerable evidence that Vanzetti may have been involved.

Bred in an atmosphere of antiforeign sentiment and nurtured on a steady diet of racist and xenophobic prejudice of the most vicious sort,

Ku Klux Klan parade in Washington, D.C., 1925. *National Archives*

the nativist movement attained maturity in a particularly ugly and dangerous manner, the revival in the 1920s of the Ku Klux Klan. Organized during Reconstruction by former Confederates as a means of resisting the civil rights actions of the period, the Klan died out after white Southerners regained control of local politics in the 1880s and 1890s. In 1915 a former Methodist circuit rider, William J. Simmons, resurrected the Klan at a rally in Stone Mountain, Georgia. Endorsing nativism, white supremacy, and Protestantism, the Klan grew slowly and by 1920, counted fewer than five thousand members. In the next five years, however, it mushroomed into a potent national organization with over five million members from all parts of the country, especially the South, the Midwest, and the Far West. In 1922, Hiram W. Evans, a Texas dentist, wrested control from Simmons and turned the Ku Klux Klan into a powerful political and social force. It attracted mainly residents of small towns who saw in the Klan the opportunity to lash out at Catholics, foreigners, blacks, and others, who they felt were undermining the foundations of America. With its mystical symbolism, its white capes and hoods affording anonymity, its secret terminology ("Imperial Wizard," "Exalted Cyclops," "Klokard"), and its clandestine meetings, the Ku Klux Klan held a powerful appeal for those persons who felt helpless against and bewildered by the demonic forces destroying American civilization.

Under Evans's able leadership and well-heeled through a professional fund-raising staff, the Klan entered the political arena and quickly won a number of impressive victories. In Texas, a Klan-backed candidate defeated the incumbent United States Senator, Charles Culberson. In Oklahoma, the Klan-dominated state legislature impeached and removed from office Governor J. C. Walton, who had tried to use the National Guard to drive the Klan out of the state. In Oregon the Klan pushed through a bill that required all children to attend public schools. This obvious attempt to destroy the parochial school system was declared unconstitutional by the Supreme Court in 1925. In Indiana, one of the Klan's national leaders, David Stephenson, totally dominated the state government. The Klan also exercised a considerable degree of political control over the state governments of California, Ohio, Georgia, and Arkansas.

The vast majority of Klan members obeyed the laws and behaved peaceably, but in an organization that thrived on racial, religious, and ethnic hatred, the ugly specter of violence inevitably appeared. With a rigidly doctrinaire moral code, the Klan considered anyone deviating from that code as an instrument of Satan. Catholics, Jews, blacks, and foreigners found themselves victims of Klan violence. In Birmingham, Alabama,

Klansmen murdered a Roman Catholic priest in cold blood. In Amite, Louisiana, six Italians were legally hanged for murdering a grocer. Many priests, nuns, rabbis, as well as blacks and Poles suffered stonings, brandings, and floggings. Divorced women received threatening letters and obscene phone calls, while bootleggers, "flappers," and immigrants were subjected to varying degrees of violence.

By 1925, many Americans had begun to fight back against the Klan. In Louisiana, Governor John M. Parker, who had the support of the state's large Roman Catholic population, waged a vigorous campaign against the Klan, and after he became governor in 1928, Huey Long in characteristically flamboyant fashion responded to a Klan leader's threat to campaign against him: "Quote me as saying that that Imperial Bastard will never set foot in Louisiana, and that when I call him a son of a bitch, I am not using profanity, but am referring to the circumstances of his birth." In such states with large Catholic, Jewish, and immigrant populations as New York, Pennsylvania, and Massachusetts, the Klan failed to gain a foothold. When David Stephenson, the Klan leader in Indiana, brutally assaulted a woman who later committed suicide, national indignation against the Klan was aroused. When Stephenson's political crony, Governor Edward Jackson, refused to intervene in the case, Stephenson publicly revealed a long list of Klan misdeeds, including political corruption and sexual misconduct. The resulting scandals damaged the Klan's reputation and lost it much public support. By 1930 Klan membership had declined drastically, and its influence in American society and politics had ended.

Another of the attempts to combat the changes taking place in society was the movement for the prohibition of alcoholic beverages. The prohibition movement arose from several sources. The large influx of German, Italian, Jewish, and Slavic immigrants after 1880 brought to the United States the drinking habits associated with those peoples. Suddenly, it seemed, bars and saloons had sprung up in almost every neighborhood, enticing men to stop by for a drink before they returned home from work. Preachers of fundamentalist persuasion discovered Biblical injunctions against drinking. Concerned with the deleterious effects of drinking on family life, women took the lead in bringing prohibition to the forefront of reform. They formed such organizations as the Women's Christian Temperance Union and the Anti-Saloon League, and made prohibition one of the leading goals of the feminist movement of the early twentieth century. Determined to break the power of the big city political machines, progressive reformers knew that the precinct captains and ward leaders often employed saloonkeepers as a major source of vote-getting. For many Populists, "Demon Rum" ranked second only to the gold standard as the source of America's social and economic problems. During World War I, the Irish and German saloons appeared to many as local centers of seditious sentiment.

Whatever their reasons, those who espoused prohibition considered it more of a moral crusade than a social experiment. Convinced of the righteousness of that crusade and exploiting the intensely emotional patriotic fervor of the war effort, the prohibitionists won ratification of the Eighteenth Amendment to the Constitution, banning the manufacture, sale, and transportation of intoxicating liquors, and they secured enactment of the amendment's enforcing legislation, the Volstead Act of 1920. As the decade of the 1920s opened, America embarked on what President Herbert Hoover would characterize as a "noble experiment."

National prohibition came at a time when America entered one of the most socially innovative eras in its history. Prohibition was an attempt to institute moral reform, an effort to purge Americans of their sinful ways, and it clashed with the new dress habits, lifestyles, and social and moral laxity of the decade. The inevitable result was widespread violation. Seldom has a law been so flagrantly and frequently flouted. The crux of the prohibition problem lay in the impossibility of enforcing it. Tens of millions of people insisted on drinking, and local, state, and federal law enforcement officials proved incapable of preventing them from doing so. Popular demand for alcoholic beverages actually increased in the 1920s, and suppliers met that demand through a national network of illegal bootlegging activities. In cities like New York, Chicago, New Orleans, and San Francisco, where public support for drinking was widespread, the law was openly violated. "Speakeasies," underground night clubs that served drinks, flourished, and in many urban areas local officials made no attempt to close them down. Formerly an exclusively male pastime, public drinking became a favorite female indulgence, as the emancipated woman of the twenties exercised her new freedom. People used all kinds of ingenious methods of obtaining illegal liquor. Women concealed flasks in undergarments, garters, stockings, and under hats. Men made their own home brews, including weak (and legal) "near beer," with less than a 1 percent alcohol content, deadly wood alcohol (methanol), and a potent concoction commonly called "white lightning." Some 1,550 federal prohibition agents made valiant attempts to enforce the law and indeed seized and destroyed more than ten million gallons of illegal booze, but their efforts hardly stemmed the innumerable violations. By 1930 it had become obvious that prohibition had failed as a national experiment in moral coercion, and in

1933, the Twenty-First Amendment to the Constitution, which repealed the Eighteenth Amendment, was ratified. Many states, especially in the South, thereupon enacted local option ordinances, which permitted individual cities and counties to remain "dry" if a majority of citizens so voted.

One of the more detrimental consequences of prohibition was the rise of organized crime in America. Because people could not obtain alcoholic beverages legally, criminal syndicates supplied them through illegal channels. With the enactment of prohibition, bootlegging rings cropped up all across the country. The most extensive and lucrative of these rings fell under the domination of criminal organizations. In Chicago, for example, the criminal empire of Alphonse "Scarface Al" Capone established itself as the most powerful underworld syndicate in the United States. Through the ruthless elimination of his rivals and through the liberal disbursement of bribes and favors to local officials, Capone built up a $75 million-a-year operation based on bootlegging, gambling, and prostitution. Although Capone was convicted of income tax evasion, his criminal empire continued to flourish. In many other cities, the mob used prohibition as the basis for establishing a very large and profitable business supplying the public with illegal services.

Of the fundamentalist revolt against the changes of the 1920s, the antievolution crusade was the most emotional. Ever since Charles Darwin published his *Origin of Species* in 1859, many people considered his biological theories of evolution as atheistic attempts to belie the story of creation in the Book of Genesis. But it was not until the 1920s that antievolution grew into a potent social force. In 1920 the former presidential candidate and secretary of state, William Jennings Bryan, began a concerted campaign to purge America's schools of the advocates of evolution. Bryan spoke on college lecture circuits, organized the support of fundamentalist sects, and lobbied state legislatures for the enactment of antievolution laws. He and his followers won their first significant victory in 1921 when the University of Tennessee fired five faculty members for teaching evolution. With none of his oratorical talents diminished by old age, Bryan gained much popular support in the South. Declaring that it is "better to trust in the Rock of Ages than to know the age of rocks," Bryan persuaded several southern states to enact laws prohibiting the teaching of evolution as a truth, and he convinced school boards to censor textbooks recognizing Darwin's theories. Ably assisted by such fundamentalist stalwarts as Rev. J. Frank Norris, the influential Southern Baptist minister from Fort Worth, Texas, Bryan scored his most impressive victory in 1925 when Tennessee enacted a law prohibiting the teaching of any theories which denied the Biblical account of creation or which suggested that man descended from the lower animals.

The Tennessee law clearly threatened the principles of free speech, academic freedom, and separation of church and state, so the American Civil Liberties Union offered to pay the legal expenses of any Tennessee school teacher who volunteered to test the law. In Dayton, a small rural community, a high school biology teacher, John T. Scopes, accepted the offer and had himself arrested for teaching evolution. The July 1925 "Monkey Trial," as it was depicted in the press, became one of the most highly publicized court cases in American history. Throngs of journalists, evangelists, and spectators poured into Dayton for the trial. The sweltering heat and the heated controversy over evolution provided several enterprising purveyors of lemonade, Bibles, hand fans, and rubber monkeys a ready market for their products.

Technically, the legal issue had already been decided before the trial began. Scopes freely admitted that he had broken the law, so the verdict was never in doubt. The main courtroom issue, made more dramatic by the confrontation between Bryan, who served as an assistant prosecutor, and Scopes's defense attorney, the renowned lawyer Clarence Darrow, centered on the validity of the law itself. A self-professed agnostic, Darrow denounced the law because it negated the most reliable findings of contemporary biologists. Bryan defended the literal interpretation of creation in Genesis. Scopes, of course, was found guilty, and the Tennessee Supreme Court later upheld the conviction as well as the constitutionality of the law. Bryan died a few days after the trial ended, and his death seriously weakened the antievolution cause. Some ardent antievolutionists continued the crusade, and in Arkansas in 1928, they succeeded in winning one of the more curious victories of the democratic process. By a popular vote, the sovereign people of Arkansas decided that Genesis was right and Darwin wrong.

Intellectual Trends

In the 1920s American intellectuals advocated ideas and theories which challenged those currently prevailing. The relativist movement resulted from an attempt to apply the scientific theories of Albert Einstein to human society. According to Einstein, common notions of such concepts as time and space are not absolute, but are governed by their relationship to the environment. Time, for example, is an artificial concept designed to provide a convenient framework within which people can regulate their daily activities. The twenty-four-hour day and seven-day week exist only because people invented them. In reality, Einstein asserted, the ultimate determinant of time is the speed of light, 186,000 miles per second, a rate at which time literally stands still. A thirty-year-old person travelling at the speed of light could begin a journey through space in the year 1920. When he returned to earth in the year 2020, he would still be thirty years old!

Such bewildering ideas challenged many of society's most cherished principles. If such fundamental notions as time and space were relative, then so must more abstract ideas as morality and ethics. Intellectuals applied the concept of relativity to academic disciplines. In history, for example, the predominant school of historiography maintained that through the scientific, objective uncovering of factual data, the whole historical truth about a past event or personality would become known. First enunciated by German historians in the nineteenth century, this scientific school emphasized the amassing of facts. The new relativist school, propounded by such historians as Carl Becker, asserted that such absolute accuracy was impossible to attain. The very act of doing research was relative to such variables as the historian's age, race, sex, political persuasion, religion, and innumerable other factors which tempered objectivity. Historical facts themselves, the relativists argued, would inevitably be interpreted according to the time in which the historian wrote and to the prevailing political, social, economic, and cultural ideologies. Thus, employing the identical data about the American Revolution, a British historian and his American counterpart would write quite different accounts of it.

Relativism profoundly influenced many fields of human endeavor. In education, John Dewey's theories envisioned the schools as miniature societies preparing children for the "real world" outside the classroom. Therefore, schools must discard the traditional classical curriculum and teach "practical" subjects to enable children to compete in human society. In the 1920s Dewey and his disciples persuaded school systems to implement his theories of "progressive education." The old classical subjects— Latin, Greek, philosophy, etc.—gave way to the more "practical" home economics, typing, and shorthand. The traditional emphasis on rigorous intellectual discipline was replaced by a democratic approach to learning in which the classroom became a social laboratory teaching children to develop their creativity.

Literature and the Arts

In American history certain eras have featured the flowering of literary and artistic endeavor of unusually high quality. The 1840s and 1850s, for example, produced such giants as Edgar Allen Poe, Herman Melville, and Nathaniel Hawthorne. The 1920s also produced a succession of writers whose works compare favorably with the finest in the nation's history. The great outpouring of literary quality came primarily from what many writers have called the "lost generation" of the 1920s, a group of intellectuals who rebelled against the monumental tragedy of World War I by expressing either a cynical approach to human nature or an attempt to revive traditional human values. These people also denounced the excessive materialism of the twenties and the reactionary fundamentalism of the antievolutionists, the prohibitionists, and the nativists.

The "lost generation" thesis does not adequately explain the literature of the era. More often than not, such writers as F. Scott Fitzgerald and Ernest Hemingway adapted their writings to the popular sentiments of the American people. The "lost generation" condemned traditional moral values, but so, in a sense, did the American people. The literary emphasis on sex, materialism, cynicism, and relativism was not a revolt against the popular values of the 1920s, but an accommodation to them. If most of the heroes of the great novels of the twenties led dissolute lives, so, too, did many of the heroes of the public. Babe Ruth and the Great Gatsby had more things in common than they did differences.

One of the most popular writers of the 1920s, Sinclair Lewis, wrote novels that depicted the drabness, sterility, and moral decadence of small town America. His main works, *Main Street* (1920), *Babbitt* (1922), *Arrowsmith* (1925), *Elmer Gantry* (1927), and *Dodsworth* (1929), ridiculed the business civilization of the decade. Most of Lewis's characters appear ensnared in a net of intellectual sterility, and their only escape lies in active participation in business and civic affairs. Their lives lack moral force, and they surrender their individuality to the socially acceptable mores of their neighbors and colleagues. Another acclaimed writer of the twenties was Ernest Hemingway, whose simple, straightforward writing style won public and critical praise. In *The Sun Also Rises* (1926) and *A Farewell To Arms* (1929), Hemingway expressed popular disillusionment with the war and its unfulfilled ideals. His principal characters seem unable to cope with wartime and postwar society, and they drift aimlessly in a world of sex and meaningless human relationships. F. Scott Fitzgerald carried these

Eugene O'Neill, by common consent, America's greatest playwright, 1927. *National Archives*

themes even further in *This Side of Paradise* (1920) and *The Great Gatsby* (1925). In these works, Fitzgerald portrayed characters whose entire lives lacked moral strength and direction. His graphic symbolism and depiction of the moral dissolution of his characters drew much criticism from fundamentalist organizations. In *Look Homeward, Angel* (1929), Thomas Wolfe related the story of a youth who rebelled against the materialistic values of his mother and against the narrow provincialism and prejudice of his North Carolina home.

Lesser writers included John Dos Passos, whose *Three Soldiers* (1921) vividly depicted the horrors and futility of war. Theodore Dreiser's *An American Tragedy* (1925) reflected a morbid interest in the seamier sides of human existence. One of the finest woman writers of the 1920s, Willa Cather, described the majesty and glory of the enduring human spirit in *Death Comes For The Archbishop* (1927). James Branch Cabell's *Figures of Earth* (1921) and *Something About Eve* (1927) aroused the indignation of many because of their very strong emphasis on sex.

In the field of poetry three of America's most renowned poets produced some of their most famous works during the twenties. Robert Frost wrote *New Hampshire* (1923) and *West-Running Brook* (1928), in which he pursued his lifelong themes of respect for nature and for humanity. Robinson Jeffers wrote a number of poems which expressed his deep-rooted antipathy toward the vile aspects of human nature and his devotion to the natural world. A native of St. Louis, T. S. Eliot gained recognition as one of the leading poets of the twentieth century. Eliot grew up in the Midwest and was educated at Harvard, but after the war, he moved to England and spent the rest of his life there. In *The Wasteland* (1922), Eliot wrote what many authorities consider the greatest poem of this century. A complex indictment of the emptiness of contemporary existence, *The Wasteland* conveys the author's conviction that faith is an essential ingredient for a person to lead a meaningful life.

Dramatists also flourished in the twenties. Eugene O'Neill, universally regarded as America's greatest playwright, dominated the field. His plays, most notably *Desire Under The Elms* (1924) and *Strange Interlude* (1928), emphasized the psychological tensions which made modern life so complex. Other notable dramatists of the period included Maxwell Anderson, Marc Connelly, and Elmer Rice. By 1930 the quality of drama produced in America equalled that in Europe.

In music, the 1920s witnessed the flowering of that unique American art form, jazz. The music evolved from slave spirituals, gospel hymns, and African tribal music. In the latter part of the nineteenth century and in the first two decades of the twentieth, jazz thrived in Storyville, the legal "red-light district" of New Orleans ("jazz," a slang expression for sexual intercourse, was applied to the music played in the Storyville cabarets). It also flourished in flophouses, black honky-tonks, and neighborhood saloons. By 1920 the popularity of jazz had spread beyond New Orleans to such places as Memphis, Chicago, and Harlem. During the twenties, many of the most famous of the black musicians, such as Louis Armstrong, "Jellyroll" Morton, and Joe "King" Oliver, moved north to Chicago and New York, where they received the recognition and income they never gained in their native South. Jazz quickly became a favorite form of musical expression, and its artists renowned as contributing to the

"King Oliver" Jazz Band, Chicago, 1923. Note famous trumpeter Louis Armstrong (third from right). *National Archives*

development of a uniquely American cultural form. Other famous musical leaders of the 1920s included George Gershwin, whose *Rhapsody in Blue* (1924) became one of the most popular musical compositions of all time. The composers George M. Cohan and Irving Berlin, the bandleader Paul Whiteman, singers Gene Austin and Ethel Waters, and pianist Duke Ellington ranked among the public's favorites during the decade.

As the 1920s came to an end, the American people could look back on a decade of significant change in their lives. Those changes included a vastly improved standard of living, radical innovations in lifestyles, and new vistas in public outlook. It is impossible, however, to understand and appreciate those changes without a careful examination of their impact on everyday life, which was profoundly affected by the Great Depression.

4

The Great Depression

The Great Depression: even today, half a century later, the term evokes memories of one of the most traumatic and eventful eras in American history. Those who lived through that period still recall the economic collapse, the social upheaval, and above all, the human suffering. Millions of Americans lost their jobs and their homes. Industrial production, foreign trade, and national income plummeted from the prosperous peaks of 1929 to pre–World War I levels. At any given moment during the early 1930s, large numbers of people could be found wandering aimlessly in the streets, searching desperately for work they had little chance of finding. Others took to the roads and highways, seeking new lives in other parts of the country. Having lost their jobs, their homes, and most of their material possessions, these migrants scattered all over America, living out of wheelbarrows or wagons, sleeping in makeshift cardboard tents, and travelling in broken-down jalopies or on foot.

The administration of President Herbert Hoover struggled mightily with the enormous problems of combatting the depression, but it proved inadequate to the task. Although recent historical studies have argued that Hoover was a far more capable and efficient administrator than earlier studies had acknowledged, he failed to alleviate the economic distress afflicting the nation. Philosophically opposed to government intervention in the economy, temperamentally unsuited to dynamic executive leadership, Hoover did not mobilize public opinion behind his administration. His bland, pontifical pronouncements on the pressing issues of the time

President Herbert Hoover using radio. *Library of Congress*

seemed only to aggravate a deepening malaise of the national spirit. By the last year of his presidency, Herbert Hoover faced a crisis that reached beyond mere economics; the American people were losing faith in the very institutions of government.

The Election of 1928

Early in 1928 President Calvin Coolidge announced in typical direct and forthright fashion that he did "not choose to run for president" again. When the Republicans held their convention in June of that year, they nominated Coolidge's secretary of commerce, Herbert C. Hoover. The candidate had a long and distinguished record of public service; the nation was at peace; and despite a recession in 1927, the economic growth of the 1920s continued. Eight years of Republican rule had produced this excellent state of the nation, and the party had every reason to believe that the voters would reward it with a third successive victory in 1928. The Democrats made the Republicans' task even easier by engaging in a bitter, acrimonious convention dispute over prohibition. Badly divided on the issue, the delegates spent more time arguing for and against its repeal than they did in trying to unite the party for what promised to be an uphill fight in the campaign. The Democrats nominated Governor Alfred E. Smith of New York, a man strongly endorsed by the urban delegates, but whose advocacy of prohibition repeal antagonized many rural delegates.

The 1928 presidential election became a controversial one, not because of the outcome—virtually everyone expected a Hoover victory—but because of the religious factor. Smith was the first Roman Catholic to run for president, and this adversely affected his vote in certain fundamentalist regions. The first Republican since Reconstruction to break the Democratic stranglehold on the South, Hoover carried Virginia, North Carolina, Tennessee, Florida, Kentucky, Oklahoma, and Texas. Many scholars have assumed that Smith's Catholicism accounted for his defeat in these southern states, but careful studies of the election by Alan J. Lichtman and David Burner disagree. Smith actually carried the five most heavily fundamentalist states: Arkansas, Mississippi, Alabama, Georgia, and South Carolina. More important than his religion in explaining his defeat were his opposition to prohibition, his clear identification with northeastern urban interests, and his association with New York City's Tammany Hall political machine. The single most important factor in Hoover's victory was the continuing prosperity in the country.

When he took office in 1929, Herbert Clark Hoover could look back on a distinguished life. An Iowa farm boy, Hoover got a degree in engineering from Stanford, and he used his talents to earn a fortune and a respected reputation in mining. Strongly dedicated to public service, Hoover held a variety of positions in the government during World War I. His most important contribution came as the head of the Food Administration when he supervised the distribution of food to millions of displaced Europeans made homeless and hungry by the war. In the 1920s Hoover rose to a leading position in the Republican party because of his efficient administrative capabilities. President Hoover began his administration in the midst of the most prosperous and flourishing period in American history. The economic policies of the Harding and Coolidge administrations had contributed to full employment, material prosperity, and an exuberant air of national confidence. Hoover ended his administration in the midst of the worst economic depression in the nation's history. The country faced massive unemployment, financial collapse, and a deepening popular mood of pessimism and despair. Before we explore the Great Depression and its impact on the American people, we shall pause for a look at the America Herbert Hoover presided over.

America on the Brink of Depression

By almost all accounts, 1929 promised to be a banner year in American history. The nation enjoyed full employment, with factories and plants churning out record numbers of automobiles, radios, clothing, and a host of other products. Technological advances had produced an amazing increase in the standard of living, a standard measured not only by material prosperity but by other factors which, taken together, provided a reasonably accurate estimate of the quality of life. Educational opportunity exploded in the 1920s, and the nation's classrooms were filled with school children. In many sections of the country illiteracy had been virtually eradicated, and a much higher percentage of Americans of both sexes now attended high school and college. Because of rapid advances in medical care, including the successful elimination of or reduction in such feared epidemic killers of the past as yellow fever, malaria, diphtheria, and smallpox, average live expectancy had jumped from about fifty-five years in 1900 to over sixty-five in 1929, the most rapid increase in the nation's history. All across the country Americans reflected the new opportunities which life in 1929 provided by attending movies and sporting events in record numbers and by engaging in a variety of recreational activities their new way of life offered. In short, in 1929 the American people enjoyed a way of life that provided not only the hope but the reality of achieving the American dream.

The state of the nation's economy had made this possible, and a few statistics will illustrate the economic progress of that remarkable decade. Total national income rose from $65 billion in 1920 to $83 billion in 1929, a 30 percent increase. Industrial workers saw wages increase by 26 percent above the increase in the cost of living. Manufacturing establishments showed a 64 percent increase in worker productivity during the decade, and stockholders in major corporations enjoyed a 65 percent increase in dividend payments. Total savings by the American people more than doubled, from $15 billion in 1920 to $36 billion in 1929, providing banks, insurance companies, and other financial institutions with the capital necessary to invest in huge expansions in the construction, automobile, chemicals, rubber, electronics, and steel industries. No wonder Herbert Hoover defeated Al Smith in 1928. Not many voters would reject an administration and a party whose policies had reaped such prosperity.

The prosperity of the 1920s was widespread and far-reaching, but as numerous economic historians have shown, the economy displayed symptoms of economic disease which threatened at any moment to infect the entire nation. One-quarter of the population, America's farmers, did not share in the boom times. Plagued with overproduction, recurring low prices, and the lack of foreign markets, many farmers barely managed to make ends meet, and many more succumbed to the perennial evils of tenancy and sharecropping. Large numbers of workers in such failing industries as coal and textiles lost their jobs or suffered drastic reductions in wages. Some 65,000 small businesses went bankrupt in the 1920s, and the 200,000 still in operation in 1929 found it increasingly difficult to compete with the large corporations. The new technology of the twenties produced many new jobs, but it also wiped out many others. By the tens of thousands, blacksmiths, carriage makers, lathers, and numerous other artisans found the demand for their services rapidly declining. Nearly six thousand banks failed during the decade, most of them small rural institutions, and larger urban banks began to experience similar troubles. Some significant areas of industrial production fell under the domination of corporate giants, thus stifling competition and driving out of business dozens of automobile manufacturers, steel processors, and utilities concerns.

More significantly, the 1920s experienced a vast increase in financial speculation, much of it by companies and individuals lacking sound resources. From 1926 through 1929 the nation witnessed an unprecedented amount of speculation in stocks and bonds in an unregulated market. The paper value of stocks tripled in that brief period, but so did brokers' loans. Millions of people, mainly from the middle class, invested life savings in stocks and bonds. To finance their purchases, they often borrowed up to 90 percent of the face value of the security. Today, when a person buys stock, federal law requires him to pay a "margin" of security (usually at least 50 percent) of the purchase price in cash. No such requirement existed in the 1920s. Consequently, it was possible for persons and even corporations to engage in "paper" transactions on the stock market by buying stock without possessing the established credit necessary to back up the purchase. In 1927 alone brokerage house and financial investment firms floated nearly $19 billion worth of new stocks but backed this huge investment with only $3 billion in assets. Clearly, such a situation would inevitably result in a day of reckoning, but for a few years, the stock market offered to investors the Midas touch, luring ordinary people to plunge more and more money into stocks. Who could resist the temptation to buy a few shares of RCA when its value skyrocketed from $95 a share in March 1928 to $178 a share a year later? Why not buy General Motors stock which cost $99 a share in 1925 and $212 a share three years later? The perennial dream of "get rich quick" came true for many during the heady bull market boom of the late twenties. By the Fall of 1929 almost twenty million Americans owned stock, and few of them realized that the bubble would soon burst.

The halcyon days of the late 1920s were not a time for sober reflection on the state of the economy. Those few who did investigate the economy seriously soon discovered signs of fundamental weakness that would soon cause its collapse. By 1928 industrial production had become gravely overextended. The construction and automobile industries, for example, found consumer markets for their products and services significantly lower than the giddy levels of 1925. The market for new cars had become saturated, and the industry began to curtail production in 1929, resulting in a sharp decline in orders for steel, rubber, glass, and innumerable other products heavily dependent on the automobile industry for the sales of their products. The Harding-Coolidge high tariff policies had brought about a decline in American foreign trade, so much so that American companies could no longer depend on foreign markets as dumping grounds for their surplus products. By 1928 consumers began to curtail their purchases of refrigerators and electrical appliances, producing a further decline in industrial production. To the astute, these trends portended serious economic problems in the not too distant future, and at the beginning of 1929 they could see that the economy continued its upward momentum only because of the enormous amount of speculation in stocks and bonds. Since that speculation consisted mainly of paper transactions, those who recognized the danger signals began quietly shrinking the size of their financial investments by periodically selling small amounts of stocks and bonds. They saw the imminence of a financial upheaval of major proportions.

Economic Collapse

In October 1929 the stock market reached its highest level and began the steepest decline in its history. During the first three weeks of October the average price of industrial stocks fell and rose in roller coaster fashion, but few people grew concerned because many of the large financial investors continued to pour money into the market. In the final week of October, however, the price levels plunged steadily downward without the expected recovery, and a growing feeling of panic spread from within the financial community to the general public. Everyone, it seemed, wanted to sell their stocks before prices dropped any lower, but such large-scale selling served only to accelerate the price decline. On Thursday, October 24, prices fell an average of $25 a share, and investors stampeded to dump their holdings. That afternoon, J. P. Morgan and Company and other large investment institutions pooled their resources to accumulate a $240 million fund, which they promptly pumped into the stock market, but even this considerable sum failed to block the impending collapse. It came quickly, on October 29, 1929, "Black Tuesday," when the New York Stock Exchange recorded by far the single most disastrous day in its history. A record sixteen million shares exchanged hands, and the average price of fifty leading stocks dropped forty points. Pandemonium broke out, as thousands of investors desperately tried to sell before they lost everything. So volatile had the mood grown that the police were called in to prevent a riot. The next day newspapers all over the country described the horrors of the "Wall Street Crash," and in subsequent months, their sensational accounts of market activities, including exaggerated tales of stockbrokers committing suicide, contributed to the growing lack of public confidence in the nation's financial institutions.

Most economists now agree that the stock market "crash" did not touch off the Great Depression, but it did become a permanent symbol of the worst economic catastrophe in American history. A few selected statistics will provide an idea of the depth and extent of the Great Depression, which did not come to an end until after the United States entered World War II. Virtually nonexistent at the beginning of 1929, national unemployment reached an estimated total of twelve million by 1933. This figure represented one-quarter of the nation's work force and does not include the millions of Americans who still worked but at greatly reduced wages and working hours. Between 1929 and when the depression reached its worst stage, in 1933, wages declined from $53 billion to $31 billion. Farm income dropped from $12 billion in 1929 to only $5 billion in 1933, and the price of corn and wheat fell to two cents a bushel. Stock prices averaged $452 a share in September 1929; in March 1933, they averaged $58 a share. From 1930 through 1932 almost six thousand banks, with aggregate assets of over $4 billion, failed, and hundreds of thousands of families lost their life savings. Some 110,000 businesses went bankrupt, and thousands of others laid off employees and sharply reduced orders to prevent bankruptcy. Total industrial production was cut in half, and some of the largest industries, such as steel, operated at less than 20 percent capacity. The depression severely affected all areas of the country, its greatest impact falling on the heavily industrialized Northeast and Midwest. The unemployment rate reached 30 percent in New York City, 40 percent in Chicago, and 50 percent in Cleveland. In cities like Akron and Toledo, almost totally dependent on single industries, the closing of plants forced anywhere from 60 to 80 percent of the laborers out of work. From the end of 1929 through the end of 1932, over 100,000 people lost their jobs every week.

The Human Impact

Statistics hardly describe the actual day-to-day effect of the Great Depression on the American people. At its worst, it made poverty a way of life for forty million Americans. As the economic boom of the 1920s came to an abrupt end, factories laid off workers, sheriffs foreclosed on mortgages, and young people by the thousands quit school to assist their families. Misery and deprivation pervaded every region of the country and affected

Veterans bonus army camp, 1932. *Library of Congress*

every class of citizen. In New York, Seattle, Washington, D.C., Detroit, and countless other cities, "Hoovervilles" sprang up. Sarcastically named after the president whom virtually everyone blamed for the depression, these squalid communities of the homeless featured families living in miserable shanties constructed of cardboard or tin, and lacking electricity, heat, running water, and sanitary facilities. In downtown business districts thousands of vendors hawked apples, gladiolus bulbs, and other commodities. Employment agencies and personnel departments were so swamped with applicants that many hired security guards to maintain order. One economist described the depression as a "temporary dislocation of the free market." But the sight of family men and women laid off from their jobs with no unemployment compensation or pension, of former bank clerks, school teachers, and truck drivers lining city streets begging people to buy apples for a nickel apiece, of mile-long throngs of the hungry waiting for hours to obtain a bowl of watered-down soup presented more than an economic problem; it was human tragedy on a grand scale.

The depression profoundly affected every aspect of American life. Economically, it produced the most drastic deflation in the nation's history. The prices of common goods and services fell to such low levels that to many it appeared that the monetary system could not survive. The deflation

Pennsylvania "soup kitchen," 1931. *National Archives*

resulted from a classic practical application of the law of supply and demand. With millions out of work, people could no longer afford to buy the products of industry. This produced an excessive supply of almost everything from food to automobiles. With the supply high and the demand low, prices dropped. During today's era of steady inflation, it is instructive to survey prices for typical consumer items during the depth of the depression. New cars averaged $600 apiece; men's all-wool suits, $10. A twenty-six-piece set of silverplate flatware cost $5, a washing machine, $48, and a solid mahogany dining set, $47. Dentists charged $1 to fill a tooth, and doctors $2 for physical examinations. A pack of cigarettes cost fifteen cents, a new automobile tire, $6, and a gallon of gasoline, eighteen cents. A new six-room house with two garages cost $2,000, and a sixty-day tour of Europe, $500. Food prices seemed ridiculously cheap: sirloin steak, twenty-nine cents a pound; pork chops, twenty cents a pound; bread, five cents a loaf; milk, ten cents a quart; butter, twenty-five cents a pound; and coffee, twenty-five cents a pound. In 1933 a New York City neighborhood restaurant advertised the following prices: three large pork chops for thirty cents; a sirloin steak dinner for twenty-five cents; and a leg of mutton dinner for twenty cents.

These prices, typical of those which prevailed during the worst years of the depression, appear almost impossibly low, yet most Americans had barely enough money to afford even the most essential items. The Federal Reserve Board aggravated the problem by pursuing a tight-money policy, which caused a further decline in the amount of currency in circulation. Coupled with the huge unemployment rate, this had the effect of an even more forceful downward tug on the economy. Businesses constantly reduced prices to sell their products, but people still could not afford them. Because of the scarcity of money, many people resorted to the ancient barter system for the exchange of goods and services. It was not unusual to find people paying their bills with chickens or repairing a house in return for food. Municipal and state governments suffered a serious loss of tax revenues, and many public employees received scrip, state or local government I.O.U.s, instead of U.S. dollars in pay. Neighborhood groceries and department stores often allowed their regular customers to charge their purchases on the promise that they would eventually pay for them (which the vast majority did).

By 1932 hard times had become a permanent part of the lives of millions of Americans. Although few people, if any, actually starved, large numbers went hungry, and many more existed on such meals as the "Kraft dinner," an inexpensive macaroni and cheese dish. Every day families

Depression prices, an A&P ad, New York City, 1933.
National Archives

made do without the meat they could not afford. In countless towns and cities throngs of people stood for hours in line to receive handouts of bread and soup distributed by the Salvation Army and other charitable organizations. Farmers slaughtered sheep and dumped wheat in city streets because they had no markets. In 1932 alone thirteen million bales of cotton went unsold, even at the absurdly low price of three cents a pound. Weak from lack of food, some teachers and school children fainted in the classrooms. On a single day in April 1932 one-fourth of the entire land area of the state of Mississippi was sold at sheriffs' auctions because the owners could not keep up the mortgage payments. Hundreds of thousands of families spent the winter of 1932–1933 without gas, electricity, and in some cases, running water, because they could not pay their utility bills. It is little wonder that under such conditions, an ugly mood of militancy began to pervade certain groups of Americans. Led by rabble-rousing orators, midwestern farmers organized protest movements that sometimes erupted into violence. In Wisconsin, Iowa, Kansas, and Nebraska, farmers' groups fought pitched battles with sheriffs' deputies, assaulted lawyers trying to foreclose mortgages, and poured milk and corn in gutters and ditches. In Washington and Kentucky, angry citizens destroyed government buildings and smashed company windows. In Idaho, Wyoming, and Minnesota, state legislatures enacted special laws prohibiting foreclosures and sheriffs' sales of confiscated property. The term "depression" came to characterize not only economic conditions, but the mood of America as well.

The Causes of the Depression

No event as complex and traumatic as the Great Depression can be explained in simplistic terms, nor can its causes be attributed to individual

Oklahoma tenant farmer, 1931. *Library of Congress*

events or personalities. The historiographical debate over the causes of the depression revolve around three central theories. The first, espoused by historian Arthur Schlesinger, Jr., blames the policies of neglect pursued by the administrations of Warren Harding, Calvin Coolidge, and Herbert Hoover. Schlesinger contends that the laissez-faire economic policies of these presidents nullified the progressive reforms enacted under Theodore Roosevelt and Woodrow Wilson and permitted such institutions of economic control as the stock market and the large corporations to follow policies of economic expansion free from the restraints of government control. Consequently, unscrupulous speculators in stocks and bonds bilked millions of their savings; corporate profits rose much faster than wages; and the genuine needs of the poor met with inattention by the Republicans. The unfettered speculative boom of the twenties came to an end with the collapse of the stock market, and with it, the whole national economic structure dissolved.

A second explanation, offered by economist John Kenneth Galbraith, holds that the enormous increase in productivity throughout the 1920s was not matched by a corresponding increase in wages. During the decade wages rose only half as rapidly as did productivity, thus resulting in an impossible economic situation of supply outpacing demand. Consumers simply did not have the money necessary to fund the continued expansion of domestic productivity, and by late 1928, industries faced huge stockpiles of unsold goods and began to curtail production. The collapse of the highly inflated stock market wiped out the reserves of capital needed to fund further industrial expansion. This, in turn, led to plant closings and unemployment, which quickly spread throughout the entire economy.

A third view, currently becoming popular, is that of the noted conservative economist, Milton Friedman. The Friedman, or monetarist, school argues that the stock market crash brought uncertainty to the large financial investors, who withheld their capital from the marketplace. The Federal Reserve Board aggravated this problem by following a policy of severe restrictions on the money supply. In the three years from 1930 through 1932, the nation's money supply declined by one-third, at the very time when the economic situation demanded an expansion of that supply. This tight-money policy lowered public confidence in financial institutions, and the drastic reduction in capital caused a rapid acceleration in bank failures in early 1933. By that time, what began as a readjustment of the stock market and of the excess of supply over demand had deteriorated into a full-fledged economic depression which quickly spread to most of the highly industrialized nations of the world.

The Hoover Response

It was a personal misfortune for Herbert Clark Hoover to preside over the nation during this era of crisis. During ordinary times, he might have retired from the presidency with a reputation as an above average chief executive. But because he governed during the Great Depression, Hoover has earned a reputation as one of the most inept and impotent presidents in American history. This assessment of Hoover stems primarily from his failure to deal successfully with the multitude of problems the depression posed. In recent years Hoover scholars have restored his reputation somewhat by their appreciation of his administrative abilities and by their crediting him for initiating many of the programs which formed the nucleus of the New Deal.

Elected in 1928 by a landslide margin over Al Smith, Hoover lost to Franklin Roosevelt by a landslide only four years later, and he left office the object of public derision and contempt. One reason for this dramatic reversal in Hoover's popularity lay in his unbending faith in the capitalistic system. Not a blind devotee of classical laissez-faire economics, Hoover did support government regulation in the public interest, but he refused to endorse any proposals extending the influence of the federal government into private sectors of the economy. He also believed, almost as an article of personal faith, that private initiative provided the most efficient and desirable method of restoring prosperity. Hoover distrusted the federal government and believed that the most responsive level of government lay at the local and state levels. Therefore, he opposed attempts to assume federal responsibility for alleviating the severe economic distress caused by the depression. Finally, Hoover felt a genuine sympathy for the unemployed and poverty-stricken, but he maintained that the relief of their suffering must originate from private charitable and philanthropic organizations.

The most immediate problem Hoover faced at the onset of the depression was the rapid decline in agricultural income, which had persisted throughout the 1920s. To remedy this situation, Hoover pushed the Agricultural Marketing Act of 1929 through Congress. The act established the Federal Farm Board, whose primary function was to stabilize the nation's agriculture through the use of a $500 million appropriation. The board would lend money to farmers' cooperatives to enable them to find more efficient means of marketing their products. The board also was empowered to purchase surplus crops and to store them in government warehouses to maintain prices at a profitable level. The Agricultural Marketing Act was the most ambitious and far-reaching attempt at direct government intervention in the economy in the nation's peacetime history. By purchasing large quantities of cotton and wheat, the Federal Farm Board artificially raised domestic prices to levels higher than those which prevailed on the world market. Hoover's experiment failed because the worldwide depression had dried up markets for American crops and because the policy of buying up surpluses without accompanying crop control legislation only served to stimulate higher production. The board also lacked sufficient funding to maintain prices at permanently high levels, and by 1932 it had incurred a deficit of over $350 million. Hoover's experiment failed to prevent continuing declines in domestic prices, but his program did lay the foundation for the New Deal's agricultural policies.

A second phase of Hoover's efforts to cope with the depression in agriculture came in his tariff policies. The Hawley-Smoot tariff of 1930 raised the import duties on agricultural products by 70 percent over their previous levels. Obviously intended to stop foreign products from competing with American ones on the domestic market, the Hawley-Smoot tariff aggravated an already serious decline in American foreign trade. To America's foreign competitors, the new tariff signalled an era of economic nationalism, and they responded by raising their own customs duties against the importation of American farm products. The opponents of Hawley-Smoot pointed out this obvious foreign retaliation to Hoover, but he succumbed to pressure from the farm bloc and signed it anyway. The resulting decline in American foreign trade contributed to the deepening of the depression throughout 1931 and 1932.

Contrary to many historical accounts, Hoover did not simply sit idly by, hoping that the stock market collapse would prove temporary. Less than two months after "Black Tuesday," he inaugurated a series of meetings with leaders of finance, industry, labor, and local government, in which he urged them to cooperate in a national campaign for economic recovery, and he succeeded in securing a voluntary program of cooperation. From business leaders, he obtained promises to maintain current levels of employment and wages. From labor leaders, he received pledges to continue working at current salary levels. From local government leaders, he won assurances of increases in spending for public works projects. By April 1930, it appeared that Hoover's voluntary program might succeed. Industrial production and employment remained stable, and heavy increases in local, state, and federal expenditures for public works pumped over $4 billion into the economy. The following month, however, the Federal Reserve Board again reduced the supply of money in circulation, and this action terrified many business leaders. Fearful of a further drop in consumer demand caused by the reduction in the money supply, they curtailed production and laid off hundreds of thousands of employees. The impact on the economy proved disastrous, and every index of economic activity declined sharply for the rest of 1930. As the incumbent president, Herbert Hoover naturally bore the brunt of voter resentment, and in the congressional elections of November 1930, the Democrats scored impressive gains. By the time the new Congress convened, in January 1931, several Republican representatives had died, leaving the Democrats in control of the House, and an insurgent Democratic-Republican coalition in control of the Senate.

The international economic situation influenced the course of the Great Depression in the United States, and several financial crises affecting foreign banks and governments in 1931 worsened the problem in America. In March, France demanded that Germany and Austria pay their short-term debts in full, but the two countries, having themselves over $4 billion in overdue credits from other countries, were unable to pay their debts to France. Although the United States and Great Britain assisted, it was not enough, and in May, the Kreditanstalt, Austria's largest bank, failed. A panic ensued, as mobs of people withdrew their gold from German and Austrian banks, depriving both countries of the capital necessary to continue paying reparations to France. President von Hindenburg of Germany appealed to Hoover, and Hoover responded with a proposal for a one-year moratorium on the payment of all German and Austrian debts. Although France eventually agreed to the moratorium, its initial reluctance to accept it led to a massive withdrawal of gold from French and British banks. By September 1931, England, Germany, Austria, and several other European countries had repudiated the international gold standard, and these countries demanded that the United States pay them the $1.5 billion in European gold it held. All of this led to the dumping by European investors of large quantities of stocks on the New York Stock Exchange, further depressing prices and bringing international trade to a virtual standstill.

These international economic developments had catastrophic consequences in the United States. Between May and December 1931 nearly two thousand banks failed, employment dropped by 12 percent, and wages fell by over 30 percent. Terrified by the international financial crisis, investors hoarded their funds instead of pumping them into the badly depressed economy. The panic spread to depositors, who made runs on banks to withdraw their funds, thus causing more failures. In December 1931 President Hoover took radical steps to combat the emergency. He called for a massive public works program costing $2.25 billion, a federal home loan bank to shore up the faltering mortgage industry, and an emergency reconstruction corporation to assist business. The public works program was the most ambitious and costly federal project in American history. The construction of the gigantic Hoover Dam on the Colorado River and other projects represented a departure from Hoover's rejection of government spending to assist the economy, and, ironically, it provided Franklin Roosevelt with ammunition for his 1932 campaign against Hoover because of Hoover's increasing reliance on deficit spending.

In January 1932 Congress gave President Hoover the most significant of his antidepression measures, the Reconstruction Finance Corporation (RFC). With an initial appropriation of $500 million and the authority to borrow an additional $1.5 billion in tax-free bonds, the RFC loaned vast sums to railroads, banks, savings and loan associations, insurance companies, and other financial institutions to enable them to preserve their financial integrity. During 1932 the RFC loaned over $1.5 billion and helped lessen the financial panic which gripped the nation at the beginning of the year. Two other 1932 measures assisted the hard-pressed monetary market. The Glass-Steagall Act made government bonds legal collateral for federal reserve notes, thus enabling the Federal Reserve Board to expand the monetary supply and banks to pay their foreign debts in gold. The Federal Home Loan Bank established home-loan banks with assets of $125 million to lend to banks and mortgage companies as a means of obtaining cash without foreclosing on mortgages. Congress also provided $2 billion to state and local governments in public works funds.

In the end, Herbert Hoover became the scapegoat upon whom the American people placed the blame for the Great Depression. Early historians of the New Deal also fault Hoover for contributing to the severity of the economic crisis. In reality, Hoover did not merely continue the free enterprise policies of his predecessors. Instead, he embarked on a program both ambitious and innovative to end the depression. His agricultural programs, Reconstruction Finance Corporation, and public works policies represented a sharp break with the past and contradicted his own philosophy of noninterference by government in the economy. Hoover's policies did assist in saving the nation's financial structure, but he failed to provide sufficient direct relief to the millions of poor, hungry, and unemployed Americans. He also failed to appreciate the deep-rooted hostility with which the American people viewed the business community, and his repetitious statements about the basic soundness of our economic institutions fell on deaf ears. Above all, Hoover lacked the qualities of personality and leadership necessary to preside over the nation during this crisis. There is some evidence that the Hoover program was beginning to work, for the economic indices did begin to move upward in the first three months of 1933, but for Herbert Hoover, it came too late. He had lost the faith and confidence of the American people, and it would fall to his conqueror in the 1932 presidential election, Franklin D. Roosevelt, to guide the nation toward the "new deal" he had promised.

5

The First New Deal

As the year 1933 began, the mood of the nation alternated between despondency and militancy. Already three years old, the Great Depression showed no signs of relaxing, and indeed would plummet to its worst level in the first three months of the year. Unemployment, poverty, and hunger afflicted millions of Americans. All over the country, people existed in a state of despair as they saw their dreams and aspirations crushed by the economic disaster that befell them. In some areas, people refused to accept their fate meekly, and in actions that were more the result of frustration than of lawlessness, poured milk on the streets and attacked deputies foreclosing on unpaid mortgages. These acts of defiance, however, were isolated, and the majority of Americans simply existed as best they could through the hard times.

When Franklin Delano Roosevelt took the oath of office as President of the United States in March 1933, he knew that his only mandate from the voters was to combat the depression. He did not disappoint them. From the very beginning of his administration, Roosevelt steered the nation on an irreversible path of massive government intervention in the economy. Through his magnetic personality and forceful leadership, Roosevelt restored public confidence in the institutions of government, and through his New Deal program, he committed the federal government to the unprecedented role of responsibility for the welfare of its citizens.

The Election of 1932

The experts predicted that the year 1932 would prove a banner one for the Democratic party, for President Herbert Hoover and his Republican party bore the brunt of public blame for the Great Depression. For three years, Hoover had failed to alleviate the terrible economic calamity, and with some justification, Americans perceived him as a person of callous indifference to the mass economic suffering the depression had engendered. In reality, Hoover sympathized deeply with the unemployed and poverty-stricken, and he had tried desperately to cope with the problems that overwhelmed his administration. Hoover's bland personality alienated people at the very time they needed inspiration, and his unconvincing promises of the imminence of economic recovery failed to convince the jobless throngs whose empty wallets spoke more eloquently of their real plight. Nothing symbolized Hoover's public image more than his response to the veterans' bonus march in the late spring and summer of 1932. A large number of World War I veterans marched on Washington to lobby Congress for passage of a bonus bill. When the Senate, under strong pressure by Hoover, defeated the bill, most of the veterans went home. Some five thousand remained and encamped in ramshackle shanties at Anacostia Flats, Maryland. After some of the veterans clashed with the District of Columbia police in July, Hoover ordered the United States Army to disperse the veterans. Personally led by Chief of Staff Douglas MacArthur, the Army forced the veterans out of Washington and burned their settlement. To many Americans, this excessive use of force symbolized an administration more concerned with an imaginary threat to law and order than with providing assistance to needy people.

When the Democratic National Convention opened in late June, the party's mood of exuberance over its all-but-certain victory in the November election was tempered by the heated dispute over the selection of its presidential nominee. The convention delegates split among the three leading contenders: Franklin D. Roosevelt, the governor of New York; Alfred E. Smith, the party's 1928 nominee; and John Nance Garner of Texas, the Speaker of the House of Representatives. At the beginning of the year, it appeared certain that Roosevelt had the nomination cinched, but his losses to Smith in party primaries in New England and to Garner in the California primary eroded his support. The first three ballots showed Roosevelt with a strong lead over his rivals but more than one hundred votes short of the two-thirds delegate majority necessary for nomination. After the third ballot, many Roosevelt delegates threatened to switch to either

Army Chief of Staff, Douglas MacArthur (right), 1932.
National Archives

Smith or Garner, and it took a considerable amount of persuasion by the Roosevelt campaign team to hold them in line. Because of the deadlock, the convention adjourned, and in the next few hours, Roosevelt picked up the support he needed. Garner threw his support to Roosevelt and persuaded William McAdoo, the head of the powerful California delegation, to do the same. This touched off a stampede of Garner delegates jumping on the Roosevelt bandwagon. The reasons for Garner's defection are unclear. Some historians have suggested that Garner's party loyalty overrode his personal ambition, while other, more cynical writers, have intimated that Garner made a deal with Roosevelt's campaign manager, James A. Farley, to throw his support to Roosevelt in return for the vice-presidential nomination, which, in fact, Garner did receive. Whatever his reasons, Garner gave Roosevelt the delegate votes he needed, and the fourth ballot saw the New York governor win an easy nomination victory. One of those instrumental in keeping southern delegates behind Roosevelt was Senator Huey P. Long of Louisiana, later one of the president's most persistent nemeses.

In his acceptance speech, given for the first time in convention history by a nominee in person, Franklin Roosevelt pledged the Democratic party and himself to a "New Deal" for the American people, a slogan that would characterize his domestic policies. Since Hoover's unpopularity all but guaranteed his defeat, Roosevelt did not campaign on a radical program. In fact, his campaign speeches hardly forecast the New Deal. They combined vague assurances of economic recovery with guarantees of fiscal responsibility. He promised a farm program that would assist the farmer, but one which would not cost the government any money. He pledged federal assistance to the needy, but also promised to reduce overall federal spending by 25 percent. Historian Arthur Schlesinger, Jr.'s contention that Roosevelt's 1932 campaign spelled out the basic ingredients of the New Deal is not supported by the evidence. If anything, Roosevelt's campaign speeches carried an essentially conservative undertone, as he criticized Hoover for reckless spending and promised to balance the budget. The central issue of the campaign, however, was not a conservative versus liberal debate, but a masterful exercise in political compromise by Roosevelt. He made promises to all major interest groups because his main concern was to win the election. And win he did. Roosevelt and the Democratic party scored an overwhelming victory over Hoover and the Republicans. Roosevelt carried forty-two of the forty-eight states, and the Democrats won large majorities in both houses of Congress.

Franklin Delano Roosevelt

The man who would be president for the next twelve years and who would determine the future course of American history in both domestic and foreign affairs was born in 1882 at Hyde Park, New York. A member of the wealthy and respected Roosevelt family, Franklin received a proper education at Groton and Harvard. He settled in New York City in 1904 and attended Columbia Law School. After marrying his distant cousin, Anna Eleanor Roosevelt, in 1905, Franklin joined a law practice two years later. In 1910, Franklin won election to the New York state senate. For the next two years, he led the Democratic party's progressive wing in opposing the party's domination by the Tammany Hall political machine. In 1912, he strongly supported the presidential nomination of New Jersey Governor Woodrow Wilson. After his victory in the 1912 election, Wilson rewarded Roosevelt with appointment as the assistant secretary of the navy, where he served for seven years. In 1920 Roosevelt became the Democratic nominee for vice-president, and even though his ticket lost, he gained influence and prominence in the national party hierarchy. In August 1921 Roosevelt was stricken by polio, and had to undergo a very difficult three-year recovery. For the rest of his life, Franklin would be unable to walk without assistance, but he refused to let the handicap destroy his political career. By 1924, Roosevelt had recovered sufficiently to nominate Al Smith at the Democratic National Convention, a performance which he repeated four years later. Although he could stand only with great difficulty, he refused to allow himself to be seen in public on crutches. In 1928, Roosevelt ran for governor of New York, and despite the Hoover landslide, defeated his Republican opponent. As governor, Roosevelt won public approval for his program of heavy state spending on public works projects to assist people rendered jobless by the depression. He won a landslide reelection victory in 1930, and by 1932, had become the nation's most popular governor.

An extraordinarily complex man, Franklin Delano Roosevelt cannot be easily and simply characterized. He had a magnetic personality, able to charm even determined political opponents. He was a sparkling conversationalist and often regaled his listeners with stories and tales so captivating that they frequently forgot the context of their original meeting with him. He possessed an instinctive grasp of the needs, aspirations, and feelings of the American people, and he employed that grasp to great political advantage. Like his distant cousin Theodore, Franklin felt a deep sense of noblesse oblige, a responsibility to assist his fellow Americans. Lacking any preconceived set of philosophical ideals about economics and politics, Franklin Roosevelt was a supreme pragmatist, willing to forgo his campaign goals for a more workable and feasible approach to the nation's problems. He took advice from many persons of differing political viewpoints, but his ultimate decisions came as much from intuition as from scholarly recommendation. During his twelve years as president, Roosevelt proved a poor administrator, but his rejection of typical bureaucratic red tape often resulted in action being taken much more rapidly than normal.

The First One Hundred Days

Historians use the term "New Deal" to denote the domestic programs and policies of the Roosevelt administration. That term is misleading, for it implies a carefully planned and structured series of programs designed to combat the Great Depression. In reality, the Roosevelt programs resulted more from expediency and improvisation than from long-range planning. Although Roosevelt did consult with his celebrated "brain trust" of college professors, he usually made decisions on the spur of the moment, or because he believed them urgent and imperative. Furthermore, Franklin Roosevelt did not classify himself as a "liberal" or "conservative." Rather, he was a pragmatist, always doing what he considered the most appropriate thing to do.

By the time he became president, on March 4, 1933, Franklin Roosevelt faced a serious crisis. The nation's banking system tottered on the verge of collapse. Every day, people withdrew tens of millions of dollars from their checking and savings accounts. In forty-seven of the forty-eight states, banks operated under severe restrictions imposed by state governments fearful of a national financial disaster. National confidence in the banking system appeared destroyed. Therefore, as one of his first actions as president, Roosevelt declared a four-day bank "holiday," to permit his administration to devise an emergency solution to the banking problem. The result was the Emergency Banking Act, enacted by Congress within four hours on March 9, 1933. The act shored up banking assets by authorizing Federal Reserve banks to issue more currency, requiring the Reconstruction Finance Corporation to buy banks' preferred stock, and directing the Treasury Department to reopen the banks according to their relative soundness. Most significantly, the act prohibited the private hoarding and exporting of gold, thus debasing the currency and permitting a much larger amount of money to enter into circulation.

The Emergency Banking Act had a magical effect. Less than a month after its enactment, people had pumped more than $1 billion back into the nation's banks. The subsequent Economy Act of 1933 slashed more than $500 million from the federal budget and restored the confidence of the financial community in the federal treasury. These measures, coupled with Roosevelt's signing of a bill which legalized the sale of weak beer, gave the American people the impression of an administration on the move, of a government that at last was attempting to deal with the serious problems facing it. By taking these actions and by justifying them to the public in the first of a series of "fireside chats" on the radio, President Roosevelt

Union Bank failure, New York City, 1933. *National Archives*

restored public morale and confidence in the government at a time when apathy and despondency seemed to pervade the popular mood.

During the first three months of his presidency, Franklin Roosevelt faced considerable pressure from numerous interest groups demanding that he take action to ameliorate their economic distress. Among the most pressing of these groups were organizations of farmers. The secretary of agriculture, Henry A. Wallace, conferred with farm leaders and devised an agricultural program that revolutionized federal farm policy. The Agricultural Adjustment Act (AAA) of May 1933 was designed to shore up farmer's income to the point where it matched that of the stable period 1909–1914. To accomplish this goal, the AAA imposed various controls on the production of certain staple commodities. By curtailing production, the AAA would maintain a steady supply of farm products, thereby raising prices in a period of increasing demand. For example, the AAA persuaded southern farmers to destroy 25 percent of their 1933 cotton crop in return for benefit payments, and the AAA purchased over six million pigs for slaughter, thus greatly reducing the nation's supply of pork. Later legislation incorporated these programs into permanent policy. The Bankhead Cotton Control Act of 1934, for example, imposed prohibitive taxes on cotton produced in excess of severe quotas, resulting in a 25 percent reduction in cotton production in just one year. The establishment of the Commodity Credit Corporation in 1934 enabled farmers to borrow money against their crops and to hold them until prices rose to reasonable levels.

In effect, the AAA subsidized American farmers at the expense of consumers and taxpayers. By paying farmers not to grow a significant portion of their crops, the Roosevelt administration brought about a revolution in traditional federal agricultural policy. The AAA had an immediate beneficial effect. National farm income catapulted from $2 billion in 1932 to $4.6 billion in 1935, and total farm indebtedness fell by $2 billion in the same period. Recent studies by such scholars as William D. Rowley, David E. Conrad, and Van L. Perkins have shown that the AAA did not come without detrimental effects on the national farm situation. For example, the drastic reduction in cotton production put over 300,000 poor black and white sharecroppers out of work. The large numbers of subsistence farmers did not benefit from the price supports paid to large farm corporations. And it appears that droughts, floods, dust storms, and similar natural disasters had more influence in reducing agricultural production than did the AAA. Finally, the AAA failed to arrest the continuing decline of the farmer as a significant element in American life. If anything, the AAA accelerated the rapid disappearance of the small farmer, as several million Americans left the farming life forever during the 1930s, primarily because the depression in American agriculture did not end until the onset of World War II.

During its first three months, the Roosevelt administration also enacted a series of laws designed to shore up the badly weakened stock and bond market and the housing industry. One act authorized the Reconstruction Finance Corporation to provide financial assistance to banks, most of the money eventually to be invested in the stock market. The Truth-in-Securities Act required brokers to furnish prospective buyers of stock with accurate and complete information about the financial condition of the companies offering the stocks. The housing industry received a desperately needed boost through the establishment of the Home Owners Loan Corporation, a federal agency authorized to borrow up to $4.75 billion to refinance the mortgages of homeowners unable to keep up their payments.

One of the most spectacular and radical of Roosevelt's proposals made during his "One Hundred Days" legislative spree was the Tennessee Valley Authority (TVA). The TVA would build dams in a seven state area, with its center on the Tennessee River. The dams would assist in flood control through a network of reservoirs and would generate cheap hydroelectric power for the residents of the Tennessee valley. The TVA would also

Tennessee miner's family, 1939. *National Archives*

manufacture fertilizer, build a navigation channel from Knoxville, Tennessee to Paducah, Kentucky, and foster soil conservation and reforestation throughout the area. Denounced by critics as a "socialistic" experiment, the TVA actually helped to rejuvenate a decaying region of the United States. Its flood control, reforestation, soil conservation, and other projects, as well as its production of abundant electric power gave the Tennessee valley a new lease on life. The region became the center of new industrial development and its agricultural production made it one of the most self-sufficient areas of the country. However, as recent scholars have shown, the TVA planners forcibly removed thousands of families from their homes, and it failed to cope with the perpetual poverty of the Appalachian region.

Other than devaluation of the dollar, the Roosevelt administration had no program for industrial recovery, and it was not inspired to formulate one until the Senate passed a bill sponsored by Senator Hugo L. Black of Alabama to limit the work week of all laborers in America to thirty hours. Philosophically opposed to government intervention in the economy, Franklin Roosevelt was appalled by the Black bill, and he ordered three members of his "brain trust," Raymond Moley, Hugh S. Johnson, and Rexford G. Tugwell, to devise an alternative to Black's radical proposal. The result was the National Industrial Recovery Act (NRA), passed by Congress in June 1933. The objectives of the NRA were to end ruinous competition, raise prices by limiting production, guarantee a minimum work week and wage, and assure the right of organized labor to collective bargaining with employers. To implement these objectives, the NRA would devise codes of management-labor practice, and businesses would be encouraged, but not required, to adopt the codes.

Under the guidance of director Hugh Johnson, the NRA became a visible symbol of the administration's attempts to cope with the depression. Gigantic NRA parades were held in many cities. The NRA's symbol, a blue eagle, was displayed everywhere, and highway billboards, radio commercials, and newspaper advertisements promoted the virtues of belonging to the NRA. Over seven hundred codes were adopted, with provisions for price-fixing, production controls, and minimum wage and maximum hours. Associations of businessmen enforced the codes and received administration exemptions from antitrust litigation. After Johnson decided that the codes unfairly discriminated against small businesses in favor of the large corporations, he attempted to force the corporations to relax the standards for the small businesses. The corporations vigorously objected, and the NRA became ensnared in a web of petty animosities between businessmen and federal bureaucrats. President Roosevelt tried to overhaul the NRA, but his efforts proved unsuccessful. The entire question was settled in May 1935, when the Supreme Court declared the NRA unconstitutional.

Although the NRA did produce substantial benefits for workers, it failed to achieve its goals. Businessmen tried to manipulate the NRA codes to eliminate their competitors, and labor unions tried to use the codes to force nonunion employees off the job. More fundamentally, the NRA acted upon a false assumption—that industrial recovery would result from an elimination of competition and a curtailment of production. In reality, the depressed economy demanded a massive increase in production to bring about prosperity, and the suppression of free competition in the marketplace stifled one of the most vital elements of economic recovery.

With the exception of the banking crisis, Roosevelt's most urgent problem lay in providing emergency relief for the masses of unemployed Americans. The financial resources of city and state governments could not cope with the six million persons on their relief rolls. The Federal Emergency Relief Act created the Federal Emergency Relief Administration (FERA) to provide financial assistance to impoverished city and state governments to continue their unemployment relief programs. Under its director, Harry L. Hopkins, the FERA immediately began distributing money to the mayors and governors. Within two days, Hopkins, cutting government red tape to a minimum, had distributed over $5 million and would distribute $500 million shortly thereafter.

One of the most original of the New Deal programs and one personally devised by Franklin Roosevelt was the Civilian Conservation Corps (CCC). With an initial appropriation of $300 million, the CCC enrolled some 250,000 young men between the ages of seventeen and twenty-one in 1,500 camps located throughout the United States. These young men were directly employed by the federal government to work in the nation's forests, planting trees, preventing soil erosion, increasing the productivity of the land, and controlling flooding. Under the direction of the War Department, the camps were operated along military lines, and the men were organized into platoons, companies, brigades, etc. They received salaries of $30 a month, with $25 sent home to their parents, and $5 for pocket spending money. During its nine years, the CCC employed almost three million young men, and by all accounts, was one of the most successful of the New Deal programs.

The adjournment of Congress in the middle of June 1933 brought an end to the most productive three-month period in the history of the executive and legislative branches of the government. During that period, the federal government accepted responsibility for the welfare of the millions of needy Americans; revitalized the national currency and banking system; revolutionized the nation's agricultural programs; embarked on a new and radical experiment in regional planning; protected the mortgages of numerous homeowners; and began a bold new policy in government-business cooperation. More significantly, the first one hundred days made it clear to the American people that their new president was trying to help them by utilizing the full resources of the government to combat the depression. Franklin Roosevelt had made the term "New Deal" more than a campaign slogan; he made it a symbol of the restoration of faith and confidence in the institutions of government and in the commitment of that government to the needs and aspirations of its citizens.

The first one hundred days, however, had not lessened the disastrous consequences of the Great Depression. A brief economic recovery in the spring and summer of 1933 ended by the onset of fall, and all economic indicators strongly suggested that the winter of 1933–1934 would prove as catastrophic as the previous one. Federal economic assistance was not getting to those who needed it nearly as quickly as Roosevelt had hoped. One of the provisions of the NRA set up a Public Works Administration (PWA), with an initial appropriation of $3.3 billion for public works. The administrator of the PWA, Secretary of the Interior Harold L. Ickes, a cautious and cost-conscious man, determined to oversee the expenditure of every cent of the PWA's funds to ensure that they would be spent wisely and efficiently. Consequently, Ickes had hardly made a dent in the available funds by October 1933. Eventually, Ickes's painstakingly slow methods would result in the construction of some of the New Deal's most worthwhile projects, but at that moment, the immediate need was for instant action.

Sometime near the end of October or the beginning of November— accounts differ on the exact date—Harry Hopkins had lunch with President Roosevelt and suggested that the federal government simply hire the unemployed during the winter at all sorts of part-time jobs ranging from raking leaves to repairing highways. Roosevelt asked Hopkins the number of jobs that could be created, and Hopkins replied with a quick estimate of four million. Roosevelt calculated that this would cost $400 million, and he ordered the money to be taken from the PWA funds and placed in a new Civil Works Administration (CWA) under Hopkins. In this unplanned and off-the-cuff manner was born another of the New Deal's innovative approaches to public policy, the concept of direct federal hiring of the unemployed.

A frail, sickly individual, Harry Hopkins nevertheless was a man of remarkable energy. Like Roosevelt, Hopkins understood little of economic theory, but he possessed an intuitive, instinctive grasp of the basic problem facing the administration: the need for immediate action. Therefore, he plunged into his responsibility as CWA administrator with an aversion to bureaucractic red tape as powerful as Ickes's addiction to it. Within the incredible space of one month, Hopkins had hired over 2.5 million people at 40 cents an hour for unskilled labor and $1 an hour for skilled. Within another month, he had achieved his goal of four million CWA workers. With virtually no planning and a complete lack of controls over the expenditure of CWA funds, some projects fully deserved the new term for wasteful federal spending, "boondoggle." Hopkins hired people to research the history of the safety pin, and he paid one hundred workers to walk the streets of Washington to scare starlings off federal buildings with balloons. Yet compared with certain federal projects of today, the CWA turned out to be a model of efficiency. CWA workers renovated over 500,000 miles of roads and highways, restored over 40,000 school buildings, and constructed over 150,000 outdoor privies in the South. The CWA spent 86¢ out of every dollar on wages, 11¢ on supplies, and only 3¢ on administrative costs, a record of bureaucratic management that would astonish the most cost-conscious policy planner in the nation's capital today.

Franklin Roosevelt tried other experiments to fight the depression. In October 1933, he implemented the economic theory which advocated government purchase of gold in order to stabilize the dollar and shore up domestic commodity prices. Each day, the president would set the price of gold by announcing the rate the government would pay for the metal. One day, Roosevelt told economic advisor Henry Morgenthau, Jr. to set the day's price at twenty-one cents over that of the previous day because 21 was a lucky number, "three times seven," as Roosevelt explained. According to Morgenthau, this was the manner in which Roosevelt set the daily price of gold for government purchase, more from a combination of "lucky numbers" and sheer guesses than from carefully considered policy. The gold buying did not work. Commodity prices declined, and the president incurred the wrath of both liberals and conservatives who believed his actions economically valueless. In January 1934 Roosevelt decided to end the policy, and he persuaded Congress to enact the Gold Reserve Act. This act set the price of gold at $35 an ounce, thus devaluing the dollar to 59 percent of its pre-Roosevelt purchasing power. It did, however, enable the Federal Reserve Board to increase the amount of currency in circulation, and it provided for more direct Treasury Department control over credit and currency.

In 1934, the Roosevelt administration concentrated more on refining and revising the legislation of 1933, rather than on establishing new programs. For example, the Federal Housing Administration (FHA) was established to insure mortgages for the new construction and repair of houses. In seven years, the FHA insured almost three million mortgages totaling nearly $3 billion. Contrary to popular opinion, the FHA did not insure the homeowner against default. It insured the mortgage company against default by the homeowner. Another new act was the Indian Reorganization Act of 1934. This act attempted to provide for self-government by the Indians living on reservations. It provided for tribal legislation to govern behavior, and allowed tribal customs to determine social mores. Administered by the Bureau of Indian Affairs, the programs gave Indian tribes a measure of control over their own destinies, but because of their abject poverty, they frequently became totally dependent upon government largesse and regulations.

The New Deal proved as much of a political program as an economic one. To implement many of its policies, the 1933 legislation called for a large degree of participation by local interests. The AAA, for example, permitted millions of farmers, including previously disfranchised southern blacks, to vote in crop referendums. More than 100,000 members of local committees administered the AAA's production-control policies. Representatives of business and labor sat together on local boards to oversee the implementation of NRA codes. Hundreds of thousands of local residents participated in the TVA's regional planning experiments. This "grass-roots democracy" possessed the obvious advantage of allowing full citizen participation in many of the main policy decisions of the New Deal, and for Franklin Roosevelt, it gave him an enormous source of political support at the grass roots level. As William Leuchtenburg has observed, it also created innumerable interest groups whose lobbying efforts often forced the president to expand the ever-increasing federal programs at a time when they were no longer needed. In 1942, the farm lobby actually won the administration's support for 110 percent parity during a time when farm profits were high.

The conflicts between the administration's policy of participatory democracy in the management of its programs and the selfish demands made by parochial interest groups was clearly demonstrated in the innumerable petty quarrels and clashes among the groups affected by the NRA. Designed to boost industrial production, increase profits, and reduce unemployment, the NRA achieved none of these goals. Consumers complained about high prices; businessmen protested against government red tape; conservatives argued about the decline of competition; and liberals railed against the lack of effective government controls. In March 1934, President Roosevelt appointed a National Recovery Review Board headed by Clarence Darrow to investigate these complaints and to make recommendations about improving the NRA. The Darrow probe found that large corporations dominated the NRA code boards and used them to stifle competition. Darrow himself advocated government ownership of industry as the solution.

New Deal scholars agree that the Darrow investigation was too biased and inconsistent to correct the NRA's deficiencies. Nonetheless, Roosevelt perceived the NRA's numerous shortcomings. The agency acquiesced in price-fixing by certain businesses, a policy stoutly defended by the businesses and condemned by NRA bureaucrats. The NRA devoted too much time and energy to regulating inconsequential businesses and not enough to regulating the important ones. The NRA's policy of voluntary cooperation with the codes simply did not work. The NRA's fundamental problem lay in the fact that it relied on an idealistic conception of human nature. Those persons directly affected by the NRA, businessmen, laborers, and consumers, all saw the agency as one which should benefit themselves at the expense of the others. Thus, large businesses saw the NRA as an opportunity to eliminate their competitors. Small businesses saw it as an opportunity to exploit labor. Labor saw it as an opportunity to win wage and working-hour concessions. Consumers saw it as an opportunity to establish a permanent system of government-imposed low prices.

Despite its defects, the NRA could not be viewed as a total failure. Its employment programs provided jobs for over two million people. Its pricing policies ended the disastrous deflationary trend of the previous four years. It set national standards for minimum wages and child labor. It produced the first national policy of a maximum work week. Perhaps most significantly, Section 7(a) of the NRA established the principle of collective bargaining between business and organized labor. That section also outlawed the "yellow-dog contract" and prohibited the practice of requiring employees to join company unions. As a consequence, labor union membership in the United States increased by a million people during the NRA's two years of existence. To be sure, Section 7(a) did not legalize collective bargaining, and many companies used methods ranging from legal harrassment to violence to discourage union growth. But the NRA did lay the foundation for future actions of the Roosevelt administration which would enforce the principles of union practice it established.

The AAA provided another example of the conflict between ideal and reality in the New Deal. Under the direction of Agriculture Secretary Henry A. Wallace, the AAA quickly became embedded in the national consciousness because of its initial programs of crop destruction and animal slaughter. Faced with the immediate and urgent problem of a vast oversupply of cotton, Wallace took the only action possible to save several million southern cotton farmers from ruin. He ordered the destruction of some ten million acres of cotton throughout the South, in return for which the AAA paid farmers over $100 million in benefits. In addition, Wallace ordered the slaughter of over six million pigs to shore up pork prices. When squealing pigs overflowed the Chicago stockyards and ran through the city's streets, a horrified nation protested this seemingly senseless and inhuman action.

The AAA, however, proved more than an unfeeling bureaucratic monstrosity. Henry Wallace was an agricultural expert, a noted geneticist and agricultural economist, and he appreciated the desperation with which the nation's farmers appealed to him for assistance. Although he would later turn to the radical left in American politics, Wallace approached the AAA with a decided conservative philosophy, one that cherished the traditional free market policy. Personally opposed to government intervention, Wallace found himself under severe pressure by numerous farmers' organizations to institute compulsory regulation of all aspects of American agriculture. Wallace did not support Senator John Bankhead's bill for compulsory cotton crop reduction, but strong support for the bill by farmers won it congressional passage and presidential approval.

Agriculture Secretary Wallace also had to cope with a serious ideological conflict within the department itself. One faction, headed by AAA administrator George Peek, strongly opposed federal intervention and advocated a free-market approach to agricultural policy. At the opposite end was a faction headed by the assistant secretary, Rexford Guy Tugwell, and by the department's general council, Jerome Frank. Frank had assembled a number of brilliant lawyers who urged massive federal interference. These men included Adlai Stevenson, Thurman Arnold, Abe Fortas, Alger Hiss, and John Abt. Ultimately, the Tugwell-Frank faction prevailed, and the Wallace policies resulted in the removal from cultivation of huge areas of farmland.

The First New Deal: An Assessment

By the end of the year 1934, it had become obvious that the New Deal was essentially a series of political compromises rather than a carefully structured economic program. Franklin Delano Roosevelt had entered the White House with as little commitment to a specific ideological base as possible. He knew little of economic theory and even less of the implications of the policies he espoused. His only goal as president was to combat the Great Depression with whatever measures it took to win the struggle. With an uncanny ability to gauge public opinion, Roosevelt knew that the restoration of public confidence in the institutions of government constituted his most immediate objective. His decisive action in the first one hundred days of his administration fulfilled that objective. For the American people knew that, finally, here was a president who was trying to help them survive the greatest economic calamity in the nation's history.

As Roosevelt biographer James M. Burns observed, the first New Deal was basically a series of compromises designed to satisfy the major interest groups in America. The NRA, for example, specifically geared its policies to the interests of industrialists, and the AAA did the same for farmers. Roosevelt did not intend, nor did he ever attempt, to overthrow any of the existing power structures in America. On the contrary, his New Deal policies during the first two years of his administration were geared toward maintaining that power structure. Thus, the president rejected all suggestions for radical reform, such as nationalization of the banks or the thirty-hour work week. Because of political opposition, Roosevelt also gave little support to such reforms as slum clearance, civil rights for blacks, and redistribution of the national wealth.

If the New Deal maintained the existing social, political, and economic structure of America society, it nevertheless opened avenues of opportunity that had previously been closed. It extended the "single interest" policies of the 1920s to government based on multiple interests. It gave such groups as farmers and labor unions a voice in government that they had never possessed before. It created a new interest group, the federal bureaucracy, that eventually would dominate all the others, for the large numbers of young college graduates who streamed to Washington in 1933 and 1934 brought fresh ideas and a commitment to reform that resulted in programs and policies which broadened the original scope of the New Deal. Finally, as William E. Leuchtenburg remarked, Franklin Roosevelt came to acknowledge the fact that the public interest, as expressed in the government of the United States, overrode all others.

The specific and immediate results of the first New Deal proved mixed. A year after he took office, Franklin Roosevelt could point with pride to the fact that the country had survived the serious recession of 1933 and was beginning to recover. Business activity had climbed by 20 percent, and unemployment had declined by an equal percentage. But in the last eight months of 1934, it appeared that the New Deal had not ended the depression. Business activity faltered and did not improve at all. Industrial production actually declined, and national income stood at only slightly more than half its 1929 level. Over ten million Americans were still unemployed, and the Roosevelt coalition appeared to be coming apart at the seams. By the winter of 1934, the Roosevelt administration faced mounting public disenchantment, the organized opposition of most large businesses, and the very real danger of the possibility of national economic collapse. Consequently, the president and his advisors decided that a new series of reforms would have to be enacted to extend and expand the original New

Deal and to solidify the administration's political position. In early 1935, therefore, the Roosevelt administration began a new program that historians would term the Second New Deal.

Major New Deal Measures

The First 100 Days

March 6, 1933	Bank Closing (by Executive Order)
March 9, 1933	Emergency Banking Relief Act
March 22, 1933	Beer and Wine Revenue Act
March 31, 1933	Unemployment Relief Act (creates Civilian Conservation Corps—CCC)
April 19, 1933	Abandonment of Gold Standard
May 12, 1933	Agricultural Adjustment Act (AAA)
May 18, 1933	Tennessee Valley Authority Act (TVA)
May 27, 1933	Federal Securities Act
June 13, 1933	Home Owners' Refinancing Act (HOLC)
June 16, 1933	National Industrial Recovery Act (NRA; PWA)
June 16, 1933	Glass-Steagall Banking Reform Act (FDIC)

Later New Deal Measures

November 9, 1933	Civil Works Administration (CWA) (by Executive Order)
June 6, 1934	Securities and Exchange Act (SEC)
June 28, 1934	National Housing Act (FHA)
April 30, 1935	Resettlement Administration (by Executive Order)
May 6, 1935	Works Progress Administration (WPA)
July 5, 1935	National Labor Relations (Wagner) Act
August 14, 1935	Social Security Act
February 16, 1936	Second Agricultural Adjustment Act
June 25, 1938	Fair Labor Standards Act

6

The Second New Deal

In the first two years of his presidency, Franklin Roosevelt had brought about a decisive shift in the role of the federal government from a passive to an active one. Roosevelt had won election by promising to do something to combat the depression, and once in office, he fulfilled that promise. In doing so, he shifted the burden of responsibility for the welfare of the American people from private to public shoulders, and he used his magical powers of persuasion to convince the public to accept that historic shift. Although the years 1933 and 1934 witnessed an unprecedented flow of legislation from Washington, most of these early New Deal measures reflected Roosevelt's determination to preserve the capitalistic economic system and mainly took the form of stopgap actions designed to tackle immediate economic crises.

In 1935, the New Deal took a decided swing to the left. Facing mounting opposition from big business, under increasing attack by popular spokesmen of both right and left wing persuasion, seeing the heart of his legislation ruled unconstitutional by the Supreme Court, and knowing that the depression had by no means ended, Roosevelt sought to regain the momentum the first one hundred days of his presidency had generated. Consequently, he and his advisers fashioned a series of new programs whose overall impact on American life proved so significant that historians have given this phase of the New Deal a completely different designation from the earlier ones. Such policies as social security, the Works Progress

Administration, and unemployment compensation committed the Roosevelt administration and its successors to the principles of Keynesian economics and to the permanence of the federal government's role as the single most influential element in American life. So popular was this second New Deal with the electorate that in his bid for reelection in 1936, Roosevelt won by one of the largest majorities in American history.

Thunder on the Right

By the summer of 1934, President Franklin D. Roosevelt's support had begun to decline. The first signs of dissatisfaction came from a coalition of disgruntled businessmen called the American Liberty League. Founded in August 1934, the League was dominated by northern bankers and industrialists who opposed Roosevelt's deficit spending and regulatory policies. Alarmed by such legislation as the Securities and Exchange Act and the Federal Communications Act, these businessmen feared the extent to which Roosevelt intended to regulate their activities. The Liberty League included such anti–New Deal Democrats as Al Smith and John J. Raskob, an officer in the Dupont Chemical Company and a former national chairman of the Democratic party. The League conducted public education programs, disseminated propaganda, and waged a vigorous campaign of newspaper editorials, the general thrust of which asserted that the New Deal constituted a serious threat to fundamental human liberties. Urging a return to the laissez faire policies of the past, the League posed a potential threat to Roosevelt, not because of its mass support, but because of the influence of its members.

Another source of opposition to Roosevelt came from a most unexpected source, a member of the Roman Catholic clergy, a Detroit priest, Father Charles Coughlin (although Coughlin did believe in nationalization of the banks, his anti-Semitism, virulent anticommunism, and vehement opposition to Roosevelt have led most historians to include him with the right wing). By 1934, Coughlin had become America's favorite radio star, his weekly program attracting an estimated forty million listeners. With a rich melodic voice and simplistic solutions to most of the nation's problems, Coughlin appealed to many. His attacks on big business, communism, and the "international conspiracy" struck responsive chords among the jobless and homeless, who found in the priest's broadcasts numerous scapegoats on whom to blame their troubles. Originally a New Deal supporter, Coughlin in 1934 turned to increasingly strident anti-Roosevelt tirades. His denunciations of such presidential advisers as Felix Frankfurter and Henry Morgenthau were delivered under a flimsy veneer of sincerity masking a strident anti-Semitism. As an alternative to the New Deal, Coughlin advocated a vague economic structure resembling the fascist state of Mussolini's Italy. Roosevelt did not fear Coughlin, but he did worry that the popular priest might join forces with his even more dangerous opponents on the left.

Storm Clouds on the Left

Of all of Franklin Roosevelt's political enemies, none proved more sensational than the senior senator from Louisiana, Huey P. Long, Jr. Born in the rural community of Winnfield in 1893, Long grew up in an atmosphere of Populist sentiment. Only twenty-five years old at the time of his election to the Louisiana Railroad Commission, which regulated public carriers and utilities, Long quickly won a reputation as a champion of the poor against the monied interests. Elected governor in 1928, Long destroyed his political opposition through a combination of bribery, intimidation, and disregard for the accepted ethics of democratic politics. Elected to the United States Senate in 1930, Long remained in Louisiana until 1932 because he wanted to consolidate his control at home before he took on the Washington establishment.

The "Kingfish," as Long was commonly called, established in Louisiana a political dictatorship so extensive that he personally controlled state politics to the level of justice of the peace. Huey Long employed methods never before witnessed in American politics. On one occasion, he had an opponent kidnapped to prevent him from disclosing information damaging to the Long machine. On another, he sent several hundred National Guardsmen, armed with Thompson submachine guns, to "supervise" an election in New Orleans. Journalists soon began comparing him to Adolf Hitler. At the same time that he destroyed the checks and balances of the democratic process, Huey Long retained the support of the people of Louisiana because he provided them with certain benefits long overdue: roads, bridges, hospitals, and schools. Unlike many other southern demagogues, whose performance in office proved as empty as the fullness of their campaign promises, Huey Long made good on his promises. On the campaign stump and at press conferences, Long often played the part of a clown and buffoon, but underneath this facade lay one of the most dangerous and sinister forces ever to gain power in America.

Long backed Roosevelt in the 1932 election but broke with him soon after. In Franklin Roosevelt, Huey Long saw the most formidable obstacle to his own aspirations to the White House, and he did everything possible to obstruct the passage of New Deal legislation. At first, Roosevelt paid little attention to the "Kingfish" because Long's opposition appeared as futile as the solo filibusters he staged against the president's bills. By 1935, however, Long had built up a large national following through his Share Our Wealth program, which called for a limitation on the maximum wealth permitted anyone. All excess wealth would be confiscated by the government and the revenue generated would be used to provide every family with a house, a radio, and an automobile, the elderly with a pension, and "worthy boys" with a college education. Despite its faulty economics, Share Our Wealth had enormous appeal, and by early 1935, Long claimed a total membership of over seven million in his 27,000 Share Our Wealth clubs. Although the claim was undoubtedly exaggerated, no one doubted Long's growing popularity, and a poll commissioned for the Democratic party revealed that in the 1936 election, Long might draw enough third-party votes away from Roosevelt to swing the election to the Republicans. Long's assassination on September 8, 1935 removed this threat from Roosevelt's plans for reelection.

Another left-wing critic of the New Deal was Dr. Francis Townsend of Long Beach, California. In January 1934, Townsend and a real estate promoter, Robert Clements, proposed that every citizen over the age of sixty be paid a pension of $200 a month, provided he retire from work and spend the money in the United States. The pension would be financed by a 2 percent tax on business transactions. Townsend claimed that the program would provide jobs for the young through the retirement of the old and that the pension funds would shore up the economy. Townsend's proposal won widespread support, and the doctor posed another potential hazard to Roosevelt's chances for reelection.

A New New Deal

Although Coughlin, Long, and Townsend won public support, the vast majority of Americans remained loyal to the president. The depression had not ended, but Roosevelt had instilled public confidence in himself and his programs. His New Deal had remained in the mainstream of American political history, following a moderate, middle-of-the-road path between the extremism of the right and left. The congressional elections of 1934 supplied a concrete example of Roosevelt's continuing popularity. Misinterpreting the massive publicity given to Coughlin, Long, and Townsend, many political "experts" predicted that the Republicans and anti-Roosevelt Democratics would score impressive gains. Instead, the election results showed the Democrats gaining thirteen seats in the House and nine in the Senate, an unprecedented gain for a president in the middle of his first term in office.

Despite this mandate, Roosevelt realized that more needed to be done. With his intuitive flair for sensing the public mood, the president knew that the voters' patience would not last forever and that in the forthcoming 1936 election, he might find himself, like Hoover, in the position of not being reelected. The main reason for this apprehension was that somehow the New Deal was not working. The PWA, CCC, FERA, and CWA had not succeeded in turning the tide against the Great Depression. Millions of Americans remained jobless, and the prospects for recovery appeared dim. All over the country, the signs of popular discontent grew more and more ominous. In 1934, labor unions staged a series of destructive strikes, many of them bloody and violent. In the Midwest, farmers' cooperatives organized violent protests against the continuing depression in agriculture. In Congress, a host of radical bills was introduced, offering revolutionary solutions to the nation's economic maladies.

Amidst this atmosphere of growing discontent, Franklin Roosevelt and his advisors in 1935 turned to a new and much more comprehensive attempt to restore prosperity by enacting a series of programs that historians have labeled the second New Deal. The distinction between the two New Deals deserves attention. In 1933 and 1934, the Roosevelt administration faced emergencies almost daily. When Roosevelt took office, the nation's banking system was on the verge of collapse. The unemployment and housing crises had grown to disastrous proportions. Despondency and despair pervaded the public spirit. The first New Deal, therefore, comprised a series of programs designed to meet existing emergencies and resulted from a sense of urgency, rather than from attempts to institute a new economic philosophy. Roosevelt never intended that these New Deal programs would be anything but temporary expedients designed to provide short-term assistance to needy persons. In addition, Roosevelt had a mandate for action and believed that it was essential for him to demonstrate to the American people his commitment to that action. He believed experimentation necessary, even if the experiment failed. The essence of the first New Deal, then, lay in action, experiment, and immediacy. The second New Deal originated out of a more sustained attempt to chart the nation on a permanent course of avoiding depression. Instead of the make-work, stop-gap measures that characterized the first New Deal, the second New

Deal comprised policies designed to effect a permanent change in the traditional non-interventionist role of the federal government. By 1935, Roosevelt had come to accept the inevitability and desireability of deficit spending as an effective device to combat depression. He also discarded his personal antipathy toward government welfare and supported the concept that in the federal government lay the ultimate responsibility for the well-being of its citizens. With the exception of the WPA, the second New Deal measures were carefully planned and deliberately designed to make permanent the crucial role the federal government played in national policy.

Of all the New Deal programs, none had as extensive and immediate an impact as the Works Progress Administration (WPA). Authorized under the Emergency Relief Appropriation Act of 1935, the WPA resulted from the continuing crisis in the unemployment situation. With an ingrained opposition to the idea of a government dole, i.e., direct assistance to the jobless, Roosevelt threw his weight behind a massive public works program designed to provide employment to some three and a half million Americans. The president believed that since the private sector could not employ these people, it was the duty of the government to hire them. The act gave him the largely discretionary authority to spend over $5 billion in public works funds. To administer the program, he selected his mercurial, chain-smoking assistant and most trusted confidante, Harry L. Hopkins.

As he had with the earlier CWA, Hopkins reduced the red tape to a minimum and used his abundant energy to get the WPA started as soon as possible. Within two months after its inception, the WPA employed over a million people in public works projects of an almost incredible variety. During its seven years of existence, the WPA built or renovated over 2,000 hospitals, 6,000 schools, 1,000 airports, and 13,000 playgrounds. These figures scarcely begin to tell the story of the WPA, whose scope was enormous and whose projects reached into almost every community in America. Few Americans had not heard of the WPA, and fewer still did not benefit from some of its projects. Altogether, the WPA employed over seven million persons, with an average of 2.1 million working at any given moment. It spent over $11 billion on over 250,000 projects. WPA crews paved streets and sidewalks, refurbished dilapidated government buildings, and constructed such federal facilities as the Mall, the Museum of Science and Technology, the National Archives, and the Jefferson Memorial in Washington, D.C. Its projects ranged from the frivolous to the grandiose, and they included footbridges over isolated streams to the massive Triborough Bridge in New York City. The WPA's impact extended far beyond the obvious economic one. Many of the jobs taught new skills to people who would put those skills to use during World War II. Many of the WPA's subagencies performed invaluable tasks. The Historic Records Office uncovered and preserved millions of priceless manuscripts and documents. Unemployed historians interviewed some 3,000 former slaves still living, and the transcripts of those interviews, the WPA slave narratives, offer a unique and precious repository of oral history sources on the institution of slavery. The Rural Electrification Administration (REA), established by the president in 1935, employed WPA labor in extending electrical power to over 40 percent of the nation's farms by 1940 (fewer than 10 percent had electrical power in 1934). The Federal Writer's Project employed hundreds of young scholars, who published a host of well-written and innovative local and state guidebooks. The Federal Theatre hired unemployed actors, directors, and stagehands to bring plays and other theatrical productions to millions of people all over the country. The Federal Art Project gave work to artists and sculptors to create public statues, murals, and paintings. The National Youth Administration (NYA) hired over two million high school and college students for jobs ranging from filing papers to constructing observatories. Such renowned Americans as the writers John Cheever and Richard Wright, and the artists, Jackson Pollock and Stuart Davis, first came to critical attention through their participation in WPA projects.

Impressive as were its accomplishments, the WPA never came close to fulfilling Roosevelt's goal of providing jobs for all the able-bodied unemployed. At its peak, the WPA employed only three million of the ten million jobless Americans. The jobs provided were temporary and paid little more than the dole. For millions who worked in WPA projects, once their projects were completed, they once again joined the ranks of the unemployed. To cut costs and to expedite work, the WPA did not plan its projects carefully and paid little attention to aesthetics. Consequently, America was covered with a uniformly stale pattern of dull grey government buildings and red brick schoolhouses. Nevertheless, more than any other New Deal program, the WPA changed popular attitudes about the responsibility of government to its citizens in need.

Social Security

In August 1935, Franklin Roosevelt signed into law the most far-reaching piece of legislation of his New Deal, the Social Security Act. Ever since his inauguration, Roosevelt had been urged by some of his advisors, most notably Secretary of Labor Frances Perkins, to promote a nationwide system of retirement income for the elderly. In June 1934, the president appointed a Committee on Economic Security headed by Perkins to devise a national social insurance program. With little dissension, the committee formulated a plan for old-age and survivors' insurance to provide federal assistance to those categories of Americans most in need. After much controversy, the committee also adopted a plan for unemployment compensation, jointly financed and administered by the federal and state governments. Roosevelt incorporated the committee's recommendations into the Social Security bill and presented it to Congress in January 1935. Conservatives denounced the bill as an unnecessary display of federal largesse, and liberals attacked its lack of substantial funding, but such administration supporters as Senator Robert Wagner of New York steered it through to passage.

The Social Security Act established a national system of compulsory taxation, unemployment compensation, and old-age pensions. The old-age pension section of the act covered persons sixty-five years old and over, who would receive a monthly pension financed by taxes on employers' payrolls and employees' paychecks, with equal sums paid by each. With the exceptions of federal, state, and local government employees, domestic servants, farm laborers, merchant seamen, and employees of nonprofit institutions, all workers in America and their employers were required to belong to the system. The taxes would start at 1 percent of income under $3,000 through 1939 and would increase to 1.5 percent through 1942, to 2 percent through 1945, and up to 3 percent through 1948. The pensions, which would not begin until 1942, would range from $10 to $85 per month, depending on wages earned, the amount paid into the system, and the total number of years the retiree had been covered by Social Security. For older Americans not eligible for Social Security, the measure provided that they be paid pensions averaging $20 per month. Because workers outnumbered retirees by twelve to one in 1935, the system's actuarial experts estimated that the excess of taxes collected over pensions would have built up a trust fund of almost $50 billion by 1980.

Another main feature of Social Security was a nationwide system of unemployment compensation to assist those people temporarily unable to find work. The program provided for payments of $15 to $18 per week for a maximum of twelve to twenty-six weeks per year. The financing for unemployment came from a tax on employers of 3 percent of payroll. Of the revenue generated, 90 percent would go to federally approved state unemployment systems, and 10 percent would go to the federal treasury. The federal sum would, in turn, be distributed to the states to help finance their programs during periods of heavy unemployment. Each state was allowed to supplement the federal payments with its own funds.

The Roosevelt administration viewed the key feature of social security, the old-age pension, as a measure designed to supplement retirees' income, and not as the main source of those incomes. Roosevelt, however, did not present the program to the American people in that manner. Instead, he trumpeted social security as the panacea for the financial ailments of older Americans. The government also promoted social security as an insurance program (its official title was Old Age and Survivors' Insurance). People were misled into viewing the program as identical to one offered by a private insurance company, in which each individual pays premiums, which are kept in a personal account and accumulate over the years to pay the amount of money stipulated in the policy. Social security contained none of these features. What the government euphemistically called "contributions" were, in fact, mandatory tax deductions from wages and payrolls. The government advertised the rate of taxation as 1 or 2 percent, when the actual figure was double that, since employers and employees paid equal sums. Unlike private insurance, social security did not have individual accounts, and beneficiaries were not automatically entitled to benefits. In addition, the maximum taxable wage was $3,000, making the tax a regressive one, thus confiscating a far higher percentage of the income of the poor, while the pensions, based on income, rewarded the wealthy. The founders of social security also badly miscalculated future demographic trends, which by 1982 had reduced the ratio of workers to retirees to three to one, thus jeopardizing the system's financial integrity. Finally, social security quickly turned into an irresistible political magnet attracting future administrations, including Roosevelt's second, in 1939, to expand benefits. and recipients without providing the funding necessary to pay for them.

Nevertheless, social security constituted a true watershed in the history of social responsibility in America. It established as a cardinal principal of social policy that certain categories of Americans—the elderly, widows, orphans—had a fundamental right to receive assistance from their government. Social security may have, as some of its critics alleged, made the welfare state a permanent part of United States domestic policy, but it was a policy overwhelmingly endorsed by the American people. Social security also brought the United States into the modern world, as it was the last major industrial country in the world to inaugurate such a program.

The New Deal and Labor

Working men and women strongly supported Roosevelt, and he endorsed their demands for higher wages and better working conditions. Roosevelt knew that his prospects for reelection in 1936 rested on his ability to retain their support. For most of the nation's workers, such programs as FERA, PWA, and WPA were popular and necessary measures to cope with the immediate and urgent problems of the depression. But these and other New Deal programs did not treat the fundamental problems faced by labor: low wages, long working hours, and unacceptable conditions in the workplace. For many, the answer lay in joining unions, but when Roosevelt took office, organized labor appeared powerless to achieve its ends. Early in his presidency, Roosevelt tried to invigorate organized labor. The famous Section 7(*a*) of the NRA sanctioned collective bargaining, but the NRA's voluntary nature and the personal antipathy toward labor by its director, Hugh Johnson, obviated serious government enforcement of the section. After a series of wildcat strikes in 1934 and early 1935, Roosevelt appointed two labor boards, one headed by Lloyd Garrison, the dean of the Wisconsin Law School, the other by Francis Biddle, a Philadelphia attorney, to investigate the issue. Both men held that Section 7(*a*) mandated employers

Police and hired thugs fight with union strikers, Pittsburgh, 1933. *Library of Congress*

to bargain in good faith with union representatives and that the union chosen by the majority of workers in a plant serve as the official representative of all that plant's employees. Most leading industries simply ignored these edicts, and Garrison and Biddle had no power to enforce them.

The year 1934 witnessed a large number of violent strikes. Angered by management's unyielding opposition to collective bargaining, large groups of union members staged sitdowns, strikes, and other more violent and visible signs of labor discontent. In Milwaukee, streetcar operators deliberately wrecked dozens of the vehicles. In Philadelphia, New York, and other cities, rioting taxi drivers burned hundreds of cabs. In Des Moines, electrical workers sabotaged the city's main power plant, plunging the area into total darkness. A massive textile workers' strike shut down plants in twenty states. In Minneapolis, striking Teamsters staged sitdowns and demonstrations which erupted into open violence. The ensuing riots left four dead and sixty-five injured. In California, longshoremen initiated a general strike that paralyzed the city of San Francisco. John L. Lewis's United Mine Workers threatened bloody action against the coal industry.

By the early spring of 1935, Roosevelt decided to stand firmly behind the unions and endorsed the National Labor Relations Bill. With the president's support, the bill passed Congress and became law in July 1935. Commonly called the Wagner Act because of its vigorous support by Senator Robert Wagner, the measure established the principle of collective bargaining and made labor unions, as distinguished from company unions, the official bargaining agents of all industry employees. It outlawed such management practices as blacklisting or firing employees who attempted to organize unions, and it gave the majority union in a factory the exclusive bargaining authority for all the factory's employees. Finally, it set up a National Labor Relations Board to arbitrate labor-management disputes and to force companies to give official recognition to unions. A milestone in the history of organized labor in America, the Wagner Act placed the full weight of the federal government behind the union movement and enforced the longtime goal of unions to represent America's laboring classes.

Most labor unions belonged to two national labor organizations. For many years, the American Federation of Labor (AFL) served as the only national organization. But when its longtime leader, Samuel L. Gompers, died in 1924, the AFL leadership split into two factions. The majority endorsed the efforts to recruit such craft and trade workers as plumbers, electricians, and carpenters, and refused to support the unionization of industrial employees. Because of the AFL's intransigience, John L. Lewis, the fiery head of the UMW, and Walter Reuther, the aggressive recruiter for the United Automobile Workers (UAW), led the drive for a national organization of industrial unions. Their efforts resulted in the November 1935 creation of the Congress of Industrial Organizations (CIO). By 1940, the CIO included in its ranks unions representing steel workers, miners, automobile workers, longshoremen, and clothing employees. The establishment of the CIO helped boost union membership in the United States from about three million in 1930 to almost ten million in 1940.

No other event better illustrated organized labor's newly won independence than the unionization of the automobile industry. In 1936, the CIO incorporated the recently founded United Automobile Workers, and the union tried to negotiate a bargaining agreement with General Motors. After several fruitless sessions with management representatives, it became apparent that the company refused to act in good faith. In 1937, most General Motors employees staged a massive sitdown strike, which helped convince the company to capitulate and formally recognize the UAW as the official bargaining agent for all its blue collar employees. The union won similar concessions from Ford and Chrysler. In like manner, unions won bargaining control over such industries as steel, rubber, shipping, and textiles. The Wagner Act and Roosevelt's strong support won for him and his Democratic party the electoral support of organized labor, support that has been of critical importance in making the party the majority one in American politics for most of the time since the New Deal.

The 1936 Election

The second New Deal was immensely popular with the American people and Franklin Roosevelt and the Democratic Party looked forward to the presidential election of 1936 with eager anticipation. At the Democratic National Convention, President Roosevelt and Vice-President Garner were renominated by acclamation. The Republicans nominated Governor Alfred "Alf" Landon of Kansas for president and newspaper publisher Frank Knox for vice-president. Although much of the national press endorsed Landon and a *Literary Digest* poll showed Landon winning, most observers did not hesitate to predict a Roosevelt victory. A master campaigner in his own right, Roosevelt capitalized on public support for the New Deal, and the voters rewarded him with one of the most resounding landslide victories in American history. Roosevelt carried every state but Maine and

Vermont and led Landon in popular votes by 27 million to 16 million and in electoral votes by 523 to 8. The Democrats won huge majorities in both houses of Congress and relegated the Republicans to virtual political extinction.

The New Deal and the Supreme Court

By the time of his inauguration in January 1937, Franklin Roosevelt saw his great electoral mandate threatened by the United States Supreme Court. Because of the New Deal's revolutionary reversal of the historic laissez faire role of the government in the economy, it came as no surprise that numerous businessmen filed lawsuits challenging the constitutionality of such measures as NRA, SEC, FCC, etc. Mainly conservative advocates of a continuation of the policies of the past, those who brought suit found a willing ally in the Supreme Court. Dominated by its conservative majority, the court clung to the traditional judicial reluctance to authorize the federal government to regulate the economy. In January 1935, the court provided an indication of things to come when it invalidated Section 9(a) of NRA, which conferred regulatory powers with the force of law on certain federal agencies. The court held that the provision gave legislative authority to the executive branch and thus violated the separation of powers principle of the Constitution. In May 1935, the court struck down the Railroad Retirement Act on the grounds that it deprived railroad companies of property without due process of law.

New Dealers were alarmed by these decisions, but they were astounded by three handed down on May 27, 1935, a date they would call "Black Monday." In one case, the court nullified the Farm Mortgage Act because it deprived creditors of property without due process. In another decision, the court ruled that the president could not remove a member of the Federal Trade Commission because independent regulatory agencies were extensions of legislative, rather than executive powers. The most far-reaching of the "Black Monday" decisions was the famous Schechter case (*A.L.A. Schechter Company* v. *U.S.*) The Schechter brothers, poultry wholesalers from Brooklyn, were convicted for violating the NRA's Live Poultry Code by selling diseased chickens and by disregarding the NRA's wage and hours regulations. The court overturned their conviction on two grounds. First, the Schechter Company operated solely within the state of New York and thus could not be regulated by Congress because Article I of the Constitution gives Congress the power to regulate only interstate commerce. Second, the regulatory powers conferred on the president acting through the NRA agencies exceeded his constitutional authority. The decision in effect invalidated the NRA since all of its provisions regulating business activity fell under the Schechter guidelines.

Outraged by the Schechter decision, President Roosevelt publicly denounced the Supreme Court, but the justices refused to submit to this pressure. In January 1936, they made another momentous decision by ruling the AAA unconstitutional because the production of farm goods did not fall under the accepted definition of interstate commerce. In May 1936, the court prohibited the federal regulation of coal mining, and in June, it outlawed a New York law mandating a minimum wage for women and children.

Upset by these decisions and armed with the mandate of his landslide reelection victory, Franklin Roosevelt turned in January 1937 to his "court-packing" scheme. Determined to overcome judicial opposition to the New Deal, the president proposed a Judiciary Reorganization bill to Congress. The bill gave the president the authority to appoint a new federal judge whenever an incumbent judge failed to retire within six months upon attaining the age of seventy. The bill limited the number of his appointments to fifty and the maximum number of new Supreme Court appointees to six. The measure was nothing more than an unsubtle attempt to fill the federal courts with pro–New Deal judges, and it aroused a storm of opposition throughout the country. Liberal Democrats joined conservative Republicans in denouncing Roosevelt's scheme to upset the delicate constitutional separation of powers through executive manipulation in the judicial branch. Despite warnings by his congressional floor leaders that the bill had no chance of passage, Roosevelt persisted and did not agree to its tabling by a House committee until the Senate rejected it by the overwhelming vote of 72 to 20. The Supreme Court won the battle, but the New Deal won the war. In 1937, many of the justices reversed their anti–New Deal stance, and the court affirmed the right of Congress to regulate wages and hours, and it greatly expanded the interpretation of interstate commerce. Within two years, five justices retired, and Roosevelt replaced them with such men as Hugo Black and William O. Douglas to give the court a decidedly liberal majority.

Several historians, including Arthur Schlesinger, Jr., and Arthur S. Link, have condemned Roosevelt's "court-packing" scheme as an unwarranted attempt to control the judiciary. At the same time, these historians have sympathized with Roosevelt's frustrations with a Supreme Court seemingly bent on destroying the New Deal. In reality, the court faced a difficult constitutional dilemma: whether to carry on the traditional strict-constructionist interpretation of the Constitution, or to broaden its view of the law. At first, the court chose the former alternative, but indicated its willingness to accommodate the law to changing circumstances. The retirement of the five conservatives perhaps reflected their realization that a new generation of jurists must cope with the legal problems raised by the New Deal.

The Passing of the New Deal

In the congressional sessions of 1937 and 1938, President Roosevelt submitted the last of his New Deal proposals, most of which were enacted. The Bankhead-Jones Farm Tenancy Act reorganized the Resettlement Administration into the Farm Security Administration, which extended rehabilitation loans to farmers and helped migrant workers to relocate. It also launched rural medical cooperatives and assisted farm cooperatives in purchasing grain elevators. Of greater significance was the second Agricultural Adjustment Act of 1938. It provided financial aid to farmers who curtailed production, and it set up quotas for cotton, corn, wheat, tobacco, and rice. This second AAA, sustained as constitutional by the Supreme Court, established the fundamental policies for future federal agricultural programs: federal subsidies to farmers who curtailed production; crop and acreage reduction; and the purchasing of surplus crops by the government according to a "parity" formula. A final measure in 1938 was the Fair Labor Standards Act, which set a national minimum wage of twenty-five cents an hour for most workers (to be gradually raised to forty cents), limited the work week to forty-four hours, and outlawed child labor in all businesses engaged in interstate commerce.

For the supporters of the New Deal, 1938 proved a disappointing year. Roosevelt faced mounting opposition from a Congress increasingly dominated by a coalition of southern Democrats and northern Republicans, which succeeded in blocking many of his proposals. Weakened by a severe recession, the economy remained sluggish, and it became apparent that the American people no longer regarded the New Deal with the same enthusiasm as in the past. In the November 1938 congressional elections, the Republicans gained eighty-one seats in the House, eight in the Senate, and thirteen governorships. At the beginning of 1939, Franklin Roosevelt, his attention now focused more on foreign than domestic issues, declared an end to any further New Deal legislation.

The New Deal in American History

The New Deal had an enormous impact on American history and has attracted considerable attention from historians. The earlier writings about the New Deal generally came from former Roosevelt associates such as Frances Perkins, who portrayed him with unadulterated admiration, and Raymond Moley, who criticized the leftward tendencies of the second New Deal. The more serious scholarly studies also often fall into the pro- and anti-Roosevelt categories. For example, Arthur Schlesinger, Jr.'s trilogy clearly reflects his liberal Democratic bias, while recent studies by younger revisionist historians reflect their overall cynicism about all phases of American history. The most balanced accounts describe the era of the New Deal as the confused, contradictory, and momentous period that it was. The following is a general overview of the New Deal according to the most authoritative studies by such scholars as William E. Leuchtenburg, James MacGregor Burns, and Frank Freidel.

In less than six years, the administration of President Franklin Roosevelt dramatically and permanently reversed the historic paths taken by the federal government for the previous century and a half, gave a new direction to American life, and graphically demonstrated the meaning of government responsibility. In an unprecedented display of federal action, the Roosevelt administration turned out legislation at a dizzying pace and implemented it with even greater alacrity. For the first time in American history, the poor and neglected masses received attention and concrete assistance from their government. The bold strokes of New Deal legislation unleashed social, economic, and political forces that would dictate the main trends of American life for the next half century. The New Deal laid the foundations for the Fair Deal, the New Frontier, and the Great Society, and not until the administration of President Ronald Reagan has anyone dared challenge the New Deal's basic assumptions about the proper role of government.

None of this would have been possible without Franklin Roosevelt, and any attempt to place the New Deal in historical perspective must begin with a review of his personality and character. Roosevelt was a great paradox of a man: bold and timid, candid and deceptive, a master planner who lacked organization, the architect of the modern bureaucracy and a poor administrator. By making the presidency the center of national attention, he started the movement toward what certain scholars call the modern "imperial presidency." Through his remarkable and uncanny sense of the popular mood, he swayed and manipulated the public to support him and his policies. Through his magnetic personality, he became the idol and hope of millions at a time when despair gripped the national psyche. Through his adroit use of patronage and persuasion, he dominated Congress to an extent unmatched since the days of Thomas Jefferson. Essentially a pragmatic person, Roosevelt often had no idea of the consequences of his actions, but he grasped the reins of power as firmly as has any president, for he knew that, above all, he must act decisively during that time of extreme national emergency. Perhaps most significantly, he provided America with the leadership it so desperately needed and in so doing, he helped to preserve the basic institutions of American society.

Richard Hofstadter, Eric Goldman, and Arthur Link are among the many historians who have portrayed Franklin Roosevelt and the New Deal as the fruition of the great Progressive reform movement championed by Theodore Roosevelt, Robert La Follette, and Woodrow Wilson. In their view, Roosevelt, himself a product of the Progressive era, carried on the work begun by these and other earlier reformers, and the New Deal was not so much an innovation, as a continuation of the policies of the past. The AAA, for example, simply refined an agricultural program that had been advocated by William E. Borah and other Progressives. The TVA was an obvious stepchild of George Norris's power proposals. The New Deal welfare and public works programs borrowed heavily from earlier Progressive experiments with such private arrangements as Jane Addams's Hull House. And the New Deal regulatory agencies built on the Progressive models of the Food and Drug Administration, the Federal Reserve Board, and similar agencies.

Some recent historical studies concentrate on the less beneficial aspects of the New Deal. Paul Conkin and Edgar Robinson criticized Roosevelt for his lack of serious economic planning, so evident in the makeshift manner in which many of the programs were assembled. Conkin and Robinson also fault Roosevelt for his unbridled faith in the ability of government to solve human problems. Milton Friedman and Anna Schwartz have written a brilliant critique of Roosevelt's monetary policies, and Friedman has given an incisive and critical analysis of the New Deal's "cradle to grave" philosophy of government assistance. Friedman argues that instead of solving problems, the New Deal aggravated them because it destroyed the incentives necessary to lasting prosperity. Francis Fox Piven and Richard Clowen have exhaustively studied the New Deal public works programs and concluded that they represented little more than sops to assuage public opinion.

The New Deal did not, of course, create the utopia some of its more idealistic enthusiasts expected, nor did it eradicate greed, poverty, and class division. The New Deal did not, in fact, even end the Great Depression. A serious economic recession in 1937 and 1938 destroyed much of the progress made since 1933, and some four million persons remained unemployed at the end of 1941. It has been argued that none of the New Deal measures effectively solved the nation's economic problems and that recovery resulted from the normal course of business cycles rather than from federal intervention. These conservative critics go on to assert that World War II, rather than the New Deal, ended the depression, and that the recovery measures of the Roosevelt administration provided only temporary relief. On the other hand, Schlesinger and other defenders of the New Deal point out that Roosevelt built into the economy certain stabilizers that have prevented the recurrence of a depression for over forty years, the longest such cycle in American history. They argue further that the reason the New Deal did not end unemployment was that Roosevelt did not engage in deficit spending of a magnitude sufficient to end it. The case for Keynesian economics, they assert, was made during World War II, when the enormous deficits—$18 billion in 1942 and $54 billion in 1943—produced full employment and prosperity.

The lack of careful planning was evident in many New Deal programs. The AAA, for example, did not resolve the perennial problem of low prices and overproduction. Despite its efforts to induce farmers to curtail production, the AAA succeeded only in aggravating the problem. In 1940, total farm production and total farm income was less than that in the recession year of 1937. The TVA also did not reflect careful planning. Although it did bring electrical power and flood control to one of the nation's most depressed areas, TVA displaced hundreds of thousands of persons and failed to improve significantly the economy of the Appalachian region, which remains even today a center of poverty. Some New Deal programs, on the other hand, proved bold and imaginative. The CCC not only provided employment to young men, it helped to conserve vast tracts of land and forests. The PWA became renowned for cost effectiveness and for the engineering excellence of its construction projects.

Against the plight of minorities, especially blacks, the New Deal failed to fulfill its promise of a better life for all Americans. Blacks, of course, received federal assistance, but their overall economic status actually declined during the 1930s. In establishing the New Deal programs, Congress stipulated that racial discrimination be prohibited, but Roosevelt capitulated to the demands of southern politicians that they exercise control over local projects and that southerners receive lower wages than northerners in such

Racial segregation, movie theater in Leland, Mississippi, 1939. *National Archives*

A Virginia farm family, 1936. *National Archives*

programs as PWA and WPA. This agreement inevitably resulted in severe discrimination against blacks. The AAA subsidies, for example, went to white landowners rather than to black tenants. The CCC camps in the South were racially segregated. In all New Deal projects in the South, whites received priority treatment in obtaining jobs. And the Resettlement Administration forcibly removed hundreds of thousands of black tenants and sharecroppers from the land they tilled, with no provisions for their future economic security.

Under Franklin Roosevelt, the office of President of the United States became the focus of federal authority. Through his fireside chats, his numerous press conferences, and his ability to capture headlines, Roosevelt gave the presidency an aura of respect and responsibility that it had generally lacked before. Even after the passage of the Government Reorganization Act of 1939, which created the modern White House staff, Roosevelt administered the executive branch with a minimum of bureaucracy. He gave the presidency a personal touch which brought the office permanently into the public eye.

When he took office, Franklin Roosevelt found the nation in a frantic, desperate state. By vigorously endorsing the concept of government as the instrument of the general welfare, he set the nation back on its historical path. He also, as Arthur Schlesinger, Jr., recently stated, made experimentation the method of democracy. His reference to "bold, persistent experimentation" as the key to government action expressed his view of the New Deal. Historians who link the New Deal to Progressivism or to

Sharecroppers' shacks, Laurel, Mississippi, 1936. *Library of Congress*

Keynesian economics attribute it with a philosophy it did not possess. Above all, the New Deal was a twentieth century application of the historic values of individual initiative and "Yankee ingenuity." With virtually no precedents to guide their actions, the New Dealers had to improvise and experiment. What is surprising is not that they failed to resolve all the problems confronting them, but how successful they generally were. Their ingenuity in implementing the directives of the president and Congress was evident everywhere in the nature and scope of the programs they organized and directed. Theirs was essentially a pragmatic approach, a great experiment, and they were as likely to admit their failures as they were to advertise their successes. Above all, they rejected the quick and easy solutions of the Marxists and Socialists who wanted to overthrow the existing order. Instead, they performed their great experiment within the existing social and economic structure, thus preserving and protecting American institutions against the ideologies who wanted to destroy them.

Like any significant event in history, the New Deal cannot be easily explained and categorized. Whether sympathetic or hostile, those historians who depict it in simplified fashion miss its extraordinary complexity. The temper of the times demanded action, and Franklin Delano Roosevelt supplied it with the New Deal. And through his forceful and masterly use of the powers of the presidency, he educated the American people to accept a new way of life.

7

American Life and Society: 1930–1945

During the years of the Great Depression and World War II, American society underwent many changes. The depression wreaked economic havoc, and people everywhere altered their traditional lifestyles to accommodate to the new economic realities. For several million Americans, one of those realities lay in moving. To seek better opportunity, large numbers of people moved to other parts of the country where they believed jobs could be found. The greatest changes came in the South and in the Great Plains, as hundreds of thousands of farming families fled from tenancy and sharecropping to look for work in northern industrial cities. Farmers and ranchers from the Texas panhandle and the Oklahoma plains looked to the burgeoning industries and agricultural enterprises in California as a means of escape from the giant dust storms that ravaged their communities and homesteads. The war also stimulated social mobility, as millions left small farms and rural communities to man assembly lines in the large cities.

Culturally, the 1930s and early 1940s saw an era of great productivity. Novelists, poets, and playwrights expressed the national mood of disillusionment and despair through works noted as much for their cynical approach to life as for their literary excellence. Others yearned nostalgically for an idyllic agrarian society which they imagined had existed in antebellum America. Whatever their viewpoint, these writers belonged to one of the golden ages of literature in American history. Most, however, failed to reach the masses, who turned in increasing numbers from literature to radio and the movies as their favorite forms of cultural entertainment. Both provided people with a release from the pressures and tensions of everyday life through romances, musicals, and comedies. Sports also gave people an outlet for amusement, and the era became known for its athletic heroes.

In other aspects of life, the thirties and forties also witnessed significant change. The end of the Prohibition era gave organized crime an increasing control over illegal activities. Education suffered a serious, although temporary, reversal because of drastic cutbacks in attendance and funding. Organized religion adopted a more active social conscience, and many of the nation's leading theologians questioned traditional values. During the war, the American people united in the great national effort against the enemy, but beneath the facade of national unity lay emerging forces that portended revolutionary changes in postwar America.

Social Trends

From the time the first colonists landed in the early seventeenth century through 1930, the United States had experienced a continuing population explosion. Economic, political, and social opportunity had made America seem like a Promised Land, and the abundance of natural resources and riches had attracted millions. Extremely high birth rates and mushrooming immigration had produced population increases of at least 16 percent in every ten-year census between 1790 and 1920. From 1930 to 1945, this historic trend ceased abruptly, and the population increase for the period was only slightly higher than the normally expected higher incidence of births than of deaths. The reasons were obvious. Not only had the immigration legislation of the 1920s severely restricted immigration into the United States, the depression hardly made America a desirable place to which to emigrate. Additionally, the depression had placed such severe economic burdens on people that many took advantage of the availability of birth control devices to limit family size. The war years also saw a population slowdown, brought on mainly from the departure for service in the armed forces of over ten million married men. Their return home after the war, of course, witnessed a return to normal, and the late 1940s produced what is often called the "baby boom."

American families had always been on the move. The westward movement in American history has been documented by historians as one of the most significant features of the nation's social development. By 1930, the traditional journey of pioneering families had long since ended, but the decade did observe a mass movement of the American people from one place to another. The countless factory shutdowns, mortgage foreclosures, and job abolishments forced millions of people to travel to other parts of the country. For many urban Americans, life began anew in the miserable shanties of the Hoovervilles that blighted metropolitan landscapes. For many rural families, mortgage foreclosures left them no choice but to move to new places. For southern tenant farmers and sharecroppers, black and white, the severe agricultural depression uprooted them from land their families had tilled for generations. For hundreds of thousands of farmers from Texas, Oklahoma, Kansas, Colorado, and New Mexico, fearsome dust storms buried their farms and ruined their land.

Everywhere, it seemed, Americans were leaving the traditional family home. Many were like the Kentucky coal miner who lamented leaving his home town, but felt he had no choice. With no income for six months, his family had been reduced to eating violets, forget-me-nots, and "such weeds as cows eat." Others resembled the Arkansas sharecropper, who with his wife and young son, loaded their meager belongings into two pushcarts and walked some nine hundred miles to the Rio Grande cotton fields seeking work. Many thousands of men left their families behind and sneaked rides in railroad freight cars to destinations unknown. One example was the folksinger Woody Guthrie, who left his wife and son at their small home in Oklahoma, caught a freight car, and eventually came to California. With its lush, fertile agricultural fields and booming movie industry, California appeared to many to live up to its nickname, "The Golden State." Just as news of the discovery of gold near Jacob Sutter's mill near Sacramento in 1848 had touched off the great "Forty-Niner" gold rush, so did stories, mainly exaggerated, of abundant opportunities ignite a mass migration to California in the 1930s. For much of the decade, U. S. Highway 66, which ran through the heart of America, was dotted with people in battered old "jalopies" and on foot making their way west. When they arrived, most found not permanent jobs, but temporary work as migrant laborers in the Imperial Valley, where they trekked from farm to farm, picking peas, lemons, oranges, grapes, and lettuce, for $15 to $30 a month, living in tents, cardboard shanties, and simply by the roadside.

The depression started this mass movement of the American people, and the federal government accelerated it. The New Deal's public works programs attracted millions of job seekers who left home to work in CCC camps or in WPA projects, going wherever the jobs were available. In addition, such vast programs as TVA and the Resettlement Administration forced millions of families off the farms. Social historians have just begun to assess the tremendous impact of the uprooting of tenant farmers and sharecroppers from southern farms. It appears that the impact was considerable. The majority of these people moved to northeastern and midwestern metropolitan areas, where they profoundly affected the social, economic, and political atmosphere. For example, over half a million southern whites and one-quarter million southern blacks migrated to Chicago, transforming that city's South Side into a huge ghetto festering with racial animosity and riddled with poverty. The same effect was produced in such places as New York City's Harlem and Detroit's Paradise Valley. This trend continued during World War II, as northern industries lured some two million southern blacks and whites. Within fifteen years, what had been for centuries the "central problem of southern history"—the race issue—became a national problem, and northerners found themselves as perplexed by it as southerners were. The scarcity of jobs for whites effectively prevented black access into labor unions and confined black employment to the lowest-paid and most menial positions. Strict racial segregation in housing and in public school education in the North turned that region of the country into one as racially divided as the South. Nevertheless, there emerged from the war a new social consciousness on the part of many northern whites, a feeling that black Americans should be treated as free and equal citizens of society. Joining with the NAACP, these whites threw their political influence behind the fledgling civil rights movement, and the immediate postwar era would see its cause championed by such people as Minneapolis Mayor Hubert H. Humphrey and President Harry S Truman.

Cultural Trends

The period from 1930 to 1945 saw the publication of some of the most renowned works in American literary history. In one sense, those fifteen years can be considered an extension of the great literary flowering of the 1920s, for many of the same writers worked in both periods. Yet they were very different eras. The "Lost Generation" of the 1920s began a new style of writing, more graphic and distrustful of human nature than that of its predecessors. The writers of the 1930s displayed a much more cynical and even morbid view of human nature and of society. To many of them, it appeared that the Great Depression came as a natural consequence of the injustice, the hypocrisy, and the utter foolishness of a materialistic society, and their works not only denounced, but rejected many of that society's most cherished values.

Ernest Hemingway and F. Scott Fitzgerald reflected the contrast between the writing of the two decades. In the 1920s, both had written about the pretensions and illusions of a society lacking in ideals, but they maintained a basically optimistic belief in the ability of American society to reform itself. In the 1930s, Hemingway's *Death in the Afternoon* (1933), and *The Green Hills of Africa* (1935) showed a bitter, comtemptuous attitude toward contemporary society. By the end of the decade, Hemingway, who had fought in the Spanish Civil War, had come to reject western democracy and to espouse the Communist-dominated Popular Front as the only hope for mankind. His masterpiece, *For Whom the Bell Tolls* (1940), is the story of people caught in the devastation of the Spanish Civil War and reveals his rather naive and idealistic philosophy of life. Fitzgerald's *Tender Is the Night* (1934) and *The Last Tycoon* (1941) disclose his belief that human nature is so pervaded with corruption that it has no hope for salvation.

To a lesser extent, Sinclair Lewis also showed the sharp contrast between the two literary eras. In the 1920s, Lewis wrote a series of novels sharply criticizing the business-oriented society of the decade. His most famous work of the 1930s, *It Can't Happen Here* (1935), reveals Lewis's belief that traditional American politics is doomed to failure. Inspired in part by the rise of Huey Long, *It Can't Happen Here* analyzes the weaknesses inherent in our democratic system. It is the story of the triumph and collapse of a Long-type dictator, who employs fascist-like means to gain power. Although the protagonist ultimately meets his doom, Lewis strongly implies that America in 1935 was ripe for the victory of a native Adolf Hitler.

Southern writers also depicted the evils of contemporary America. In his trilogy, *The Sound and the Fury* (1929), *Light in August* (1932), and *Absalom! Absalom!* (1936), William Faulkner told the story of a Mississippi family whose succeeding generations lapse further and further into decadence and decay. The North Carolina writer, Thomas Wolfe, also depicted the provincialism and decadence of southern society. His *Look Homeward, Angel* (1929), *Of Time and the River* (1935), and *The Web and the Rock* (1939) rebelled against the materialism and bigotry in the South. A group of southern writers, who called themselves the Agrarians, looked to the antebellum South as a means of delivering their native region from the corruption of modern society. In *I'll Take My Stand* (1930), such writers as the novelist, Robert Penn Warren, the poet, Allen Tate, and the historian,

Frank Owsley, Sr., wrote essays in which they called on the South to reject modern industrialism and return to the old-fashioned values of the past. Of lesser literary value, but far more popular, was Margaret Mitchell's *Gone With the Wind* (1936), a monumental novel which recounted the story of a Georgia plantation family before, during, and after the Civil War. The novel's hero, Rhett Butler, and heroine, Scarlett O'Hara, became two of the most popular characters in American literary history.

Other writers of note during the 1930s and early 1940s included John Dos Passos, whose two trilogies, *U.S.A.—The Forty-Second Parallel* (1930), *Nineteen-Nineteen* (1932), and *The Big Money* (1936); and *Adventures of a Young Man* (1939), *Number One* (1943), and *The Grand Design* (1949), took the reader on a panoramic tour of America from 1900 to 1940, as seen through a sarcastic and ironic lens. Another writer, John Steinbeck, captured the drama, poignancy, and hardship of the "Okies" journeying from Oklahoma to California in *The Grapes of Wrath* (1939). In *Studs Lonigan* (1932), *The Young Manhood of Studs Lonigan* (1934), and *Judgment Day* (1935), James T. Farrell wrote a trilogy about the moral dissolution of a lower-class Irish family in Chicago. *Native Son* (1940) won Richard Wright acclaim as the nation's leading black writer. Some of the leading female novelists of the era were Pearl Buck, Willa Cather, Ellen Glasgow, and Katharine Anne Porter.

Poetry and drama also flourished during the 1930s and 1940s. T. S. Eliot continued his production of critically acclaimed poems and plays, and Eugene O'Neill maintained his reputation as America's greatest playwright. Robert Frost, Carl Sandburg, and Edna St. Vincent Millay became the most popular poets in the nation, and Stephen Vincent Benét and Archibald MacLeish won recognition. In drama, Maxwell Anderson, Thornton Wilder, Marc Connelly, Lillian Hellman, and Robert Sherwood wrote plays depicting aspects of the American social scene ranging from the black predicament to the exploitation of the masses. All in all, the 1930s were one of the most productive decades in the history of the American theater.

Culture of the Masses

For Americans in the depression and war years, the movies afforded a favorite form of entertainment. No one who spent any length of time in a movie theater during the thirties would have known that America was in the midst of the Great Depression, for by the millions people laughed,

Bette Davis, two-time academy award winner, *National Archives*

cried, and identified with the celluloid escapism churned out by the Hollywood studios. By 1930, the movie industry had developed the art of making motion pictures into a major American business. Such technological innovations as sound and color film had given the industry the means to depict on the silver screen a distorted and unrealistic, yet highly entertaining portrayal of life. And the hard times of the 1930s provided the perfect atmosphere for the industry to become enormously successful. The movies gave people a pleasant and captivating diversion from reality. For the housewife concerned over the source of next week's food money, it was easy to become absorbed in the melodramas featuring Bette Davis,

Greta Garbo, and Jean Harlow. For the job seeker, an escape from economic worry could be found in the comedy of Will Rogers and the savoir faire of Clark Gable.

Each week, eighty-five million Americans, over half the nation's population, scrounged the twenty-five cents (ten cents for children) for a theater ticket. Hollywood catered to their tastes with a variety of films presenting a romantic version of what life should be. The films of the thirties were governed by a strict code of morals, rigidly enforced by the "czar" of the Hollywood censors, Will Hays. The provocative and unrestrained sexuality of the silent movie era was replaced by the "family" code of the thirties, in which passionate embraces, adultery, double beds, and seminudity vanished. Under the new code, family life became sacrosanct, and the good guys always triumphed over the bad guys. The most popular movie star of the 1930s was Shirley Temple, a little girl whose film exploits promoted the virtues of simplicity, honesty, and righteousness. For adults, the frothy, schmaltzy singing of Nelson Eddy and Jeanette MacDonald and the romanticized dancing of Fred Astaire and Ginger Rogers set the moral tone.

Under this veneer of morality, however, lurked a not-too-subtly disguised lasciviousness. Throughout the decade, Americans were thrilled with the on- and off-stage exploits of such female sex symbols as Greta Garbo, Joan Crawford, and such male sex symbols as Clark Gable, Robert Taylor, and Gary Cooper. Some films also attracted audiences for their representation of sexual themes. Mae West, W. C. Fields, and Charles Boyer were among the movie stars who laced their dialogue with double entendres. The most popular film of the 1930s, *Gone With the Wind*, released in 1939, emphasized the illicit romance between the swashbuckling Rhett Butler, portrayed by Clark Gable, and the flirtatious Scarlett O'Hara, portrayed by the English actress, Vivien Leigh. *Gone With the Wind* became the most famous and popular film ever made. Millions saw it, and some of its devoted partisans watched it over a dozen times.

From 1940 to 1945, Hollywood joined in the national war effort. Most of the films of the era were heavily laced with wartime propaganda, featuring gallant American, British, and French heroes and heroines fighting the sadistic Germans and slanty-eyed, buck-toothed Japanese. Almost every movie made during the period contained inspirational messages calling on the actors and the audiences to contribute their share in the fight for freedom and democracy. Even the very famous *Casablanca*, starring Humphrey Bogart and Ingrid Bergman, was conceived as a propaganda film. Although the general quality of these movies was low, the era did see the production of what is widely considered the greatest movie ever made, Orson Welles's *Citizen Kane,* a drama based on the life of William Randolph Hearst, the publishing magnate.

Of even greater popularity than the movies was the radio. Every weekday evening from 7:00 to 7:15, telephone use all over the country declined 50 percent; retail business dropped 75 percent; and many movie theaters closed—all because it was time for *Amos 'n' Andy.* Such devotion, engaged in even by President Franklin D. Roosevelt, to a comedy serial, in which a pair of white actors, Freeman Gosden and Charles Correll, portrayed a couple of black citizens, typified the radio audiences of the 1930s. Poverty-stricken as they may have been, most Americans still had radios and listened to them with a regularity and dedication that easily outperformed that of the religious faithful. The radio was to the American family of the 1930s and 1940s what television is today, an amusement and pastime so integral a part of people's lives that they regulated those lives around their favorite programs. During supper, the family listened to the news, then sat in the living room for the broadcasts of their programs. Since the radio set supplied only voices, people pictured in their minds the cops-and-robbers scenes of *Gangbusters,* the oriental mysteries of *Charlie Chan,* the weekly exploits of Ozzie and Harriet Nelson or George Burns and Gracie Allen. Or they might anxiously await the next installment of their favorite serial: *The Green Hornet* or *Boston Blackie.*

It is suggestive of the enormous hold of radio on the American people that on October 30, 1938, a twenty-three-year-old announcer named Orson Welles caused a panic by announcing on a program named "Invasion from Mars" that Martians had landed along the east coast of the United States. Welles's imitation of an announcer interrupting the regular program with news bulletins of the "invasion" was so realistic that thousands of people piled into their cars and headed away from the "invasion site" in New Jersey. During World War II, radio became an effective medium of information, as people every day listened to H. V. Kaltenborn, Edward R. Murrow, William L. Shirer, and other announcers presenting the latest news of the battle action.

Newspapers and magazines continued to exercise a considerable influence. During the thirties and forties, much competition existed, as most large cities possessed two or more rival newspapers competing for readers. A variety of popular magazines also vied for reader favor: *The Saturday Evening Post, Life, Look, Collier's, Time, Newsweek, Coronet, Reader's Digest,* and a host of movie, popular romance, and detective magazines. Among the favorite regular features were comic strips, featuring such characters as the prizefighter, Joe Palooka, the detective, Dick Tracy, the comical pair, Mutt and Jeff, and the Ozark hillbilly, L'il Abner.

As is the case today, public reading habits ran the gamut from sordid romances to works of literary quality. In the 1930s, popular best-sellers included Pearl S. Buck's *The Good Earth,* a somewhat idealistic depiction of Chinese Life, and *Jack Armstrong: All-American Boy,* a poorly written story based on a radio adventure series. Also popular during the thirties were stories of the science-fiction hero, Buck Rogers, and the African adventures of Tarzan, the ape-man. In the 1940s, the public turned to stories about the war. One of the leading best-sellers of the era was *See Here, Private Hargrove,* a novel about a soldier who constantly gets into trouble with the military bureaucracy. Other popular literature of the war years included Kathleen Windsor's *Forever Amber,* a fictional account of the lusty reign of King Charles II of England, and *The Robe,* a version of the plight of the Christians during the Roman persecutions.

In music, popular tastes changed dramatically during the 1930s. At the beginning of the decade, the most popular songs were those sung by such "crooners" as Gene Austin, Rudy Vallee, and Bing Crosby. Slow in tempo and romantic in theme, these songs reflected the reaction to the fast-paced trends of the 1920s. By the end of the 1930s, all America was taken up by "swing" fever. By 1935, big bands, as they were called, had become a favorite form of musical entertainment, and by 1938, these bands were playing the sound known as "swing." Popularized by such bandleaders as Benny Goodman, Harry James, Tommy and Jimmy Dorsey, and Duke Ellington, swing turned into a cult. An offshoot of jazz, swing was characterized by a very fast tempo ("faster than the human pulse," as the *New York Times* piously chided) and the improvised playing of masters of drums, saxophones, trombones, and trumpets. It gave rise to a new kind of dance step called the jitterbug and to a teenage code of behavior that brought on the younger generation of the thirties and forties as much condemnation from its elders as did rock 'n roll on later generations of young people. Many of the songs of the late thirties and early forties clearly reflected an attempt to break away from the past: "Tutti Frutti," "Three Little Fishes," and "The Flat Foot Floogee." During the war, ballroom dancing became very popular, as couples danced to the music of the Andrews Sisters and other favorite singers.

Another form of popular entertainment was provided by organized sports. Baseball continued to lead the rest, and such stars as Lou Gehrig, Joe Dimaggio, and Bob Feller became almost household words. Football increased in popularity, and the New Year's Day bowl game became an

Mildred "Babe" Didrikson Zaharias, America's great all round athlete. *Library of Congress*

American fixation. Two stars of the 1930s foreshadowed the future domination by black athletes of many aspects of the sports world. In 1936, a young man named Jesse Owens thrilled the American people with his record-breaking performance at the Summer Olympic Games in Berlin. With Adolf Hitler in attendance, Owens broke four world records in track and made the Führer's perverted racial theories seem absurd. In boxing, a young Detroit black named Joe Louis won the world heavyweight championship and through his remarkable ability in the ring and his conduct outside it, became one of America's most beloved heroes.

Crime

In the 1930s criminals became famous. A host of small-time hoodlums, as well as vicious murderers, received heavy publicity for their illegal exploits. The most famous was John Dillinger, a notorious bank-robber, who was killed by FBI agents outside a Chicago movie theater. Other famous criminals included: Lester M. Gillis, better known as "Baby Face Nelson;" George "Machine Gun" Kelly; Charles "Pretty Boy" Floyd; Arizona Clark "Ma" Barker; and Clyde Barrow and Bonnie Parker ("Bonnie and Clyde"). Most were killers, ultimately ending up as the victims of law enforcement ambushes. Because they often robbed banks and stole from the wealthy, they received much public adulation. Like the earlier western outlaw, Jesse James, these criminals were often depicted as modern versions of Robin Hood, robbing the rich and helping the poor.

Of even greater significance was the rise of organized crime. During the Prohibition era, many of the nation's large cities saw the bootlegging traffic monopolized by tightly organized criminal syndicates, collectively known as the Mafia. By the time Prohibition ended in 1933, the Mafia had come to dominate a wide range of illegal enterprises in narcotics, alcohol, prostitution, extortion, and racketeering. Under the leadership of Charles "Lucky" Luciano, the Mafia extended its influence throughout the decade. Despite attacks on it by law enforcement agencies such as the FBI and the New York City District Attorney's Office under Thomas E. Dewey, the Mafia grew stronger.

In response to this increasing criminal activity, the Federal Bureau of Investigation (FBI) developed into the nation's leading law enforcement agency. Led by J. Edgar Hoover, who assumed the bureau directorship in 1924, the FBI built a reputation for unimpeachable integrity. Virtually unknown in 1930, the FBI came into the public limelight with its successful investigation of the Lindbergh kidnapping and its vigorous pursuit of leading criminals. With Hoover attracting favorable publicity and with his "G-men" killing and capturing many of the nation's most wanted criminals, the FBI by 1940 had earned a deserved reputation for efficiency. During the war, the FBI was charged with the task of protecting the nation's internal security against enemy spies and saboteurs and generally performed a successful job.

The most sensational criminal case of the 1930s was the Lindbergh kidnapping. On March 1, 1932, the twenty-month-old son of Charles A. Lindbergh was kidnapped from the second floor of the Lindbergh home in Hopewell, New Jersey. The crime stunned the nation, and for weeks newspaper headlines recorded every detail of the case. Although Lindbergh paid a $50,000 ransom, the child was not returned, and six weeks later, the dead body of a baby boy was found several miles from the Lindbergh home. Two and a half years later, a man named Bruno Richard Hauptmann was arrested for passing some of the gold notes that had been part of the ransom money. After a sensational trial in 1935, Hauptmann was convicted and executed the following year. Although most historians accept the official version of the crime—that Hauptmann was guilty—newly discovered evidence raises many questions. Since no autopsy was performed on the body, a serious question remains as to whether the corpse was actually that of the Lindbergh baby. In addition, researcher Anthony Scaduto has uncovered evidence from the files of the New York Police Department that certain evidence against Hauptmann, particularly handwriting analysis and testimony linking the kidnap ladder to wood from Hauptmann's attic, was deliberately falsified to implicate him.

Intellectual Currents

In the 1930s and 1940s, American intellectuals found themselves confronted with circumstances that seemed to challenge some of their most strongly held beliefs. For some, the social and economic chaos wreaked by the Great Depression led them to reject traditional American democracy and to turn to communism. During the thirties, such men as the social reformers Whittaker Chambers, Alger Hiss, and John Abt joined communist cells because they saw communism as a means for undoing the damage capitalism had caused. With a naive view of human nature, these people engaged in spying and espionage for the Soviet Union. As historian Allen Weinstein has documented, several of the New Deal agencies were infiltrated with small groups of communist agents who used their positions to obtain information for the Soviets. Most of these people became quickly disillusioned with the hypocrisy of the Marxist movement and left.

The vast majority of intellectuals, of course, did not join the communist movement. Instead, many plunged into working with the New Deal to implement their ideas about reforming society for the better. These men included such persons as Adlai Stevenson, Dean Acheson, Jerome Frank, Telford Taylor, and many others. They used their enormous talents to bring about changes that would, they believed, create a more just and egalitarian America. They saw in the federal government the means to abolish poverty and injustice, and they drew up most of the bureaucratic regulations that accompanied New Deal legislation.

American intellectuals, of course, reflected the times in which they lived, and their works revealed a deep cynicism toward the historic social and economic trends in America. Historians of the 1930s, for example, colored their works with a decidedly economic theme. Such historians as Charles A. Beard and Matthew Josephson portrayed the American past as a class conflict between the rich and the poor. In other fields of economic endeavor, the social sciences, especially sociology, became much more prominent than earlier. Using modern techniques of research, such social scientists as John Dollard and Gunnar Myrdal documented the class and caste divisions in American society.

Organized religion was heavily influenced by intellectual trends. In the thirties and forties, the writings of the liberal Protestant theologian, Reinhold Niebuhr of Union Theological Seminary in New York, emphasized the essential immorality of human nature and the necessity for the churches to become actively involved in political, economic, and social reform. Niebuhr and his colleagues tried to modernize the Social Gospel movement, but emphasized the religious purpose behind church activism.

Education

The Great Depression and the Second World War profoundly affected all levels of education in America. The 1920s had witnessed a steady progress toward fulfilling the ideal of a free public education for all children. Most states had enacted compulsory attendance laws, and except for rural areas of the South and for blacks, the vast majority of children received some schooling. The depression halted this trend, as total expenditures for education in the United States dropped from $1.8 billion in 1930 to $1.5 billion in 1934. In addition, many families simply could no longer afford to send their children to school, and total school attendance for the 1930–1935 period declined by about 10 percent. Many teachers lost their jobs; others saw their salaries drastically reduced, as expenditures for books and supplies were also reduced.

This bleak picture improved dramatically between 1935 and 1940. Many of the New Deal programs, such as the WPA, stressed rebuilding America's educational programs, and vast sums of federal money were spent for constructing new buildings and providing schools with such additions as playgrounds, gymnasiums, and auditoriums. By 1940, the nation's school system had revived, and the number of students enrolled had grown by more than four million over the 1920 figure, and educational expenditures had doubled, increasing by over 50 percent in the five years from 1935 to 1940. As a measure of the impact of the educational system on America, illiteracy, for both whites and blacks, had been cut in half between 1920 and 1940.

World War II saw an increase in education, with enrollment, expenditure per student, and the number of teachers significantly higher in 1945 than in 1940. Colleges and universities saw a decline, as millions of young men of college age enlisted in the armed forces, but everyone saw this as only a temporary trend. The grammar and high schools contributed to the war effort by including heavy doses of patriotic propaganda in the curricula and by having school children engage in war collection drives for clothing, metals, and other items. The colleges and universities placed emphasis on scientific research for the development of new weapons and modern technological equipment to aid the war effort.

At all levels, the schools placed more emphasis on preparing students for careers in business and industry and less on the traditional academic curricula. John Dewey's theories of progressive education had become firmly established by 1930, and the schools began to introduce such subjects as typing, manual workshops, and home economics into the curricula. The classical academic subjects, history, foreign languages, the arts, etc., suffered corresponding declines. Some 50 percent of American high school students studied Latin in 1910; by 1940, only 12 percent did so. As Jacques Barzun concluded in his brilliant wartime study of American education, *Teacher in America,* the new emphasis on practical, rather than intellectual training, led to a general lowering of academic standards, a contention substantiated by the fact that over 40 percent of the men inducted into the Armed Forces during the war could not pass the verbal and mathematics parts of their entrance examinations.

The Impact of Technology

For the American people in the years from 1930 to 1945, certain developments were taking place that would radically change the world in which they lived. These developments came under the general label of scientific, or more accurately, technological change. Their impact, however, extended far beyond the world of the scientist, for they would bring about revolutionary changes in every level of society. Many of these innovations directly resulted from the massive scientific research effort for victory in the war, but most came from the efforts of private researchers and industrial engineers who were part of the historical tradition of technological change. Ordinary citizens were aware only dimly, if at all, of the changes taking place, but American technology in the 1930s and 1940s invented a variety of products and techniques that would alter their way of living. A few examples will suffice. Because of the necessity of producing, storing, and shipping huge volumes of food to servicemen overseas, a new method of freezing food was discovered. Using freon gas and an elaborate system of condenser coils and a compressor, the food freezer was developed. Within a few years after the end of the war, the vast frozen food industry grew into one of America's largest. A by-product of this innovation was the refining of the air conditioning industry. Available only to the wealthy in the 1920s, air conditioning would become an integral part of the living and working conditions of the American people. Another major industry was the production of synthetic materials. First perfected by the Germans in the 1920s in the nylon and rayon industries, synthetics became a large and profitable business by 1945. From synthetic rubber to plastic, the industry produced a variety of materials that drastically altered clothing styles, housing patterns, and the general physical atmosphere of the places where Americans worked and studied. Petroleum and natural gas quickly replaced coal as the main sources of America's energy. The easy availability and low cost of these fuels made possible the enormous expansion of American industry in the postwar world.

In today's world of electronic marvels, it is difficult to imagine that less than a half century ago, Americans did not have television, automatic transmissions, dishwashers, microwave ovens, and color photography. Yet all of these and numerous other common items of today were invented during the 1930s, and leaders of business and industry were quick to realize their potential. One of the most far-reaching technological developments, one whose potential is just being realized today, was the digital computer. During World War II, a team of American and British scientists used crude computers to perform such tasks as code-breaking and logistics computation. Because of the rapidity of the machine's calculations, the War Department commissioned a group of American scientists at the University of Pennsylvania to develop a faster computer. Although they did not complete their assignment before the war ended, the scientists in 1946 produced the world's first electronic computer, a massive, primitive prototype of the computers in use today. It was called ENIAC, and even though its cathode ray tubes burned out every seven minutes, the scientists knew that they had invented one of the modern world's most remarkable devices.

Looking Toward the Future

Perhaps no other event better expressed the mood of the American people than the New York World's Fair. When it opened on April 30, 1939, in Flushing Meadow, New York, at a cost of over $150 million, the New York World's Fair drew raves of admiration and astonishment from the millions of people who flocked to its exhibits. Its theme was "The World of Tomorrow," and it was dedicated to the blessings of democracy and the marvels of technology. It was gaudy, ostentatious, and commercial, but the Fair did provide the American people with a glimpse into the future, a future of prosperity, peace, and comfort.

The most popular exhibit, General Motors's "Futurama," gave Americans a look at their nation in the year 1960, a vision of America that no one doubted. America, predicted the exhibit's organizers, would be a nation of superhighways, traveled on by air-conditioned cars costing less than $250 apiece. It was a nation of green fields, pollution-free air, and abundant food for everyone. It was a nation with the best education in the world, with cancer and other dread diseases cured, and people living their extended lifetimes in perfect ease and comfort, free from crime, congestion, and economic worry.

This utopian society did not, of course, come about. Yet Americans in 1939 had no doubts that it would. They had met the challenge of the Great Depression and would shortly emerge victorious in a struggle to preserve democracy in the world. Despite their problems, they faced the future with a confident air of assurance that theirs was the greatest nation on earth, which would successfully meet the challenge of the future.

8

From Isolation to Intervention

During the first five years of his presidency, Franklin Roosevelt devoted most of his attention to domestic issues and little to foreign policy. With the exception of the "Good Neighbor" program, his foreign policy displayed a marked tendency to isolation. From 1938 on, he reversed his direction, as crises in the Far East and on the European continent led him to shift toward a policy of active involvement in world affairs. By the time of the Munich conference in September 1938, it had become apparent that Nazi Germany under Adolf Hitler posed a serious threat to world peace, and Roosevelt began to reconsider his previous isolationist position. When war erupted in Europe a year later, the president decided that the best interests of the United States would be served by backing England and France against Germany. Keenly aware of the strong opposition to intervention among the American people, Roosevelt slowly and cautiously tilted American foreign policy away from isolation. After his victory in the 1940 election, Roosevelt openly and enthusiastically urged public support for the Allies, and the United States took such actions as Lend-Lease to give them active assistance.

At the same time, the United States and Japan drifted slowly toward war. From the Japanese invasion of Manchuria in 1931 to its outright attack on the Chinese mainland in 1937, America had considered Japan the most serious threat to world peace. After 1937, the Roosevelt administration took measures to meet that threat. By early 1941, Japanese-American relations had deteriorated so sharply that both countries expected to go to war. The rest of the year witnessed futile attempts on both sides to avert that war.

The London Economic Conference

When Roosevelt took office in March 1933, the international economic system had almost collapsed. Germany had defaulted on reparations payments in 1932, and those European countries to whom the debts were owed, could not, in turn, pay their debts to the United States. In early 1933, all European countries except Finland defaulted on their payments to American creditors. The Great Depression aggravated the situation, for it affected the industrial nations of Europe as severely as it had the United States. With domestic production declining, most European countries had erected high tariff barriers against foreign products, and the resulting decline in world trade further complicated the problem.

To seek a solution to that problem, the world's industrialized nations sponsored a World Economic Conference, which opened in London in June 1933. The main issues of the conference centered on a dispute between those countries, like France, who still based their currencies on gold, and those, like England and the United States, who had repudiated that gold standard. For several weeks, the delegates wrangled over the stabilization of the dollar. The chief American envoy, presidential advisor Raymond Moley, made efforts to reach a compromise figure. But, convinced that further depreciation of the dollar was essential to economic recovery at home, President Roosevelt sent a message to the conference on July 3, which declared that the United States would not permit any agreement mandating stabilization of the dollar. Because of this message, the conference disbanded without having taken any action to combat the depression. Many scholars have criticized Roosevelt for his refusal to allow the conference to arrive at a compromise stabilization figure, but Roosevelt was only practicing what the other countries also practiced, economic nationalism. France refused to abolish the gold standard, and England refused to lower the trade barriers. Roosevelt can hardly be faulted for doing what he thought necessary to cope with his most urgent crisis, the domestic depression.

The Good Neighbor Policy

In his inaugural address, Franklin Roosevelt committed the United States to the policy of a "good neighbor" in foreign affairs. A few weeks later, he addressed the Pan-American issue and applied the phrase "good neighbor" specifically to United States relations with Latin America. In general, the policy dedicated the United States to a reversal of the belligerent, interventionist policies of the past. The president, Secretary of State Cordell Hull, and the assistant secretary of state for Latin American affairs, Sumner Welles, wanted America to pursue a policy of nonintervention and good will toward its neighbors in the western hemisphere. This policy actually had begun during the Coolidge administration and was carried forward under Hoover by the United States ambassador to Mexico, Dwight Morrow.

The Good Neighbor policy did not begin favorably. When a group of rebels overthrew the Cuban government in 1933, Roosevelt sent 30 warships to Havana as a demonstration of American power. He also refused to recognize the new revolutionary government under Ramon San Martin, and that government collapsed. To Latin Americans, it appeared that Roosevelt was continuing the imperialistic policies of the past. When the Inter-American Conference met in Montevideo, Uruguay, in December 1933, Secretary of State Hull was confronted with open hostility by the delegates and press representatives from Central and South American countries. However, Hull quickly won their support when he announced that he would vote for a resolution renouncing the right of any nation to intervene in the internal affairs of others. Hull's action led to the signing of several new treaties in which the United States joined its Latin American neighbors in guaranteeing the sovereignty of existing governments, the inviolability of national territory, and the equality of all nations. This Good Neighbor policy repudiated those of such presidents as Theodore Roosevelt and Woodrow Wilson, who had treated the western hemisphere as American territory and who had not hesitated to employ armed intervention to foster American political and even commercial interests.

This new approach received its first test in January 1934, when a government under Carlos Mendieta came to power in Cuba. The real power in the government lay in a military strongman, General Fulgencio Batista, and many Americans urged Roosevelt to remove him. But in May 1934, Hull signed a treaty in which the United States formally recognized this new Cuban government and abrogated the Platt Amendment of 1901, under which the United States had assumed the right to intervene in Cuban affairs.

The United States also negotiated treaties with Haiti, the Dominican Republic, and Panama that recognized their sovereignty and called for the end of American military presence within their borders.

By the time a new Inter-American Conference convened, in Buenos Aires in December 1936, the Good Neighbor policy had built up considerable friendship for the United States throughout Latin America. Roosevelt attended the meeting in person and was hailed as a hero by the populace and the delegates. The new atmosphere of mutual trust among equals led to agreements by the western hemisphere nations to lend assistance to each other in the event of armed aggression from outside the hemisphere and to seek peaceful negotiations of all potentially hostile differences among themselves. The Monroe Doctrine had become "Pan-Americanized."

Europe in Turmoil

During the 1930s, a series of events occurred in Europe that led to the outbreak of World War II. Foremost among these was the rise to power in Germany of Adolf Hitler. A native Austrian who had served with distinction in World War I, winning the Iron Cross, Hitler joined the fledgling National Socialist Workers Democratic (Nazi) Party shortly after the war ended. He quickly assumed leadership of the right-wing organization and used his considerable oratorical skills to build it into one of Germany's main political parties. When a succession of governments in the Weimar Republic failed to resolve such issues as reparations payments and inflation, the country's leadership turned to Hitler and the Nazis. He became Chancellor in 1933, and a year later gained dictatorial control by outlawing his opposition and by winning the support of the German army. Within a few years, Germany under Hitler mushroomed into the most powerful country in western Europe, and it embarked on a series of foreign policy maneuvers designed to expand German territory. In 1935, Hitler renounced the Treaty of Versailles and began to rearm the German war machine.

The first European overt act of aggression in the 1930s, however, came from Italy, under the dictatorship of the fascist leader, Benito Mussolini. In December 1934, a skirmish between Italian and Ethiopian troops led to open hostilities between the two countries. Mussolini's goal was the conquest of Ethiopia, and he rejected all attempts by the League of Nations to mediate the dispute. Responding to a personal plea by the Ethiopian ruler, Emperor Haile Selassie, and to strong pressure from England, the

League voted to condemn Italy as the aggressor and to impose economic sanctions against her. The collective security system established by the Allies after World War I faced its first real challenge, and it failed to meet that challenge. Coal and oil were Italy's two most urgently needed materials, and the League refused to include them on the list of embargoed items. The United States's response to the Ethiopian crisis was to invoke the Neutrality Act of 1935, which prohibited American arms shipments to belligerents. Hull called for a "moral embargo" on the shipment of certain commodities to Italy, but American businessmen ignored the request and actually increased their trade with Italy, especially in coal and oil. The western allies condemned the United States for the failure of the economic sanctions, but both England and France were more vacillating, and neither country proved willing to endorse any action entailing binding commitments.

The Spanish Civil War, which erupted in July 1936, also put the collective security system to the test. Spanish rebels, led by General Francisco Franco and supported by the Roman Catholic Church, the nobility, and the monarchists, revolted against a Popular Front government backed by republicans and communists. From the beginning, Roosevelt agreed that any escalation of the conflict might lead to a general European war and that a policy of strict nonintervention would prevent that escalation. Some two thousand Americans did voluntarily fight on the government side, but most Americans complied with Roosevelt's policy of neutrality, his embargo on trade with the belligerents, and his "moral embargo" on trade with countries actively supplying the opposing sides.

Throughout 1937, Roosevelt continued his isolationist posture. In a public address given on October 5, he did suggest that the western democracies might have to quarantine the aggressor nations. Some historians interpret this "quarantine the aggressors" speech as signalling a new awareness by Roosevelt of the impending war in Europe and as a first step in his plan to educate the American people on their responsibility of maintaining world peace. The evidence does not support this interpretation. When Roosevelt presented the address, the only aggression occurring was the Japanese invasion of China. Furthermore, in the almost two years between the speech and the outbreak of World War II, Roosevelt made no serious efforts either to implement this vague proposal or to redirect public opinion at home.

The German occupation of Austria in March 1938 marked the first step in Hitler's plan to expand German territory. A few months later, he demanded that Germany be ceded the Germanic areas of Czechoslovakia.

Anxious to avoid war, Neville Chamberlain, the British Prime Minister, and Edouard Daladier, the French Premier, met with Hitler and Mussolini at Munich in late September 1938. The allied leaders yielded to Hitler, and without consulting the Czech government, signed the infamous Munich agreement permitting German dismemberment of Czechoslovakia. The Munich accord was a victory for the forces of appeasement, who argued that peace, even at the expense of the independence of small nations, was preferable to war. Munich, of course, did not produce "peace in our time," as Chamberlain proclaimed upon his return from the conference, and the pact has been condemned almost universally as a futile attempt to placate Hitler. Yet, public opinion in France and England strongly endorsed it the Munich agreement. But in the following year, when Hitler demonstrated that he would not be satisfied with Czechoslovakia, a sharp change would occur. In the next year, both Britain and France would adopt a much stronger position toward Germany.

For the United States, Munich became a watershed in the history of its foreign policy during the 1930s. In January 1939 Roosevelt asked Congress for $1.8 billion for national defense, a relatively minor beginning in what would shortly become a massive defense buildup. It reflected Roosevelt's growing awareness of the imminence of war in Europe and of his determination to lend assistance to the allies when that war came.

Isolationism in the 1930s

During the first six years of his presidency, Franklin Roosevelt demonstrated his reluctance to get the country involved in foreign affairs. Public opinion strongly opposed binding commitments by the United States in international policy. This isolationist impulse had always influenced American diplomacy, and only during the administration of Theodore Roosevelt did the United States begin to assume the trappings of a world power. World War I reinforced this new internationalist direction, but the end of the war brought about a dramatic reversal. The refusal of the United States to join the League of Nations and the World Court and the disarmament proposals of the Washington Conference of 1921 symbolized the revival of isolation sentiment in the country. Although the 1920s saw an expansion of American business interests abroad, the general theme of American foreign policy during the decade was noninvolvement. Writers and historians at the time asserted that World War I had been a mistake, that it had not made the world safe for democracy, and that the wisest course of action for the United States lay in not corrupting herself with the affairs of other nations. The xenophobic movement of the 1920s reflected the revived isolationism of the decade.

The Great Depression injected the isolationist spirit with added vigor. The American people naturally wanted their government to devote its full energies to the domestic economic crisis. Many people were persuaded that an international conspiracy of bankers and industrialists was responsible for the depression, a theory given popular currency by demagogues of the right and the left. Many influential persons advocated American withdrawal from world affairs, an idea vigorously promoted by newspaper magnate William Randolph Hearst and by many of the leading progressives in the Republican and Democratic parties. Always quick to ameliorate public opinion, Roosevelt adopted isolation. A former proponent of American participation in the League of Nations, he reversed himself during the 1932 campaign. After becoming president, Roosevelt made a few internationalist overtures, but generally remained isolationist. In 1935, he requested that Congress authorize United States membership in the World Court, a largely ineffective guardian of international law located in Geneva. But there was so much opposition to the proposal within the major parties that it failed to secure the two-thirds vote necessary for Senate approval, one of the few legislative defeats Roosevelt suffered in his first term.

Perhaps the most widely advertised symbol of the isolationism of the thirties was the Nye Committee investigation. In March 1934, *Fortune* magazine published a scathing indictment of the American arms industry, accusing it of deliberately trying to prolong World War I to increase its profits. The article received much favorable response from the public, and the Senate appointed a committee to investigate the charges. Headed by Senator Gerald P. Nye of North Dakota, the committee operated on the premise that sensational exposés were more important than accuracy. American arms manufacturers were brought before the committee and publicly charged with manipulating the United States into the war to make profits. The committee blamed J. P. Morgan, one of the nation's leading bankers, of deliberately profiteering from the war by serving as an agent for the Allies.

The Nye Committee revelations led to a further increase in popular sentiment for isolationism. Many congressmen pressed for legislation affirming the neutrality of the United States in the event of a European war and banning the export of American arms to belligerents. Roosevelt strongly opposed the measure because it hampered his discretionary ability to use American economic strength in foreign policy. Congress, however, demanded action. In late February 1935, Senator Key Pittman of Nevada, the chairman of the Foreign Relations Committee, introduced a resolution prohibiting the export of arms and munitions during foreign wars and banning the transportation of arms on American ships. Though the bill gave the president no discretionary authority in the event of war, Congress overwhelmingly passed it. Roosevelt reluctantly signed the Neutrality Act of 1935 into law. The Ethiopian crisis led the president to seek discretionary authority to employ embargoes only against aggressors, but his proposal was rebuffed, and a new Neutrality Act, extending the old one into 1936, was passed.

In 1937, Roosevelt adopted a more isolationist posture than some of his former opponents. Senator Nye, one of Congress's leading isolationists, urged Roosevelt to lift the embargo on the sale of arms to Spain, but Roosevelt refused. A new Neutrality Act was passed in 1937, which extended the arms embargo and prohibited American citizens from sailing on belligerent ships, but it allowed belligerents to purchase certain goods from the United States on a cash-only basis and transport them on non-American vessels. This Neutrality Act of 1937 was the highwater mark of isolationism in the 1930s, and Roosevelt reluctantly supported it. For the rest of 1937, he carefully avoided any actions that might be construed as interventionist. He did, however, oppose the Ludlow Amendment. Introduced by Congressman Louis Ludlow of Indiana, the amendment stipulated that, except in case of invasion, the United States could not go to war, unless a national referendum approved the action. Clearly, the amendment would have crippled the freedom of action necessary to the successful conduct of foreign policy. But it is a measure of the extent of isolationist feeling in the United States at the time that the House of Representatives, under strong pressure from Roosevelt to vote against the measure, managed to defeat it by a vote of only 209 to 188.

The Reluctant Interventionist

The years 1938 and 1939 saw the United States edge, slowly and cautiously, away from isolation. Recognizing the Nazi peril, Roosevelt beefed up the armed forces and tried to avert a European war. He called for an international conference to settle unresolved world problems, and he wrote to Hitler asking the German dictator to renounce territorial claims against the independent nations of Europe. But events moved quickly, and the European war everyone feared did commence in September 1939. After

Germany completed its conquest of Czechoslovakia, Hitler made it plain that Poland was his next objective, and he was not deterred by an Anglo-French-Polish treaty guaranteeing Poland's sovereignty by force. On August 23, 1939, Germany and the Soviet Union signed a nonaggression pact, under which both countries agreed not to attack each other. This pact freed Germany from the threat of a two-front war, and on September 1, German armed forces invaded Poland. Two days later, England and France abided by their treaty with Poland and declared war on Germany.

President Roosevelt invoked the Neutrality Act and issued an official proclamation of American neutrality, but from the beginning, his sympathies lay clearly with the allies. He called a special session of Congress to repeal the ban on the sale of American arms to belligerents. Despite considerable isolationist opposition, Roosevelt's will prevailed, and a new Neutrality Act was passed, lifting the arms embargo, but retaining the bans against Americans traveling on belligerents' ships and on American ships engaging in arms commerce with belligerents. Roosevelt was determined to avoid the unrestricted submarine warfare that had plunged the United States into World War I, and on November 4, 1939, he declared the Baltic Sea and the Atlantic Ocean from Norway to Spain combat zones. This declaration effectively excluded American shipping from most of the European seaports and, at the same time, invited Germany to open unrestricted submarine warfare within European continental waters without the fear of American retaliation.

By the end of June 1940, Germany had conquered Denmark, Norway, Belgium, Holland, and France. The frightening speed with which the German war machine completed its conquest led Roosevelt to adopt a decidedly pro-British policy. In the spring and summer of 1940, he received from Congress over $17 billion for national defense, a huge sum for that time. He also established a National Defense Research Committee to apply the latest technological discoveries to weaponry and warfare. In July 1940, the Smith Act became effective. It required all aliens in the United States to register with the government each year and imposed stiff prison sentences on anyone who said or published anything that might lead to insubordination in the armed forces. To strengthen his administration against partisan attacks by the opposition, Roosevelt named two leading Republicans, Frank Knox and Henry L. Stimson, as secretaries of the navy and of war.

After the German conquest of France, Roosevelt committed the United States to a policy of giving direct military assistance to England. He listened sympathetically to the entreaties of the new British Prime Minister, Winston Churchill, and decided to supply England with large quantities of arms, munitions, and destroyers. He bypassed Congress and negotiated a direct exchange that would give England old American destroyers in return for British bases in the western hemisphere. In September 1940, the terms of the exchange were announced. The United States received the right to establish military and naval bases on British possessions in North America in exchange for fifty American destroyers. This historic agreement marked a turning point in American foreign policy. The "destroyer deal" was vehemently opposed by many isolationists, but Roosevelt prevailed and committed the nation to a new policy of interventionism.

The Election of 1940

For the Republican party, the presidential election of 1940 appeared as ominous as did that of 1936. The Roosevelt administration retained its strong popular backing, and the war in Europe gave the incumbent president an obvious advantage. The Republicans believed that their only hope in the campaign lay in capitalizing on the considerable isolationist sentiment in the country, and the three leading candidates for the nomination were all ardent isolationists: Senators Arthur H. Vandenburg of Michigan and Robert A. Taft of Ohio and District Attorney Thomas E. Dewey of New York. The Republican convention opened just two days after France's surrender to Germany, and the delegates feared voter reprisal if they nominated an outspoken isolationist. So they nominated Wendell L. Wilkie of Indiana, a corporation executive and a supporter of Roosevelt's policy of aid to England. Roosevelt was reluctant to run for a third term, but the urgency of foreign events persuaded him to do so. The Democrats nominated him and selected the Secretary of Agriculture, Henry A. Wallace, as his running mate.

Although the outcome of the election did not seem in doubt, Wilkie campaigned energetically. He assailed the New Deal for its failure to end the continuing depression and unemployment, but the massive increase in defense spending caused an economic upswing, depriving Wilkie of this argument. Near the end of the campaign, Wilkie charged that Roosevelt's pro-British policy was leading America towards war, and his popular support increased. Roosevelt responded with the blanket assurance that he would not send American boys to fight in "foreign wars," and "your president says this country is not going to war." Roosevelt won the election, and the Democrats retained their majority, but the president's popular and electoral totals declined from their 1936 levels.

Lend-Lease

Shortly after the election, the president decided to renew his commitment to England. Under the provisions of the Neutrality Act, England could purchase only those arms and munitions from the United States that she could pay for in cash. By the end of 1940, the British treasury was running out of money. Responding to an urgent plea from Churchill, Roosevelt requested that Congress grant him the authority to supply England with large quantities of war materials, to be paid for "in goods and services at the end of the war." Signed into law on March 11, 1941, the Lend Lease Act and a subsequent $7 billion appropriation entrusted the United States to becoming what Roosevelt called an "arsenal of democracy."

To put Lend-Lease into effect, the president approved a new policy of allowing American Navy yards to repair British vessels damaged by German U-boat (submarine) attacks, and he authorized American Coast Guard cutters to assist the British Navy in antisubmarine warfare. He also sent American ships far into the Atlantic to assist the British in the detection and evasion of U-boats. This new policy made the United States an active ally of England in everything short of outright hostilities. Realizing the risk of war this new policy entailed, Roosevelt pursued it anyway because he knew that England's only hope lay in the success of the Lend-Lease shipments in meeting her needs. The German U-boat campaign had caused massive destruction to the British fleet by sinking ships at twice the rate new ones could be built. To emphasize his commitment to a British victory, Roosevelt also declared a state of national emergency.

On the Brink of War

When Germany invaded the Soviet Union on June 22, 1941, President Roosevelt decided that the United States would participate more actively in the war against Germany. In July, General George C. Marshall, the Army Chief of Staff, asked Congress to extend the draft (in 1940, Congress had passed the Selective Service Act, effective for one year). After a heated debate, the extension bill passed the House of Representatives by only one vote, and following Senate approval, Roosevelt signed it into law. He also signed an agreement with Iceland which permitted the United States to maintain bases there and allowed the U. S. Navy to escort American and Icelandic ships sailing between America and Iceland. Roosevelt also ordered the Navy to destroy any hostile ships that threatened our shipping.

On August 12, 1941, President Roosevelt and Prime Minister Churchill met aboard the cruiser *Augusta* at Argentia, Newfoundland and signed the agreement known as the Atlantic Charter. This document stated the principles upon which the United States and England based "their hope for a better future for the world." These principles included the right of all peoples everywhere to choose the form of government they desired; the sovereignty and independence of all nations; and the right of everyone to live in freedom from fear, want, and aggression. More significantly, at the meeting, Roosevelt and Churchill agreed that British vessels could join the American-Icelandic convoys and enjoy the same protection by the United States Navy. This decision virtually ensured that the United States would enter into an undeclared naval war with Germany, since the Germans sought to destroy British shipping everywhere in the open seas. In a radio address in September, Roosevelt told the American people of the Argentia decision and also of his order to the Navy to destroy any German ships or submarines found in the shipping lanes between the United States and Iceland.

Several public opinion polls released in October 1941 revealed that while most Americans did not want to become involved in another war, they strongly supported the president's agressive new policies. In that month, Roosevelt received from Congress permission to arm American merchant vessels and authorization for them to enter the European war zone and to defend themselves against German attacks. Inevitably, this led to open hostilities. On October 17, U-boats torpedoed the destroyer *Kearny,* and eleven Americans died. Two weeks later, the destroyer *Reuben James* was sunk, and one hundred fifteen lives were lost. Such incidents had ultimately led to the American declaration of war against Germany in 1917, and in all probability, would have led to one in 1942. Franklin Roosevelt believed that the United States's best interests would be served by a British victory, and he wanted to do anything to make that victory possible. The recent publication of the secret wartime correspondence between Roosevelt and Churchill shows that the president fully expected his new policies to lead the United States into war with Germany by the middle of 1942. Events in the Far East, however, led to the outbreak of war there before Roosevelt's European plans were fulfilled.

The United States and Japan

In September 1931 Japanese armed forces invaded and occupied the northern Chinese province of Manchuria. This was the first in a series of events which led to the attack on Pearl Harbor and to United States entry into World War II. The Pearl Harbor attack resulted from the breakdown of Japanese-American negotiations and from the Japanese belief that America posed a deadly threat to their plans for predominance in the Far East. To understand the reasons behind the failure of diplomacy, it is necessary to explore in detail the complex history of Japanese-American relations between 1931 and 1941.

The Japanese invasion of Manchuria in 1931 was ignited by the impulsive seizure of a Chinese railroad by a group of Japanese soldiers, an action not planned by the civilian government, but probably by the military leaders. Once the railroad seizure took place, Japan did not rescind it, and sent large numbers of troops to occupy all of Manchuria. Ever since the end of the Russo-Japanese War in 1905, Japan had enjoyed economic privileges in Manchuria, and it used those privileges to construct a barrier against potential Russian expansion. Technically under the authority of the Chinese government, Manchuria actually lay more under the control of independent Chinese warlords who cooperated with the Japanese. When the Chinese Nationalist government under Chiang Kai-shek attempted to extend its control to Manchuria, Japan responded with belligerency. Keenly aware of the unstable popular base of Chiang's regime and fearful that Chiang would prove unable to prevent Soviet expansion into Manchuria, Japan occupied the province.

President Herbert Hoover and Secretary of State Henry L. Stimson viewed the Japanese invasion of Manchuria as an act of naked aggression. Ignorant of the complex situation that existed, Hoover and Stimson looked for means of resisting the conquest, and they soon discovered that they were powerless to prevent it. American public opinion adamantly opposed any action which might entail the use of force. The domestic problems caused by the Great Depression consumed much of the president's time and energy. Seeking help from their European friends, Hoover and Stimson learned that England opposed the use of force against Japan and that the League of Nations refused to endorse economic sanctions. The president and the secretary therefore turned to moral condemnation. In January 1932, Stimson proclaimed his famous doctrine of nonrecognition of any territorial changes brought about in the Far East which conflicted with the treaties of the United States government and which threatened the sovereignty and independence of China. This "Stimson Doctrine," which originated in a similar warning given Japan in 1915 by Secretary of State William Bryan, ignored the realities of world politics. Japan disregarded Stimson's reproach and less than a month later invaded Shanghai and massacred thousands of civilians. When the League of Nations adopted a resolution endorsing the

"Stimson Doctrine" and condemning Japan as the aggressor, Japan withdrew from the League. The Hoover-Stimson policy of nonrecognition attempted to enforce foreign policy with moral exhortation, rather than diplomatic, economic, or military coercion.

From the time of the Manchurian crisis, the United States conducted formal but cool relations with Japan. American policy in the Far East rested on friendship with China, and when a full-scale war between China and Japan erupted in July 1937, President Roosevelt openly sympathized with China, an action that culminated almost a century of cordial relations. To Americans, China seemed the embodiment of the mystique of the Orient, and the vast country offered a perfect opportunity for Americans to carry their ideals abroad. Ever since the Open Door Policy of 1900, which declared China fair game for western commercial exploitation, Americans looked on China as a marketplace for their products. Many people also detected in China's continuous political turmoil the chance to export the values and institutions of democracy. Many denominations regarded the Chinese as ripe for conversion to Christianity and sent numerous missionaries to the country. Popular works by such writers as Pearl Buck ingrained in the public mind fanciful theories about the inscrutable Orient and the land of Shangri-La. Thus, American sympathies lay clearly with the Chinese, and when the Japanese launched their invasion in 1937, the Roosevelt administration condemned it as the aggressor, but took no further action. In December 1937, Japanese planes sank the American gunboat *Panay* and three American oil tankers near Nanking. Japan apologized for the incident and indemnified the United States government and the oil company for the damages incurred.

For two years, Roosevelt paid little attention to the Far East, but in 1939, he decided that the United States must assume a larger role there. In making this decision, he was influenced by Secretary of State Hull, who acted on the advice of his main advisor for Far Eastern affairs, Dr. Stanley Hornbeck. Roosevelt also made the decision because he believed that the United States must fill the Far Eastern vacancy created by England's and France's increasing preoccupation with European matters. Roosevelt and Hull saw Japanese withdrawal from China as the key to peace in the Far East. Realizing the futility of the policy of moral condemnation, they applied economic persuasion. In July 1939, the president gave Japan six months' notice of the intention of the United States to terminate the Japanese-American Commercial Treaty of 1911, under which the two countries had agreed to trade a wide variety of products. By 1939, commerce between the two had become extensive and lucrative, and Japan imported more than 50 percent of its iron, steel, and crude oil from the United States. The American threat to abrogate the commercial treaty jolted the Japanese, and they began negotiations with the State Department. The talks, however, proved futile, for neither country would make concessions on the Chinese question. The United States viewed the Japanese presence in China as blatant aggression, and Japan viewed it as its rightful duty to try to impose order and stability in the largest country in Asia.

After a moderate Japanese government came to power in January 1940, the United States postponed the imposition of the embargo on the export of vital raw materials to Japan. In July, this moderate government fell and was replaced by a more expansionist one under Prince Fumimaro Konoye. The new Japanese government immediately began promoting what it called the Greater East Asia Co-Prosperity Sphere, under which all the nations of East Asia would join together under Japanese leadership to form an independent economic coalition, similar to the current European Common Market, an organization of Oriental peoples free from reliance on American and European commerce and determined to rid Asia of white imperialists. As the first step in implementing this concept, Japan persuaded the Vichy French government to permit it to station troops and build airfields in northern Indochina. When Japanese troops occupied northern Indochina in late 1940, the United States imposed an embargo on the export of iron ore, scrap iron, pig iron, steel, and other materials to Japan.

The American embargo split the Japanese government into two main factions: those who wanted to negotiate with the United States and those who desired war. Strongly backed by Emperor Hirohito, Prince Konoye supported those who wanted negotiations. As a basis for those negotiations, Konoye stated that in return for the lifting of the embargo, Japan would repudiate its nonaggression pact with Germany and Italy, withdraw its troops from China, and resume normal economic trade with the United States. Unconvinced of the sincerity of the proposals, Secretary Hull responded with a four-point demand that merely restated the American position that Japan withdraw from China as the basis for future negotiations. The Japanese Foreign Minister, Yosuke Matsuoka, believed that these negotiations, conducted while he was in Moscow, contained too many concessions from Japan. Therefore, he formulated a new set of Japanese demands, deliberately couched in harsh language to invoke American wrath: the termination of United States aid to England; United States pressure on Chiang Kai-shek to surrender to Japan; the lifting of the embargo; and the removal of all restrictions on Japanese immigration into the United States.

Obviously, these new Japanese proposals were unacceptable to the United States, and Hull restated the American position in unmistakable terms. Matsuoka fell from power in July 1941, but Japan continued its aggressive actions and occupied all of Indochina that month. President Roosevelt responded with the impoundment of all Japanese funds in the United States, the closing of the Panama Canal to Japanese shipping, and the calling of the Philippine militia into active military service. On August 1, he took an action which he knew might lead to further Japanese expansion in the Far East, but which he felt necessary as a demonstration of American determination. He embargoed the shipment of oil to Japan.

Not eager for war with the United States, the Japanese leadership looked for ways to safeguard their interests yet maintain peace. Prime Minister Konoye asked Roosevelt for a face-to-face meeting to resolve their differences. Just as eager to avoid war, Roosevelt favored the idea, but Hull persuaded him to adhere to a policy of firmness by making Japan agree to American demands on China before the meeting took place. The President therefore replied to Konoye that the fundamental differences on China would have to be settled before the meeting could occur. A further exchange of notes between Roosevelt and Konoye reiterated their original messages.

By the beginning of October 1941, those elements in the Japanese government favoring a militaristic policy had taken control. Led by the war minister, General Hideki Tojo, they rejected Konoye's proposal that in the interest of peace, Japan withdraw from China. On October 16, Konoye fell from power and was replaced by Tojo. The new prime minister immediately began preparations for war with the United States, but at the insistence of the emperor, resumed negotiations with the United States. Between November 17 and the outbreak of war on December 7, the Japanese ambassador to the United States, Kichisaburo Nomura, along with a special envoy sent by the Japanese government, held several meetings with Roosevelt and Hull to find some last-minute diplomatic means of averting war. The Japanese diplomats presented their government's final offer: (1) no further Japanese aggression in Southeast Asia, (2) equal access by both countries to raw materials in the Dutch East Indies, (3) resumption of normal Japanese-American trade, (4) American assistance in seeking peace between Japan and China, (5) Japanese withdrawal from Indochina after the conclusion of the Sino-Japanese peace, and (6) the immediate withdrawal of Japanese forces from southern to northern Indochina. Presented on November 20, this offer bore a striking resemblance to one drafted by President Roosevelt. The only major difference between the two proposals was American insistence on Japanese neutrality in the event the United States entered the war in Europe, a provision that the Japanese would have accepted, since they had already decided not to become involved in the war in Europe. On November 25, however, two events occurred that convinced Roosevelt not to submit his message. He received information that Japanese warships and troop transports were assembling off Formosa, and the British and Chinese governments strenuously objected to American acceptance of the Japanese proposals. The next day, November 26, Secretary of State Hull presented the final demands of the United States government to the Japanese: the immediate withdrawal of all Japanese forces from China and Indochina; and public support by Japan of the Nationalist Chinese government. Roosevelt and Hull knew that the November 26 message constituted a rejection of the Japanese ultimatum of November, but they remained open to further negotiations. Japan, however, did not. Its leaders decided on war with the United States and ordered a large fleet under Admiral Chuichi Nagumo to carry out the planned attack on Pearl Harbor. On December 7, Japanese planes attacked the naval base at Pearl Harbor, Hawaii, and the next day, the United States declared war on Japan.

The momentous events leading to the Pearl Harbor attack and the historiographical controversy it generated will be explored in detail in the next chapter. What follows is a brief summary of the main motivations behind each country's action. Japan regarded itself as the strongest force in the Far East and as the only formidable obstacle to Soviet expansion in the region. Its invasion of China was precipitated both by territorial ambition and by a desire to take the role of a world power. When Roosevelt embargoed the shipment of strategic war materials, Japan faced two choices: accept permanent status as a second-rate power; or boldly confront what it considered to be American obstinacy.

For the United States, the critical issue lay in what Roosevelt and Hull perceived as Japanese aggression in China. As the negotiations proceeded, American intelligence's deciphering of the Japanese diplomatic code provided ample evidence of Japanese duplicity. As Nomura talked, Hull knew that Japan was planning an attack on American military and naval bases in the Pacific, although he did not know that Pearl Harbor was the specific target. It is little wonder that Hull did not trust the Japanese. For his part, Franklin Roosevelt did not desire a war with Japan, for he believed that the full resources of the United States must be conserved for the inevitable struggle against Nazi Germany. Yet under strong pressure from the Chinese lobby and from the British government to maintain a hard line, the president could not bring himself to engage in a policy of appeasement. In the end, war came because neither Japan nor the United States was willing to surrender what it considered essential aspects of its national integrity.

9

World War II

The Japanese attack on Pearl Harbor plunged the United States into World War II. The Pearl Harbor controversy continues to provoke historical debate about the precise roles of the United States and Japan in the event. The subsequent declaration of war against the United States by Germany brought America into the European conflict against Germany and its ally, Italy. Throughout the war, President Roosevelt maintained close and friendly relations with the leaders of America's two strongest allies, Great Britain and the Soviet Union. Together with the British Prime Minister, Winston Churchill, and the Soviet Premier, Josef Stalin, Franklin Roosevelt formed a triumverate which determined Allied wartime policy and the constitution of the postwar world.

The first year of the war witnessed a string of Japanese and German victories. The conquest of the Philippine Islands, Singapore, the Dutch East Indies, and numerous islands in the Pacific Ocean won for Japan an empire that exceeded in area and population any of the past. The German expansion to the gates of Moscow made Adolph Hitler the conqueror of most of the European continent. The rest of the war saw a steady reversal in Axis fortunes, as the Allied armies regained the conquered territories. In the Pacific, a two-pronged attack, led by Admiral Chester A. Nimitz from Pearl Harbor and by General Douglas MacArthur from Australia, closed in upon the Japanese empire. A series of amphibious landings recaptured many islands from the Japanese Army, and a series of titanic naval engagements resulted in the destruction of the mighty Japanese fleet. In Europe the Allied forces under General Dwight Eisenhower prepared for the invasion of France with the conquest of North Africa and the assaults on Sicily and Italy. In June 1944 the D-day invasion of Normandy gave the Allies a foothold in western Europe, from which they gradually expanded eastward into Germany. On the eastern front, the Soviet armies successfully defended Stalingrad and drove the Nazi war machine back into Germany.

The final year of the war, 1945, produced the most important decisions to come out of it. President Harry S Truman authorized the dropping of the atomic bomb on two Japanese cities, a decision which quickly ended the war and ushered in the nuclear age. President Roosevelt had acquiesced in Soviet domination of eastern Europe, and agreed that the United States, Great Britain, and the Soviet Union would jointly occupy defeated Germany. By the time of the Potsdam Conference, it had become apparent that Stalin had no intentions of living up to the agreements reached at Yalta, and the war's end yielded a world as insecure as that at its beginning.

Pearl Harbor: The Continuing Controversy

Near the end of November 1941 a large Japanese fleet under the command of Admiral Chuichi Nagumo left Japan on a northeastern course that would take it far out of range of the usual Pacific shipping lanes. Spearheaded by four huge aircraft carriers, each bearing scores of torpedo and dive bombers, as well as hundreds of Zero fighters, the fleet had embarked on a momentous mission: a surprise attack on the headquarters and main base of the United States Navy's Pacific Fleet at Pearl Harbor, Hawaii. At 7:55 A.M., on December 7, 1941, the first wave of Japanese planes arrived over the base and began a series of relentless attacks on American ships and airplanes. An hour later, a second wave struck. The Japanese had scored an overwhelming success. All eight battleships moored at Pearl Harbor were either destroyed or disabled. Three cruisers and three destroyers were heavily damaged. Almost every American airplane on the island of Oahu was destroyed. Over two thousand American servicemen lost their lives, all at a cost of only twenty-nine Japanese airplanes and three small submarines.

Pearl Harbor was one of the most stunning and shocking events in American history. Constantly reassured of the readiness of the United States armed forces and believing that the Roosevelt administration had done

Pearl Harbor, 1941. *National Archives*

everything possible to avert war, the American people received the news
of Pearl Harbor with disbelief. Their initial reaction was to rally behind
the president and give universal support to his request for a declaration of
war against Japan and his reciprocation of the German declaration of war
against the United States three days later. Despite their enthusiastic support
for the war effort, many people raised troublesome questions about Pearl
Harbor. How did it happen? Who was responsible? Why were we taken
by surprise? These and other questions underscored what has become one
of the great historical debates of twentieth-century historiography, a debate
left unresolved by the seven official government investigations into the
incident. In general, the debate revolves around the question of whether
or not the Roosevelt administration possessed foreknowledge of the attack
and whether or not Roosevelt allowed the attack to take place in order to
bring the United States into the war.

The Pearl Harbor historians may be classified into three main categories: pro-Roosevelt; anti-Roosevelt; and the moderates. The pro-Roosevelt school, which includes such historians as Herbert Feis, Samuel Eliot
Morison, and Norman A. Graebner, maintains that the Roosevelt and Hull
policies of firmness towards Japan upheld the principles of democracy that
America had always championed, and that Roosevelt possessed no previous

knowledge of the attack. The anti-Roosevelt school, which includes Charles A. Beard, Charles C. Tansill, and John Toland, contends that Roosevelt and Hull adopted a policy of deliberate antagonism towards Japan and that the administration exercised extraordinary carelessness in not foreseeing the attack and defending against it.

Between these two extremes, a more balanced view has emerged. Upheld by such scholars as James MacGregor Burns, Paul W. Schroeder, and Gordon W. Prange, the moderate school shuns the partisanship and near-hysteria of the others and concentrates on the evidence. The historians of the moderate school believe that like any other momentous event in history, Pearl Harbor cannot be explained in simplistic terms. An accurate appraisal of the event must take into consideration the history of Japanese-American diplomacy, the personalities of the people involved, and numerous other factors. Because Pearl Harbor continues to excite the public imagination and because a substantial amount of previously classified information about it has been recently made available, we shall now examine the main features of the controversy.

One of the reasons for Pearl Harbor lay in the fundamental misunderstandings of the United States and Japan toward each other. To most Americans, including influential officials in the Far Eastern section of the State Department, the Japanese were the most inscrutable of the Oriental peoples. Everything the Japanese did seemed to contradict basic western values. The Japanese spoke, read, and wrote backwards. They opened their locks by turning keys to the left. They built their houses from the top down. They sat on floors. They ate raw fish. They condoned political assassination. They laughed at tragedy. They conducted themselves with an exaggerated code of manners, yet did not hesitate to treat others with extreme rudeness. They did not believe in God, yet their religion influenced every aspect of their lives. The Japanese, too, failed to understand Americans. They looked on Americans as greedy imperialists, bent on subjecting orientals to economic, social, and political domination by whites. Throughout the convoluted negotiations preceding the outbreak of the war, both sides acted from confusion and misunderstanding, neither attempting to comprehend the rationale behind the actions of the other. The Japanese considered themselves the guardians of Oriental culture, language, peoples, and territory against the onslaught of western imperialism. The Americans considered themselves the bearers of the fruits of western civilization and of the values of Christianity to the people of Asia.

China, the fundamental issue dividing the two countries, provided a clear illustration of their differing views on foreign policy. To the Japanese,

China was torn apart by a civil war between the Nationalists and the Communists, leaving the country vulnerable to Soviet expansion. At the same time, they saw in China's civil disorder the opportunity to extend their own empire. President Roosevelt and Secretary of State Hull, on the other hand, believed that Japan had violated the principle of the Open Door by engaging in clear acts of aggression in China. According to historian James C. Thompson, Jr., Dr. Stanley Hornbeck, one of the State Department's most influential policy makers in the Far Eastern section, believed the Japanese the apotheosis of evil and the Chinese the paragons of virtue. Hornbeck influenced Hull, who had no expertise in the region, to adopt an increasingly inflexible policy toward Japan.

When the Japanese government presented a new set of proposals to the United States on November 20, 1941, Roosevelt originally intended to send a favorable response. Aware that the greatest threat to American security lay in Europe, Roosevelt wanted to avert war in the Pacific, if at all possible. Hull, however, persuaded him to approve the November 26 response to Japan, demanding Japanese withdrawal from Indochina and recognition of Chiang Kai-shek. The Hull message led to the outbreak of war, but Hull certainly did not perceive it that way. Roosevelt's intended response would have led to extended negotiations between the United States and Japan, for it had a conciliatory tone, and it agreed in principle to several of the Japanese demands. The British and Chinese lobbied intensively against Roosevelt's initiative. England wanted the United States to go to war to assist her in her efforts, so her envoys in Washington pressured the president to adopt a harder line against the Japanese. The Nationalist Chinese had a powerful lobby in Washington and used it to pressure Roosevelt to withdraw his message and permit Hull to send his much more militant note. Roosevelt yielded to the pressure because he did not want to alienate such important friends as England and China.

As early as January 1941 the Japanese had formulated plans for the Pearl Harbor attack. A modern industrial nation with few natural resources of its own, Japan's survival as a world power depended on its ability to receive a regular supply of raw materials. When the United States imposed the embargo, Japan looked to the immense treasures of natural resources in Southeast Asia. The Japanese also considered themselves the defenders of oriental civilization and used that idea to justify their conquests. The documentary sources clearly establish Japan's intention to conquer China, Formosa, the Philippines, and Southeast Asia. The negotiations with the United States appear motivated more by a desire to postpone war than to avoid it.

Neither Roosevelt nor Hull had any clear idea of their goals in the Far East. They vacillated between firmness and flexibility. Neither desired war with Japan, yet neither seemed willing to enter into serious negotiations. Their reluctance to do so was prompted in part by the breaking of the Japanese diplomatic code by American intelligence. From early in 1940, Roosevelt and Hull knew the details of Japanese intentions, and they realized that the Japanese displayed treachery in their avowed desire for peace and their simultaneous secret plans for conquest. By the early morning of December 7, 1941, the Japanese diplomatic message in which they broke off relations with the United States had been deciphered, a certain indicator of war. Yet no one in authority warned the American military and naval commanders in the Pacific of this fact until it was too late.

The evidence does not establish that Franklin Roosevelt possessed foreknowledge of the Pearl Harbor attack. Two recent revelations, however, do suggest the possibility that certain officials in the United States government did receive prior information concerning the attack. In several tape-recorded memoirs, the governor of Hawaii, John A. Burns, stated that the head of the FBI office in Hawaii, Robert L. Shivers, informed him one week before the attack that the attack would come within a week. Burns did not state whether he informed officials in Washington nor did he reveal the source of the FBI's information. His extraordinary revelation, however, does raise the possibility that FBI Director J. Edgar Hoover learned of the impending Japanese attack and refused to share that information with the president. None of the available evidence from federal records or from Roosevelt's papers indicates that Hoover so informed him.

A second recently declassified document from the files of the National Security Agency also supports the foreknowledge theory. Chief Warrant Officer Ralph T. Briggs, a radio intercept operator at the Navy's electronic intercept station in Maryland, stated that on December 4, three days before Pearl Harbor, he picked up a Tokyo weather broadcast which included the phrase *higashi no kazeame* (East Wind Rain). Briggs immediately relayed the message to naval intelligence headquarters in Washington because he had been alerted to watch for it. From deciphered Japanese codes American intelligence knew that the "East Wind Rain" message meant that Japan would go to war against the United States. Brigg's account is corroborated by the story of Captain Lawrence Safford, the chief of the Navy's code and signal section, who told a congressional investigating committee in 1946 that he relayed the message from Briggs to top naval officials, who "spirited away and suppressed" the information.

There is no evidence that this information was ever presented to

President Roosevelt. Roosevelt did know that war with Japan was probable, and he was aware of the possibility of a surprise Japanese attack on a major American installation in the Pacific. Roosevelt assumed, however, that the attack would take place against the large military base in the Philippines because of its proximity to Japan. The implications of certain writers that Roosevelt deliberately allowed the Pearl Harbor attack to get the United States into the war are not supported by the evidence. His primary concern lay in assisting England in its struggle against Germany, a far more serious threat than Japan, and the basis of his Japanese policy was to prevent war to give America a free hand in dealing with the Nazi menace. When the Japanese attack came, Roosevelt was genuinely shocked, for he knew that his policy had failed and that the United States would have to fight a war on two fronts.

Early Reversals

In the first year of the war, it appeared that Germany and Japan might win by default. After the Pearl Harbor attack, Japanese naval, air, and land forces launched invasions of numerous American, British, and Dutch possessions in the Far East. In the Philippines, General Douglas MacArthur commanded a force of over 100,000 men, but it included fewer than 20,000 trained Americans, the remainder consisting largely of inexperienced Filipino recruits. Although he knew of the Pearl Harbor attack, MacArthur failed to place his forces on full alert, and a Japanese air assault on the large U.S. air base at Clark Field devastated American air power in the Philippines. This paved the way for a Japanese invasion of the islands. As the Japanese army pushed toward Manila, MacArthur declared the Philippine capital an open city and withdrew his forces to the Bataan Peninsula and the island of Corregidor. For three months, MacArthur successfully defended against Japanese attacks, but when it became obvious that his men lacked the supplies to continue fighting, he was ordered to leave. His replacement, General Jonathan Wainwright, surrendered two months later, on May 6, 1942. The Americans who surrendered were treated with the utmost cruelty by their Japanese captors during the long trek to the prison camps, and some three thousand Americans died in the infamous Bataan death march. In addition to the Philippines, Japan also conquered Wake Island and Guam, two American possessions in the Pacific. By the early spring of 1942, the Japanese had extended their conquests to the Malay peninsula, Singapore, most of Burma, Hong Kong, Borneo, the Celebes, most of New Guinea, the Dutch East Indies, the Caroline, Marshall, and Solomon Islands, as well as two of the Aleutian Islands off the Alaskan coast. Their empire extended over an area greater than that of any other country in world history.

In Europe, Allied fortunes met with equal catastrophe. German U-boats sank nearly eight million tons of Allied shipping in 1942, and they even ventured near the Atlantic coast of the United States, where they sank hundreds of thousands of tons of oil tankers and other merchant ships. Under the brilliant leadership of General Erwin Rommel, the German Afrika Korps inflicted a series of disastrous defeats on the British, and threatened to drive through Egypt and sever the Suez Canal. In Russia, a mighty German offensive drove deeply into the Ukraine, the Crimea, and the Caucausus, and the Wehrmacht drove all the way to the Volga River. To many observers, it appeared that the war had already been decided.

The Allies Hold Fast

In the second half of 1942 there was a startling reversal of Allied fortunes. In the Pacific, in Africa, and in Europe, Allied forces stopped the Axis onslaught and began to turn the tide of battle in their favor. To extend the area of their Pacific conquests, the Japanese decided to invade the small island of Midway, an outpost guarding Hawaii against attack from the west. Under the same Admiral Nagumo who had commanded the Pearl Harbor fleet, a large Japanese task force sailed directly for the island in late May. Forewarned of the Japanese intentions by intercepted code messages, Admiral Chester A. Nimitz, the commander of the American Pacific fleet, stationed a flotilla of aircraft carriers in the path of the Japanese. In a battle lasting from June 3 through June 6, dive bombers and B-17 bombers from American aircraft carriers and from Midway destroyed four Japanese carriers, a heavy cruiser, and three destroyers. At a loss of only one carrier and one destroyer, the Americans had won a spectacular victory. They saved Hawaii from possible invasion, inflicted a stunning defeat on the hitherto invincible Japanese Navy, and boosted public morale in the United States. The heroic pilots of the Battle of Midway, most of whom did not survive their missions, gave American forces in the Pacific the momentum in the war against Japan.

That momentum was not dissipated. On August 7, 1942, a large force of American marines launched an amphibious invasion of the southern Solomon islands of Tulagi and Guadalcanal. Both islands lay within easy air and sea access to vital American shipping lanes, and their capture was essential in order to continue supplying MacArthur's forces in Australia. Thus began what is commonly called the Battle of Guadalcanal, but in reality consisted of a fifteen-month long series of air, sea, and land battles resulting in the American capture of the entire Solomon island chain. That conquest did not come easily. Suffering from dysentery, malaria, and other tropical diseases, the poorly supplied marines suffered grievous losses, but managed to fend off a number of desperate attacks by the Japanese. The Navy also suffered serious losses in the many sea battles, but it also inflicted considerable damage on the Japanese.

In Africa, British forces under General Bernard Montgomery defeated Rommel's army at El Alamein in Egypt and slowly forced the Germans to retreat to the west. Shortly afterward, a large Allied invasion force under General Dwight Eisenhower landed in North Africa and attacked the Germans in Tunisia. Although initially surprised by the ferocity of the German resistance, the Allied forces under Montgomery and Eisenhower continued to press forward and fought a series of successful engagements that resulted in complete surrender of German forces in North Africa in May 1943. The Battle of North Africa not only gave the Allies control over that vital area, it also reopened the Mediterranean to their shipping.

In Russia, the German Sixth Army under General Frederich von Paulus attacked the city of Stalingrad in August 1942. Anticipating an easy capture, von Paulus unexpectedly met heavy resistance and threw larger and larger forces into the city. Under the brilliant command of General Vasili Chuikov, the Soviet Sixty-Second Army fought off the German attacks month after month. In what would emerge as the bloodiest battle of the war, Stalingrad became the scene of brutal hand-to-hand combat, with neither side giving quarter. In November over a million Red Army troops easily broke through the German flanks, inadequately defended by Italian and Rumanian forces, and surrounded the Sixth Army. With its supplies cut off, the Sixth Army held out for two months before surrendering in late January 1943. The Battle of Stalingrad became the decisive turning point in the war on the eastern front. The Germans lost a quarter of a million men, and the Russians had shattered forever the myth of the invincibility of the Nazi war machine.

Allied Offensives

In 1943 the Allies scored impressive victories over the Axis. In Russia, German and Soviet forces met in July in a titanic struggle near the town of Kursk. Over two million men, three thousand tanks, and two thousand

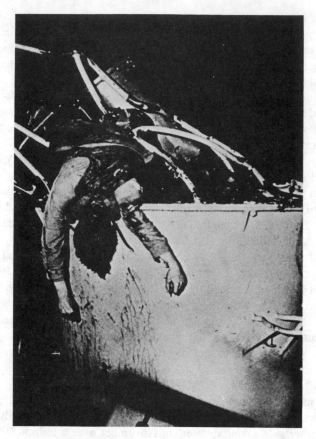

The price of war. A U.S. Navy sailor, 1944. *National Archives*

planes contested a very small area. Equipped with new and formidable Tiger tanks, the Wehrmacht launched a massive offensive against heavily reinforced Russian lines. With an enormous superiority in manpower, the Russians withstood the German attacks and forced them to withdraw from the battlefield. The Battle of Kursk crushed the German offensive, decimated their reserves, and led to a succession of Red Army counteroffensives that pushed the Germans all the way back to the Dnieper River.

In the European theater the Allies laid the foundations for the invasion of France. Through an aggressive new antisubmarine campaign, they broke the U-boats' domination of the Atlantic shipping lanes. New methods of detecting enemy submarines and of convoy shipping drastically reduced the toll taken by the U-boats. The year 1943 also saw the successful invasion and conquest of Sicily and the invasion of Italy in September. At first the Allied armies moved rapidly, but after their liberation of Rome in June 1944, fierce resistance by the Germans forced them to halt.

The Allied strategy for the campaign against Japan entailed a massive pincer operation against the Japanese-held Pacific islands. From Hawaii the Navy and Marines would retake the islands in the Gilbert, Marshall, and Marianas chains, while from Australia American and Australian forces would retake New Guinea to prepare for the invasion of the Philippines. In November 1943 the Hawaii-based command of Admiral Nimitz began an island-hopping campaign with the successful but costly assault on the Tarawa atoll in the Gilberts. Then a joint Navy-Marine operation captured the Marshall islands in the central Pacific. From his headquarters in Australia, General MacArthur started a drive through the island of New Guinea against the Japanese bases in the town of Hollandia. One of the most difficult of the war, the New Guinea campaign involved American and Australian troops hacking their way through hundreds of miles of dense jungle, fending off exotic and deadly creatures, and combatting rare tropical diseases in addition to Japanese troops. Their persistence paid off, and by February 1944 the Allies had cleared the Japanese from the northern New Guinea coast.

D-Day

On January 15, 1944, General Dwight Eisenhower, supreme commander of the Allied forces in Europe, arrived in London with the order to invade northern France and destroy the German forces in western Europe. To implement that directive Eisenhower and his staff had prepared a plan code-named Operation OVERLORD. One phase of the campaign called for an air offensive against Germany. Under the command of the Royal Air Force's Sir Arthur Harris and the United States Army's General Hap Arnold, the air offensive featured a series of terror-bombing raids against major German population centers. Protected by squadrons of fighters, American and British bombers showered thousands of tons of high explosive and incendiary bombs on German cities, causing enormous civilian casualties and tremendous physical devastation. One single air raid on Hamburg in 1943 left over forty thousand civilians dead and half the city destroyed.

Allied intelligence played a vital role in the war. Besides the usual methods of spying, the Allies relied heavily on information gleaned from British intelligence's employment of a captured German deciphering machine. Only recently declassified, the details of this "Ultra" secret reveal that the Allies obtained top secret data about German military plans, which enabled them to plan the invasion with a considerable degree of accuracy. Thousands of underground agents, mainly French and Dutch resistance fighters, also provided the Allied high command with much information about German military operations.

On June 6, 1944, the D-Day invasion of Europe began. In the largest amphibious operation in history, a quarter of a million Allied troops landed on the beaches of Normandy and within a month established an invincible beachhead in northern France. From that beachhead American, British, Canadian, and French forces moved swiftly east. Ably led by such commanders as General Bernard Montgomery, the head of the Twenty-First Army Group, and General George Patton, the head of the U.S. Third Army, the Allies overwhelmed the Germans. By the middle of September they had liberated all of France and had captured the important cities of Brussels and Antwerp. There the Allied drive stalled. Montgomery's land and airborne offensive against the city of Arnhem was repulsed, and logistics problems forced the Allies to stop. In December the Germans launched an attack against the American forces in the Ardennes area. The ensuing Battle of the Bulge resulted in heavy casualties for both sides. After being driven back by the German offensive, the Americans received reinforcements and crushed the German attack.

On the eastern front in 1944 the Soviets staged an enormous offensive in central Russia, where they surrounded and forced over 350,000 German troops to capitulate. This great victory gave the Red Army the momentum it needed to drive the Germans completely out of Russia by the end of the year. By January 1945 vast Soviet army groups were stationed along the Polish-German border and were preparing for the final offensive against Berlin.

In the early summer of 1944 the Marines captured the heavily defended islands of Saipan, Tinian, and Guam in the Marianas chain. During these island battles a huge sea-air conflict took place in which carrier-based American planes devastated a huge Japanese fleet. By this time in the war, the United States possessed such enormous technological and material advantages over Japan that the American pilots referred to the air-sea battle as the "Great Marianas Turkey Shoot." After securing New Guinea, MacArthur's forces prepared for the liberation of the Philippines. In October they invaded and captured the island of Leyte in a battle accompanied by a spectacular sea engagement known as the Battle of Leyte Gulf, which ended in the destruction of the Japanese fleet.

Victory

In the year 1945 the Allies won the war. After recovering from the German Ardennes offensive, Eisenhower's army groups moved eastward into Germany. After crossing the Rhine River, they surrounded an enormous German force of almost 400,000 and forced it to surrender. This great victory virtually cleared the western half of Germany of Nazi troops, and the Allies pushed forward against little opposition. From the east Soviet forces drove deeply into Germany, and under the masterly leadership of Marshall Georgi Zhukov, captured Berlin. On May 8, 1945 the Germans surrendered, thus ending the war in Europe.

After securing Leyte, MacArthur's forces invaded and conquered the main Philippine island of Luzon. Simultaneously, Admiral Nimitz's forces attacked and secured the Japanese-held, heavily defended islands of Iwo Jima and Okinawa. To soften Japan for the planned invasion, a massive bombing campaign against Japanese cities had been initiated. Although the bombing raids inflicted enormous casualties, the Japanese refused to surrender, and it appeared that an amphibious invasion of Japan would be necessary. However, President Harry S Truman, who assumed office after Franklin Roosevelt died on April 12, authorized the dropping of the recently produced atomic bomb. On August 6, a B-29 dropped the bomb on the industrial city of Hiroshima, and three days later a second atomic bomb was dropped on the city of Nagasaki. The catastrophic destruction caused by the atomic bombs persuaded Emperor Hirohito and the Japanese high command of the futility of further resistance, and Japan formally surrendered on September 2, 1945.

The Grand Alliance

From the time the United States entered the war, America and Great Britain agreed to fight for common goals and to coordinate their military strategy. President Roosevelt and Prime Minister Churchill frequently conferred, and the British and American high commands agreed to combine their staffs and to establish a joint military command. Since the United States would play the major role in the defeat of Germany and Japan, it was agreed that an American would command the Allied Expeditionary Force in Europe. The United States Army's Chief of Staff, General George C. Marshall, selected Dwight Eisenhower for the position primarily because of "Ike's" proven abilities in staff organization and administration. In Asia, Admiral Nimitz and General MacArthur commanded the Pacific campaign, while Admiral Louis Mountbatten of Britain commanded the Near Eastern Indian, Burmese, and Chinese phases of the war against Japan. Inevitably, such an arrangement produced personal jealousies and disputes between the Americans and British over their spheres of authority. One such dispute involved General (later Field Marshall) Montgomery and General Eisenhower. As head of the northern prong of the Allied advance in Europe, Montgomery demanded that Eisenhower award his army group priority in manpower, supplies, and air support. This, of course, brought about immediate opposition from American commanders whose forces were making swifter progress than Montgomery's. General Douglas MacArthur also complained about the Allied decision to give the war effort against Germany priority, thus leaving him with only a small proportion of the supplies he requested. On the whole, Eisenhower and General George Marshall, the Chief of Staff of the Army, performed a masterful job in soothing hurt feelings and persuading these highly individualistic commanders to sacrifice personal ambition for the greater good of the war effort.

From the onset of war, President Roosevelt and Prime Minister Churchill believed in an Allied victory, and they began to formulate plans for a postwar world that would prevent the recurrence of such a terrible conflict. Churchill desired a postwar world with adequate provisions for the security of Europe against German aggression, and he believed that the only means of accomplishing this was to divide Germany after the war. Roosevelt, on the other hand, held more idealistic views, and he argued for a postwar world based on the principles of the Atlantic Charter. The implementation of such principles, Roosevelt knew, would entail the breakup of the British Empire, and Churchill protested vehemently against this possibility. This disagreement, however, did not cause a serious rift between the two leaders, and they remained steadfast friends throughout the war.

The Anglo-American display of unity did not extend to their relationship with the Soviet Union. Although the Soviet premier, Josef Stalin, concurred in the goal of defeating Germany, he refused to endorse the principles of the Atlantic Charter and from early in the war, made little attempt to disguise his territorial ambitions for Eastern Europe. When the

British Foreign Secretary, Anthony Eden, visited Moscow in December 1941, Stalin insisted that England give formal approval to the Soviet absorption of Latvia, Lithuania, and Estonia, as well as parts of Finland, Rumania, and Poland. Eden refused to endorse these demands, and after the United States entered the war, it, too, refused to sanction any Soviet territorial gains. In May 1942, the United States, England, and the Soviet Union signed a twenty-year treaty of alliance. The treaty contained no mention of national boundaries, but it did commit the United States to providing the Russians with considerable quantities of supplies and equipment.

In October 1943 Secretary of State Hull, Foreign Secretary Eden, and the Soviet Foreign Minister, Vyacheslav Molotov, met in Moscow to discuss the postwar treatment of Germany, and the three agreed that Germany would surrender unconditionally, abolish all vestiges of Nazism, establish a democratic government, and submit to joint military occupation by American, British, and Soviet troops. So successful was the Moscow conference that President Roosevelt requested a meeting with Churchill and Stalin. The British and Soviet leaders agreed, and the three men met at Teheran, the capital of Iran, in late November and early December 1943. At the conference, Roosevelt, Churchill, and Stalin agreed on the urgency of an Allied invasion of France, and Stalin promised that Russia would enter the war against Japan as soon as Germany was defeated. They also agreed on the partition of Germany, with each country occupying one part, to prevent the recurrence of German militarism. Roosevelt also introduced the idea of the establishment of a postwar United Nations to settle future international disputes peacefully. The atmosphere of candor and cordiality in which the Teheran Conference was conducted convinced Roosevelt that he, Churchill, and Stalin would be able to create a postwar world free from the threat of war.

In 1944 the veneer of Allied unity eroded, as serious disagreements arose among the three powers. As Soviet armies rolled into eastern Europe, Stalin made clear his intentions of occupying that region. The most pressing problem area was Poland. Because of its geographical location, Poland had for centuries been victimized by German and Russian aggression. In 1939, in accordance with a secret provision of the Nazi-Soviet Non-Aggression Pact, Germany and the Soviet Union jointly invaded Poland and divided the country between them. As Soviet troops pushed the Germans out of Poland, Stalin installed a puppet regime there to establish a Soviet satellite. Under pressure from Polish exile organizations and appalled by the Soviet actions, Roosevelt and Churchill protested and demanded that Stalin permit free democratic elections to allow the Poles to choose their own form of government.

Because of the rapid pace of events—it appeared certain that the war would end in 1945—Roosevelt, Churchill, and Stalin met at Yalta in the Crimea to make final plans for the last military effort against Germany and to settle their differences over Eastern Europe. The Yalta Conference produced the main decisions regarding the fate of postwar Europe. Roosevelt, Churchill, and Stalin agreed to divide Germany into four main occupation zones, each controlled by one of the Allied powers, the United States, England, the Soviet Union, and France. They also agreed that Poland could annex certain areas in eastern Germany and that Germany would have to pay an unspecified amount of reparations. The three leaders also promised to institute a new Polish government based on the results of free, democratic elections to be held as soon as feasible after the war. Roosevelt also won British and Soviet approval of his cherished United Nations concept. The international organization would be established shortly after the surrender of Germany, and it would foster the principles of the Atlantic Charter and settle all disputes peacefully. Finally, the Russians agreed to enter the war against Japan and to give formal diplomatic recognition to the Nationalist Chinese government under Chiang Kai-shek.

The Yalta Conference has generated heated historical debate. On the one hand, Herbert Feis and other scholars argue that Roosevelt and Churchill achieved their goals at the conference, that military necessity made inevitable the Soviet domination of Eastern Europe, and that obtaining Soviet support for the United Nations and for the war against Japan were important diplomatic victories. On the other hand, Charles Tansill and other historians argue that Roosevelt "betrayed" Eastern Europe by acquiescing in Soviet domination of the area, and that he displayed an utterly naive attitude toward the Russians. The most reasonable assessment comes from historians like James MacGregor Burns, who argue that the truth lies between the two extremes. Franklin Roosevelt did exhibit an almost incredible degree of ignorance of Russian and Eastern European history, and his reliance on the advice of such amateurs as Harry Hopkins rather than on the expertise of such knowledgeable men as Averill Harriman led him to place an unjustified faith in the promises of the Soviet dictator. Roosevelt, however, did realize that Stalin's aggressive intentions in Eastern Europe represented more than merely the expansionist desires of a communist leader. The Soviet Union had carried by far the heaviest burden in the war against Germany, with over twenty million Russian lives lost. To prevent the recurrence of such a catastrophe, Stalin wanted to construct a barrier of Soviet-dominated states between his homeland and Germany. By the time the Yalta Conference convened, the Red Army already controlled much of Eastern Europe, and the only way to force it to withdraw was to go to war against our own ally, a notion unacceptable to the public in America and Britain. At the time of Yalta, the Soviet agreement to enter the war against Japan was a considerable diplomatic achievement. And Roosevelt sincerely hoped that the United Nations would be able to resolve whatever disputes still divided the Allies in the postwar world.

The Election of 1944

In early 1944 Franklin Roosevelt decided that he would seek reelection to a fourth term as president. The decision came despite his rapidly deteriorating health and the advice of his physicians not to run again. Roosevelt apparently considered himself indispensible to the war effort and to the grand alliance he had formed with Churchill and Stalin. Although the American people were unaware of Roosevelt's cardiovascular problems, many of the Democratic party's leaders knew that he might not survive a fourth term. Therefore, they considered the choice of a vice-presidential running mate as crucial. The incumbent vice-president, Henry A. Wallace, had considerable support from ardent New Dealers but even larger opposition among party bosses and southerners. Roosevelt proposed giving the vice-presidential nomination to James F. Byrnes, the head of the Office of Economic Stabilization, but Sidney Hillman, a vice-president of CIO and a leading spokesman for the organized labor-progressive wing of the party, declared Byrnes unacceptable because of his support for racial segregation. Roosevelt thereupon threw the nomination open to a contest between Wallace and Missouri Senator Harry S Truman. On the third ballot, Truman was nominated primarily because he proved an acceptable compromise choice to the convention. The Republicans nominated Governor Thomas E. Dewey of New York for president and Governor John W. Bricker of Ohio for vice-president.

The campaign lacked the excitement of previous Roosevelt campaigns. The nation was in the midst of war, and the traditional political ballyhoo seemed out-of-place during such a time. Roosevelt's reelection appeared certain. Not only had he retained popular support, the election year witnessed a string of impressive Allied victories over Germany and Japan. Dewey campaigned vigorously, but he gave the voters little choice, for he endorsed virtually all of Roosevelt's domestic and foreign policies. The outcome came as little surprise. Although he suffered further erosion in his popular and electoral vote totals, Roosevelt easily defeated Dewey, and the Democrats retained control of Congress for the twelfth consecutive year. Although Roosevelt had campaigned actively and seemed to regain some of his earlier vigor, the constant pressures of office, aggravated by the long days of travel to Yalta and the taxing diplomatic negotiations of the conference proved too much of a strain on the president, already suffering from serious circulatory disorders. During a brief vacation at his resort in Warm Springs, Georgia, Franklin Roosevelt suffered a massive cerebral hemorrhage and died on April 12, 1945. That evening Harry S Truman took the oath of office as the new president.

World War II in Retrospect

With the advantage of hindsight, it becomes relatively easy for the historian to look back on past events and to suggest what should have been done to prevent mistakes. It should be kept in mind that the decisions made and the actions taken during the war did not result from carefully formulated policies. Rather, they came in the context of the pressure of time and events, of human beings attempting to cope with problems affecting the entire planet, problems made immensely more difficult by the enormous complexity of wartime politics, economics, diplomacy, and military affairs. In this light, one can criticize some of the actions and decisions taken during the war, yet sympathize with and appreciate the difficulties faced by those who made those decisions and took those actions.

Probably the most controversial decision of the war was President Truman's authorization of the dropping of atomic bombs on the Japanese cities of Hiroshima and Nagasaki in August 1945. Widely criticized because of the horrors of nuclear war, Truman's decision came from a sincere and completely justified belief that the employment of atomic weapons would bring the war to a speedy end. In addition, General George Marshall had informed President Truman that the only alternative to dropping the bombs was an invasion of the Japanese mainland, an invasion that could cost over a million American casualties. The recently ended Battles of Iwo Jima and Okinawa had cost almost 100,000 casualties, with American soldiers and marines flushing death-defying Japanese troops from heavily defended caves, and American sailors facing the terrors of the *kamikaze* suicide attacks on our ships. The prospect of invading the Japanese main-

Atomic destruction, Hiroshima, 1945. *Library of Congress*

land itself, defended by several million troops eager to give their lives for their emperor, was a horrifying prospect. To avert this chilling possibility, the atomic bombing of two cities seemed a less destructive alternative. Placed in proper perspective, the atomic bombs did not even cause the greatest loss of life in the war. That dubious distinction belongs to the Allied fire-bombings of Dresden, Germany, in February 1945 and of Tokyo, Japan, the following month, although it required thousands of incendiary bombs to produce the same destructive effects as one atomic bomb.

Another controversial decision was that of President Truman and General Eisenhower to allow the Russians to capture the German capital, Berlin. By early April 1945, Allied armies had crushed German opposition on the western front, and as we now know, could easily have marched directly east and taken Berlin before the Russians. Winston Churchill, George Patton, and others urged Eisenhower to order the Allied armies to drive as far east as possible to restrict the area of postwar Soviet domination. Truman supported Eisenhower's refusal to accept the advice. First, the consensus of Allied intelligence was that an Allied drive to Berlin would cost many thousands of casualties. Second, at the Yalta Conference, Roosevelt and Churchill had agreed to a Russian capture of Berlin, and Truman and Eisenhower felt obligated to honor the agreement. Thus, when American and British forces reached the Elbe River, the line of demarcation between themselves and the Russians, they halted, allowing the Red Army to move deeply into Germany, Czechoslovakia, and Austria. The decision not to take Berlin thus had untold consequences for the future of eastern Europe, but it was a decision made under the most difficult of circumstances and made to save American and British lives.

World War II unleashed forces which still play a significant role in world affairs. In Asia, the war gave impetus to the desire for independence from colonialism of the subjugated peoples of the area. In India, for example, the end of the war saw the renewal of the mighty independence movement led by Mahatma Gandhi, a movement which resulted in the total British withdrawal from the subcontinent three years after the war ended. In Indochina, the war helped instill new vigor in the anticolonialist movement led by Ho Chi Minh against the French. In such places as Malaya and Indonesia, popular guerilla campaigns against colonial rulers were begun. In Europe the barbarities and atrocities of the Nazi concentration and extermination camps generated a strong measure of public support for the Zionist goal of an independent Jewish nation in the Middle East, and in 1948, the nation of Israel was created out of the old British protectorate of Palestine. In China, the Communist Chinese under Mao Tse-tung renewed their civil war against the Nationalist forces under Chiang Kai-shek in 1945. Despite massive American military and economic assistance, Chiang's faction steadily lost popular support. Ironically, the end of World War II produced a map of Europe strikingly similar to that at the beginning, with Poland and other eastern European countries lying under the domination of a foreign power. The war was the last great crusade for a world based on peace, democracy, and mutual trust among nations, and it failed to achieve those goals. Nazi Germany had been defeated, but in its place an even greater menace to world peace, Soviet Russia, now dominated the same areas of the continent as had Germany at the beginning of the war. Consequently, the United States faced a new challenge, one that would entail a radical change in its historical policy of noninvolvement in world affairs. The Cold War would bring America permanently into active involvement in the world through the new policy of containment. This, however, would pose a problem for postwar America. For the generation of World War II, America had successfully met the challenge facing it, both on the battlefields of Asia and Europe and on the home front.

10

The Home Front

During World War II, the American people faced one of their most difficult challenges, and they met that challenge through an unprecedented display of national unity. Because of the virtually unanimous support for the war effort, the government was able to meet its goals in industrial production, manpower, finances, and all the other areas that the war demanded. Aided by bipartisan support for the war and for the way in which he was handling it, President Franklin D. Roosevelt provided the country with the same type of dynamic leadership he had given during the depression.

Because of the enormous demands the war effort made on America's human, natural, and industrial resources, the federal government operated a heavily managed economy. Numerous federal agencies dictated wage and price standards, regulated economic activity in minute detail, and imposed a national system of rationing that encompassed such integral commodities of everyday life as food, gasoline, and clothing. At the same time, people survived this increased regulation of their lives with a minimum of discomfort and little complaining. Millions managed to evade the government-imposed controls and obtained their luxuries through the inevitable black market. Most people, however, voluntarily complied with the demands, as evidenced in the large measure of cooperation between management and labor.

The war generated a social revolution in America. Large numbers of blacks left the rural South, as they made their way to the centers of industrial production in the North and Midwest. Millions of women took over traditionally male jobs and demonstrated their capacity for performing as well as men in occupations ranging from welding to steel production. These and other minority groups experienced for the first time the bountiful opportunities that had hitherto been reserved for white men, and the seeds of the future movements for racial and sexual equality were planted during the war.

America on the Eve of War

At the beginning of December 1941, the United States had just begun to recover from the Great Depression. To be sure, the economic crisis had not yet ended—there were still some 4 million people out of work—but the beginning of the Christmas season unveiled a new mood of optimism and confidence about the future. That mood was tempered by the realization that America might be dragged into the war, and a recent Gallup poll had revealed that a substantial majority of the American people supported the ᵣ Roosevelt administration's policies of assistance to England and the Soviet Union and of firm resistance to Japanese demands in the Far East. Knowing full well that such policies might propel us into war, Americans nevertheless believed that their government stood on the side of righteousness and that if war came, we would win it.

Assisted by a record $8 billion in federal spending for national defense, the economy showed signs of vigor and strength. Most people now held jobs, and although they took home an average of only $40 a week, they ate well and maintained a standard of living that enabled most to afford a few luxuries. Not since the boom years of the 1920s had the economy displayed so many symbols of growing prosperity. The gross national product in 1941 stood at more than double its depression low. National income reached an all-time record of $95 billion, and total industrial production exceeded its 1939 level by two-thirds. The automobile industry experienced its most profitable year since 1929; its total retail sales of $54 million exceeded the 1929 level by over $6 million. Farmers enjoyed their most prosperous year since the mid-1920s, as food prices climbed to record highs. Counterbalancing this rosy picture was the continuing impoverishment of millions of American families. Blacks did not share in the overall prosperity and remained the most neglected group of citizens. Almost four million families earned average annual incomes of only $300, a sum which by any standards meant abject poverty. Over seven million workers earned less than the legal minimum wage of forty cents an hour, and many earned less than fifteen cents an hour. Tenant farmers and sharecroppers, coal miners, domestic servants, and many other categories of employees found little opportunity to rise above the lowest economic class. Most people still could not afford to buy cars, and the great majority had little hope of fulfilling the cherished dream of owning their own home.

Despite these sobering facts, there was an air of exuberance about America in 1941. The American people had come through one of the most disheartening and difficult travails in their history, and they had done so remarkably well. Christmas shoppers reflected this new, confident mood by purchasing items considered unreachable luxuries in the past: nylon stockings, wool suits, and a variety of new toys. The entertainment business flourished, as more Americans went to movies, night clubs, and dance halls than even during the flourishing twenties. If the Japanese attack on Pearl Harbor shattered this optimistic national mood, it did not weaken the resolve of the American people as they made ready for what everyone knew would be a long, difficult, and costly struggle.

Manpower

After the outbreak of war, one of the most pressing problems facing the Roosevelt administration was the mobilization and recruiting of the armed forces. The Selective Service Act of 1940 and its renewal the following year had already provided the War Department with over a million men in the Army and Navy. Most of these recruits were given hasty and inadequate training and were equipped with surplus materials left over from World War I. Yet they represented the nucleus of what would become by far the largest military organization in American history. One of Congress's first actions after the declaration of war was a new Selective Service Act that required all men between the ages of twenty and forty-four (in 1942, the minimum age was lowered to eighteen) to register with their local draft boards. The act also required all men between forty-five and sixty-five to register for potential domestic employment in vital industries. This largest draft in American history worked smoothly. The overwhelming majority of eligible men complied with the law. During the war, almost ten million men were drafted, and an additional five million volunteered. In general, younger men and those without families of their own were drafted first, but the enormous manpower demands eventually found the great majority of those between eighteen and thirty-five called into active duty. A few categories of men received exemptions from the draft: certain politicians, those engaged in vital occupations, and male farmers who did not have adult assistance on the farm. Those who were called up for service had to pass fairly rigorous mental and physical examinations, and approximately one-quarter failed one or more of the tests.

The problems of training, housing, feeding, equipping, and providing for the innumerable other needs of this mass of men placed tremendous strains on the nation's resources. On the whole, the government managed to handle those problems with considerable success. Those men inducted into the Army were sent to one of several large military camps where they received a sixteen-week basic training course, in which they were given intensive drilling in the fundamentals of military life: physical fitness, weapons handling, strategy and tactics, etc. One such base was located at Fort Polk, Louisiana, where, in 1940, a brigadier general named Dwight Eisenhower received the praise of the Army's General Staff for his brilliant organization and handling of war games maneuvers. Similar camps were located at Fort Hood, Texas, and Fort Dix, New Jersey for the Army, Quantico, Virginia, and Paris Island, South Carolina, for the Marines, and San Diego, California for the Navy. The air forces were organized under the Army, Navy, and Marines. They did not have a separate branch of their own. After the basic training, the recruit was sent to one of many advanced camps, where he was given specialized instruction in such fields as infantry, armor, and logistics. The government built over a thousand military bases in the United States. Hastily constructed, these bases became the temporary home for the American "GI" (after Government Issue) until he was called to overseas duty. The ubiquitous Quonset Hut and wooden barracks facilities were the most obvious features of these bases. Most were located near towns and cities, and weekends and furloughs became occasions for the servicemen to invade the nearest communities to engage in the "hell-raising" activities that universally accompany war.

Most of the recruits were young men, many without a high school education, and few with a college degree. They came from every town, village, and city in America, and the bases to which they were sent became miniature melting pots, with men from every social, economic, and regional subdivision congregated together. Within time, the raw recruit was turned into a proficient fighting man, capable, as he would demonstrate, of holding his own with the fearsome warriors of the dreaded German Wehrmacht. Upon his arrival at boot camp, he was made instantly familiar with the differences between military and civilian life. He learned the language of the unit to which he belonged (in the Marines, a latrine was a "head," field boots were "boondockers," coffee was "dough," etc.). His typical day consisted of an hour of calisthenics, an hour and a half of close order drill, an hour of long-distance running, training in weapons handling and firing, more drilling, more fitness training, and a couple of hours of propaganda. He led a gruelling existence and went to bed each night exhausted, but he emerged from the ordeal a tough and thoroughly prepared soldier.

Financing the War

World War II cost the federal government more money than any other event in American history. The total cost of the war was the enormous sum of $321 billion, less than half of which was raised through the traditional means of taxation. The remainder, some $220 billion, was raised through borrowing, increasing the total national debt from $40 billion at the beginning of the war to $260 billion at the end.

From the onset of war, there was a national consensus that no one should profit unduly from the struggle. Therefore, the Roosevelt administration adopted the principle that the greatest burden of wartime taxation would have to be born by the wealthy. However, the need for revenue proved so heavy that it soon became obvious that taxes for all income groups would have to be raised. In 1940 Congress had passed two revenue acts which raised income and corporate taxes and imposed a graduated excess profits tax on business revenue. In 1941, Congress again raised these taxes, but the income tax structure weighed so heavily on the upper classes that most wage earners escaped paying federal taxes altogether. In October 1942, Congress passed a Roosevelt-endorsed measure that revolutionized the national income tax system. It increased the corporate tax to 40 percent, placed a 90 percent rate on excess profits, and drastically increased estate and gift taxes. The Revenue Act of 1942 also reduced exemptions to $500 for single persons and to $1,200 for married couples and it raised the regular income tax from 4 to 6 percent of income. The act also imposed a surtax of 13 to 82 percent on all taxable income and placed a "victory tax" of 5 percent on all income over $624 a year. Under this act, tax rates were much steeper for upper income groups than for lower income people. A person earning $500,000 a year had to pay 88 percent in taxes, while a person earning $3,000 paid only 9 percent. This produced a dramatic decline in the proportion of total national income retained by the wealthy.

To make up for the deficits in revenues, the Roosevelt administration promoted the sale of war bonds. In war loan drives, the government staged propaganda campaigns to persuade people to purchase bonds. Movie stars, leading sports heroes, and other celebrities were employed to travel the country promoting the bond drives. Most of the bonds were purchased by corporations, insurance companies, and large financial institutions. A considerable amount was sold in the form of $25 and $50 series "E" bonds, which could be afforded by the average American family. The bond drives were quite successful. People bought them for patriotic reasons and for the profits the bonds promised. The combination of bond sales and the large increases in income tax revenues provided the government with sufficient money to finance the war effort with little serious financial burden on the American people.

The Mobilization of Industry

One of the nation's most pressing needs was the transformation of American industry from a peacetime to a wartime production basis. The Roosevelt administration had already made provisions for this massive transformation of the nation's industrial production, and through its prewar defense spending, had provided the capital necessary for a thorough beginning. From 1939 through 1941, American industry underwent the change with relative ease, for the depression had so seriously weakened its productive capacity that idle factories and unemployed men could be utilized in defense production with no serious disruption of the normal domestic production of automobiles, appliances, etc.

In 1939, President Roosevelt established a War Resources Board headed by the United States Steel magnate, Edward R. Stettinius, Jr., to advise him on industrial mobilization for war. The board lasted only two months and was dissolved because of criticism of its domination by giant corporations. The War Resources Board did present a plan for the mobilization of industry that called for virtual dictatorial powers to be exercised by an administrator. The plan proved too drastic, and Roosevelt ordered another one to be drawn up by Bernard M. Baruch, who had performed brilliantly as the chairman of President Wilson's War Industries Board during World War I. Baruch's plan provided a more feasible approach to the problem and essentially outlined the steps necessary for the gradual transition of the national economy from one based on peace to one based on war. At first, Roosevelt ignored the Baruch plan, but after the fall of

France in June 1940, he established the Advisory Committee to the National Defense Council. The council recommended, and Congress enacted, legislation that provided for Reconstruction Finance Corporation funding for the construction of defense plants and for income tax benefits for businessmen who invested in defense industries.

In 1941, the president replaced the Advisory Committee with two agencies that would exercise a substantial degree of authority throughout the war. The Office of Production Management (OPM) and the Office of Price Administration and Civilian Supply (OPA) were given the power to oversee war production and to maintain reasonable price levels on industrial products. The OPM performed a yeoman task in coordinating American and British production and in providing assistance to the automobile companies in converting their plants to the production of tanks and airplanes. Because of severe shortages of many essential raw materials, Roosevelt reorganized the OPM in August 1941. The basic agency responsible for the critical allocation of national resources between the armed forces and the civilian economy was the Supplies Priorities and Allocations Board under Donald M. Nelson of Sears, Roebuck. Nelson, however, failed to arrange an equitable system of dividing the natural resources, permitted the military to determine production priorities, and gave the large corporations an almost exclusive monopoly on war production. In October 1942, Roosevelt appointed Supreme Court Justice James F. Byrnes head of the new Office of Economic Stabilization. Byrnes immediately established a plan of allocations that quickly ended the disruption and shortages created by Nelson. Byrnes proved so successful that Roosevelt appointed him head of the Office of War Mobilization in May 1943 and gave him dictatorial control over nearly every aspect of the national economy.

The national industrial needs during the war were enormous, but industries more than met their quotas of tanks, planes, guns, and other necessities. The aircraft industry, for example, only employed some 46,000 persons and produced fewer than 6,000 planes in 1940. By 1944, it had a work force of over two million and produced 96,000 planes. The shipping industry produced over fifty-five million tons of shipping. Overall, American industrial production during the war doubled its 1939 total, and the total of agricultural production increased by one-fifth. The greatest incentive for this tremendous increase was the huge amount of money pumped into the economy by the federal government. In 1944, the year of heaviest wartime productivity, the government spent over $90 billion in wartime goods and services, an amount almost half the total gross national product that year. One beneficial result of this increase in national productivity was full employment. By 1944, over fifty-four million men and women held jobs, and the demand for laborers was so great that anyone who wanted to work could find a good job with relative ease.

Labor and the War

To cope with the problem of mobilizing the work force and regulating wages, hours, and working conditions, President Roosevelt established the War Manpower Commission (WMC) in 1942. The WMC drew up an elaborate set of guidelines governing labor, the most significant of which was a rule prohibiting defense workers from leaving their jobs for the duration of the war. The WMC also proposed legislation to draft men for wartime work. Strongly opposed by organized labor, the proposed legislation did not receive congressional approval before the end of the war.

In January 1942, Roosevelt created the War Labor Board (WLB), an agency whose primary responsibility lay in mediating labor disputes. Soon after its creation, the WLB discovered that it had to establish an overall national labor policy for the duration of the war to reconcile the opposing interests of management and labor. Some spokesmen for management suggested a wartime moratorium on the right of collective bargaining and a suspension of unionization drives, but the WLB stood firmly by the principles of the Wagner Act. To encourage unionization, the agency developed a "maintenance of membership" plan whereby unions retained the right of collective bargaining for all employees of a particular factory during the life of the work contract, but the unions had to agree to surrender the closed shop in those states where it was legal. Under the WLB's aegis, union membership expanded by almost five million during the war.

The WLB's greatest concern was preventing inflation by keeping union wage demands to a reasonable level. The agency proclaimed labor's right to a standard of living compatible with the general standard that existed at the outbreak of war. When wage demands exceeded that standard, the WLB revoked pay raises granted by industry. In general, wages during the war rose slightly more than did the cost of living. Because the WLB operated fairly, organized labor cooperated with it and the AFL and CIO promised President Roosevelt that they would not strike. The vast majority of unions abided by this pledge, but several did not. In May 1943, the United Mine Workers (UMW) under John L. Lewis called a nationwide coal strike because the WLB refused to grant coal miners excessive pay increases. Roosevelt seized the mines, but the UMW struck again. After

Roosevelt threatened to draft them, the miners returned to work. When Lewis threatened to call a third strike, Roosevelt capitulated and granted the UMW large wage increases. Lewis's actions and the threat by railroad workers to call a rail strike in 1943 appeared to many Americans as an insult to their patriotism and resulted in public clamor for restraints on labor's freedom. In June 1943, Congress passed the Smith-Connally "War Labor Disputes" Act, which empowered the president to seize struck industries and required labor to wait thirty days before executing a strike. Many state legislatures also passed antilabor legislation that outlawed such practices as the closed shop and secondary boycotts.

On the whole, American workers prospered during the war. Because of the enormous demands, industry operated at full capacity, and many workers earned overtime, weekend, and holiday pay that doubled their regular salaries. The WLB encouraged industry to intitiate special incentive programs designed to increase productivity. A model experiment was set up at the Grumman aircraft plant in Long Island, New York. Grumman had a special incentive pay system, by which workers who produced more than their allotted quotas would receive bonus pay. The company deliberately ran its production lines at normal speed to relieve the threat of worker exhaustion evident at many other plants. It also established a number of fringe benefit programs to provide its employees with additional incentives. For example, Grumman provided special services ranging from repairing automobiles to running errands. The Grumman experiment proved successful in every respect. Worker morale remained high, with only a 1 percent turnover rate and a 3 percent absenteeism rate, and the plant exceeded its production quotas each year of the war.

Women and Labor

By the end of the war, the symbol of "Rosie the Riveter" had become a staple ingredient of government wartime propaganda. Throughout the country, government films and posters praised the selfless devotion of American women who left their traditional household duties, discarded their aprons and donned coveralls and goggles to fill the gaps in the labor force which were created by the manpower needs of the armed forces. This stereotyped image obscured the real story of American women during the war. In 1940, some twelve million women held jobs, and women made up over 25 percent of the nation's work force. During the war, about four and a half million additional women joined the work force. Since over twelve million steadily

A welder, one of many women in the war industry, 1943. *Library of Congress*

employed men joined the armed forces, nearly three-quarters of the deficiency was made up by men. Of those women who did work, about one-quarter worked in industry, the rest holding jobs in agriculture and in clerical positions. Almost 70 percent of all adult women in America did not work throughout the war. Of those who did work, the vast majority, over 85 percent, had no children at home, and almost half were not married.

Nevertheless, the contributions made by American women to the war effort were great. Women worked at jobs that had previously been reserved for men: as riveters, welders, hydraulic press operators, crane operators, bus drivers, train engineers, bellhops, lifeguards, lumberjacks, or "lumberjills," as they were called, and in a variety of other positions far removed from the traditional female occupations in clerical, teaching, and nursing. By all accounts, women performed as well as their male counterparts, and by the end of the war, had become accepted as valuable, although temporary, components of the American economic spectrum.

However, sexual discrimination prevailed. Most industries paid male workers considerably more than females. During the war, women who worked in heavy industry received an average of 40 percent less pay than did men. Women did not receive the same opportunity to advance to higher positions, and most companies awarded men seniority much quicker than women. In November 1942, the War Labor Board did issue an order that permitted employers to raise women's wages to the same level as men's, but few complied with the order, and the federal government did not enforce it. Heavily dominated by men, organized labor vigorously opposed any actions that would bring about equality of economic opportunity. When the war ended and men began returning home from service, female employees were laid off to provide openings for these men. During the last half of 1945, over 1.3 million women were dismissed from their wartime positions, and by September 1946, that figure had risen to over two million. As a consequence, despite the demonstration of their potential as vital and productive members of the labor force, American women were relegated to their traditional status as soon as the wartime emergency ceased.

Blacks and the Home Front

For American blacks, World War II proved a time of hope and frustration, advancement and regression. With the noble ideals expressed in the Atlantic Charter, the war gave blacks the hope that their historic status as second-class citizens would end. The civil rights movement, long frustrated by the hostility of local, state, and federal governments, gained impetus during the war, as many Americans came to champion its goals. Such black leaders as Roy Wilkens of the National Association for the Advancement of Colored People (NAACP) and A. Philip Randolph, the president of the Brotherhood of Pullman Porters, helped to persuade the Roosevelt administration to take steps in the direction of racial equality. After a threatened march on Washington by fifty thousand of Randolph's men, Franklin Roosevelt issued an executive order in June 1941 that directed that blacks be admitted to job training programs, prohibited racial discrimination, and established the Fair Employment Practices Commission (FEPC) to investigate charges of discrimination in employment. During the war, the FEPC held public hearings, conducted investigations into allegations of racial discrimination in defense plants, and issued orders that the antidiscrimination clauses in defense contracts be enforced. For the first time since the end of Reconstruction, the United States government made an effort to upgrade the lives of its black citizens. By 1945, almost two million blacks worked in defense industries and were paid an average of almost $2,000 a year, a remarkable increase over their 1940 average of less than $500.

Despite the federal programs, blacks did not receive the treatment they desired. The armed forces remained racially segregated throughout the war, and black troops were given largely menial and service tasks. In wartime employment, blacks were paid, on the average, one-third less than whites for the same jobs. The FEPC did not possess either the legal authority or the manpower necessary to enforce its provisions, which were ignored or violated by the majority of war industries. By 1944, blacks held only 7.5 percent of the jobs in war industries, and those they did hold were usually less lucrative than those held by whites. Organized labor vehemently opposed equality of opportunity in hiring, and many of the most powerful of the unions either excluded blacks entirely from their membership or permitted only a token representation.

The most highly publicized racial incident during the war was the bloody and violent Detroit race riot of June 1943. Because of its existing automobile industry, Detroit became one of the nation's leading centers of industrial production. Job opportunities abounded, and from 1940 until the time of the riot, some sixty thousand blacks and four hundred thousand whites from the South had migrated to the city. For at least a year, racial tensions had festered in the congested city, as racist propaganda from the likes of Father Charles Coughlin, the Reverend Gerald L. K. Smith, and J. Frank Norris flooded the city's white population. Also, antiwhite propaganda was disseminated among the black population. The two races competed for jobs and housing, and throughout 1942 and the first six months of 1943 racial violence intensified. On the night of June 21, 1943, a fight between a white sailor and several black youths suddenly erupted into an open confrontation between the races. Originally confined to a small bridge, the clash spread to several white and black areas of Detroit, as exaggerated rumors of the conflict reached more and more people. By five o'clock the following morning, mobs of blacks and whites roamed the streets, attacking innocent bystanders, destroying private property, and ignoring pleas to end the violence. Throughout the day, some ten thousand whites marched down the main thoroughfare in the city's black section shooting, knifing, and beating lone Negroes they happened to capture. Negro mobs retaliated. Governor Harry F. Kelly of Michigan finally had to request federal assistance, and President Roosevelt sent a battalion of troops into the city. By noon on June 22, order was restored.

An official inquiry by the city government resulted in a report that placed the blame for the violence squarely on Detroit's black community. However, the evidence clearly shows that whites bore an equal, if not greater, responsibility for the bloodletting. Of those killed in the riots, twenty-five were blacks and only nine were white. Over 80 percent of the injured were black, and three-quarters of the property damage was inflicted on black-owned businesses and residences. The city police made no attempt to suppress the white violence, yet reacted with fury against black rioters. Other racial incidents occurred in Mobile, Alabama, Beaumont, Texas, and in the Harlem section of New York City.

The riots reflected the fact that America remained a racially divided nation, a fact thoroughly documented in 1944, with the publication of Gunnar Myrdal's *An American Dilemma*. In painstaking detail, Myrdal analyzed the discrimination that prevailed in the country. Wendell Wilkie, Eleanor Roosevelt, and other white leaders pleaded for better treatment of America's blacks, but their pleas went unanswered. In Congress, Senators Theodore G. Bilbo of Mississippi and Allen Ellender of Louisiana led southern segregationists in successful filibusters against such bills as an antilynching law, the repeal of the poll tax in federal elections, and the strengthening of the FEPC.

The Fate of the Japanese Americans

After the attack on Pearl Harbor, the public demand for revenge against the Japanese was understandable. That thirst for revenge, however, extended to some 125,000 American citizens of Japanese descent. Most of these people were born in America (and were called *Nisei*), although about one-quarter had emigrated from Japan *(Issei)*. The vast majority lived on the West Coast, mainly in California. The Japanese Americans made up about 1 percent of California's population, but their Oriental features made them a highly visible group of people. The shock, rage, and terror ignited by the Pearl Harbor attack made the Japanese Americans natural targets for the popular mood, succinctly expressed by Lieutenant General John L. DeWitt, the commanding officer of the Army's Western Defense District: "A Jap's a Jap. It makes no difference whether he is an American or not." Within days after Pearl Harbor, white Californians began taking actions that indicated their feelings. Banks froze all funds held by Japanese Americans and refused to cash their checks. Grocery stores, service stations, and other commercial establishments refused to do business with them. The state of California revoked their licenses to practice law and medicine and fired them from civil service positions.

Quick to sense the public mood, politicians and editorial writers joined the swelling chorus demanding that the Japanese be evacuated from the West Coast. Perhaps the most influential newspaper columnist in America, Walter Lippmann, threw his prestige behind the movement for mass evacuation. Succumbing to the pressure, President Roosevelt signed on February 19, 1942 the infamous Executive Order No. 9066, authorizing the Secretary of War to remove "any and all persons" from official military areas. The entire West Coast was declared a "military area," and with brutal swiftness, 110,000 Japanese Americans were forcibly removed from their homes. Over $1 billion in property—houses, businesses, farms and equipment—was confiscated, and the Japanese lost half a billion dollars in annual income. These people were transported to "relocation centers" and then to a dozen internment camps located in eight western and southeastern states. These camps, located on federal land, were operated by the War Relocation Authority, and provided primitive living conditions for the internees. In general, each camp consisted of a series of wooden barracks providing an average of five hundred square feet of living space for a family of six persons. These apartments had no cooking, washing, or lavatory facilities and were poorly heated. Few even had running water.

The Nisei and Issei accommodated themselves to their new life. Within a short time after their arrival, they transformed the camps into model communities. They organized work battalions to raise crops, cook, do the laundry, and other chores. They operated camp police and fire departments, established post offices, and even opened tailor, beauty, and barber shops, held religious services, conducted weddings and funerals, educated their children, and did everything communities ordinarily do.

Nisei (second generation Japanese Americans) evacuees bound for a relocation camp, 1942. *National Archives.*

Much has been written about the gross violation of the civil liberties of these Japanese Americans. Such noted champions of civil rights as Supreme Court Justice Hugo Black and the Attorney General of California, Earl Warren, vigorously defended the removal. Perhaps the most tragic aspect of the story is that there was no justification for the removal. No evidence was ever produced to justify even the remotest suggestion of disloyalty among these people. Many Nisei served in the armed forces. The Nisei 442nd Regiment, which served in the Italian campaign, became the most decorated military unit in American history. Not a single Nisei soldier deserted, while the desertion rate for non-Nisei soldiers averaged 10 percent. Throughout the war, the beginning of each day in the internment camps was marked by a salute to the American flag and a pledge of support for the war effort. In Hawaii, where the proportion of the Japanese population was much higher than in California, the Japanese Americans were not removed, and many served in highly sensitive positions in the Pacific Fleet headquarters.

The treatment of the Japanese Americans must be considered in historical perspective. Although unjustified and marked by obvious racism, the relocation of these people resulted from genuine, though exaggerated fears. The Pearl Harbor attack came as such a surprise and as such an insult to national honor that Americans looked for a target on which to vent their fury. In the Japanese Americans, they found that target. During the hectic months following Pearl Harbor, when the United States could not yet retaliate, all sorts of fears and rumors swept the country. At any moment, people believed, the Japanese would attack the West Coast, and it was imperative to prevent it. Even Franklin Roosevelt allowed himself to fall victim to the mass hysteria. Some writers have likened the removal of the Japanese Americans to the Nazi removal of European Jews to the concentration camps, but such a comparison is highly misleading. Despite their ill-treatment, the Nisei and Issei did not suffer genocide. The vast majority survived the camps and returned to their home towns after the war, where they were quickly assimilated into American society. Today, Japanese Americans make up the most highly educated, longest lived, and economically prosperous of all of America's ethnic groups.

Rationing

For a people accustomed to peacetime living, War Production Board Directive No. 1 to the Office of Price Administration in January 1942 came as a shock, for that directive inaugurated the practice of rationing. Because the war effort constituted the highest priority, the Roosevelt administration decided that consumer needs must be allocated on the basis of supply. Since the supply of many items, ranging from gasoline to rubber, fell below wartime and consumer demand, the government was forced to institute rationing, the restriction of consumer purchases of specified items to a limited quantity per household. By the middle of 1942, ration offices had been opened in every state, and over thirty thousand volunteers had been recruited to handle the administration of controlling prices and consumer allottments of more than 90 percent of the merchandise sold in six hundred thousand stores. Ration books containing coupons were issued for every man, woman, and child in the nation.

Rubber became the first item rationed. Because of the Japanese conquest of Malaysia and Indonesia, the entire national source of rubber had fallen into enemy hands. The United States had a stockpile of only six hundred thousand tons, scarcely enough to meet domestic consumer demand for one year, not to mention the huge demands made by the military. As a consequence, the government banned the civilian purchase of new and recapped tires. For the duration of the war, Americans had to make do as best they could, either by drastically reducing their driving or by paying exorbitant prices for tires on the black market. Gasoline rationing soon followed. Most automobile owners were issued "A" coupons, which entitled them to purchase four (later three) gallons of gasoline per week. Certain categories of occupations, including doctors, workers in essential industries, and policemen were given "B" and "C" coupons, which enabled them to supplement the meager amount allowed for the "A's." The gasoline rationing resulted from the German U-boat attacks on American oil tankers off the Atlantic Coast and also from the severe rubber shortage. The rationing had an immediate impact. Automobile driving declined greatly from the prerationing level, and by 1943, the nation's highways were being used at only 20 percent of their capacity, compared with 60 percent before rationing went into effect.

While the rubber and gasoline rationing caused disruptions, food rationing had the most direct impact on the American people. Almost everything that people liked to eat and drink—sugar, meat, cheese, coffee, butter—was strictly rationed by a point system that caused endless confusion and complaining. Housewives had to contend with ration books containing such instructions as: "All RED and BLUE stamps in War Ration Book 4 are WORTH 10 POINTS EACH. RED and BLUE TOKENS are WORTH 1 POINT EACH. RED and BLUE TOKENS are used to make

CHANGE for RED and BLUE stamps only when purchase is made. IM-
PORTANT! POINT VALUES of BROWN and GREEN STAMPS are
NOT changed." When a woman went to the grocery, she had to pay for
her food purchases with stamps and cash, carefully calculating her weekly
allotment of stamps so she would have enough to get the most essential
items. Each month, grocers handled three and a half billion stamps worth
fourteen billion points. To obtain credit, they had to turn the stamps over
to their wholesalers, who deposited the stamps in banks. The banks then
gave the wholesalers a sufficient amount of credit to buy more foodstuffs.
Inevitably, the bureaucracy of administering the ration program led to
delays, confusion, and frustration. Almost daily the OPA changed its point
value system, forcing people to scour their daily newspapers for such
official notices as: "Tomorrow: Coffee coupon No. 25 expires. Last day
to use No. 4 "A" coupon, good for four gallons of gasoline." The OPA
bureaucrats devised countless indecipherable regulations about the exact
nature of the food, especially meat, people bought with the coupons. The
regulations about beef ran over forty thousand words, informing butchers
in minute detail how they should cut T-bone steaks and grind chuck.

It is difficult to assess the effectiveness of wartime rationing. Genuine
shortages of certain goods did exist, and the government imposed rationing
to ensure that shortages of others did not surface. As the war progressed
and the public complaints about bureaucratic inefficiency increased, the
OPA did attempt to ameliorate conditions. The OPA director, Prentiss M.
Brown, made herculean efforts to minimize the red tape. However, the
system never did perform as its advocates hoped. Black market trade in
rationed commodities flourished throughout the war. For the right price,
people could obtain virtually anything they wanted. The theft and coun-
terfeiting of ration coupons became a national scandal, which the government failed to end. By the end of the war, over two thousand people had
been convicted of black market activities in gasoline, and almost five
thousand service stations had lost their licenses for violating the rationing
regulations. The actual violations greatly exceeded these small numbers.
The OPA admitted that 5 percent of the nation's gasoline supply was
purchased with counterfeit coupons, and the government estimated that
over one million gallons of gasoline were illegally sold each week. While
the majority of Americans complied with the system, millions used money
or influence to evade it. A final inequity in the system consisted of its
failure to bring about a fair and practicable program of allocation. In some
parts of the country, surpluses of scarce items existed, while in other areas,
scarcity was the rule. In some places, meat, gasoline, and other rationed

commodities sold for as much as 50 percent more than in other areas. America's first experience with full-fledged government manipulation of the law of supply and demand had mixed results.

Fighting Inflation

Besides being a means to conserve scarce items, the rationing system was one of the federal government's main tools in the attempt to keep wartime prices from rising beyond reasonable expectations. With numerous consumer goods in short supply, with organized labor demanding higher wages, and with manufacturers seeking profits, the wartime economic situation contained all the ingredients for the most sustained increase in wholesale and retail prices since the Civil War. If prices were allowed to rise to their natural marketplace level, they would, the Roosevelt administration feared, make the production of essential war materials prohibitively expensive. Therefore, the president took steps to prevent runaway inflation by artificially controlling prices and wages for the duration of the war.

The most important cog in the anti-inflation machinery, the OPA, was granted the authority to fix maximum prices and to impose rent controls by the Emergency Price Control Act of 1942. Agricultural prices, however, could not be controlled until they reached 110 percent of parity. Farmers took advantage of this provision to increase food prices by 11 percent in 1942 alone. The sharp rise in the price of food naturally generated demands by labor for corresponding wage increases. By September 1942, the situation threatened to get out of hand, so Roosevelt received the authority under the Anti-Inflation Act to freeze all wages and prices at their levels of September 15. Under the vigorous leadership of Prentiss Brown, the OPA in 1943 forced a reduction in food prices and held the line against other unwarranted price increases. These efforts, combined with those of the Office of Economic Stabilization under James F. Byrnes, held the increase in the cost of living during the last two years of the war to only 1.5 percent.

The Technology of War

World War II ushered in a new age of armed combat, an age in which technology and science joined to make war more sophisticated and deadly than ever before. For the United States, it was imperative to produce weapons more advanced than those of the enemy. The Japanese, for example, used a Douglas Aircraft prototype to develop the famed Mitsubishi "Zero" fighter plane, which was faster, more maneuverable, and more accurate than any possessed by the Allies at the beginning of the war. The Japanese also developed torpedo dive-bombers capable of destroying American ships with ease, as the Pearl Harbor attack graphically demonstrated.

Germany, however, posed a much more serious threat, for German scientists developed during the war a variety of modern weapons systems that almost gave their fatherland the technological edge it needed for victory. Some of the German weapons included the Stuka dive-bomber, which provided powerful air support for the massed tank attacks of the Wehrmacht; the 88mm. gun, which served both as an effective rapid-fire antiaircraft gun and as the most destructive antitank gun of the war; the JadgTiger tank, a monstrous, seventy-five-ton machine with great speed and maneuverability and outfitted with infrared firing sights; and the electronically operated U-boat, which wreaked havoc among Allied shipping. Of far more serious consequences for the Allies was the German research in jet propulsion, rocketry, and atomic fission. By the end of the war, German scientists had produced the world's first jet plane, the fearsome Messerschmidt 262 fighter, which easily outmaneuvered and destroyed large numbers of Allied planes. The Germans under Dr. Werner von Braun, a brilliant young physicist, also invented the V-1 and V-2 rockets. Launched from bases in Holland and Germany, these rockets, carrying heavy bomb loads, landed in London and caused much loss of life and property damage. German scientists also conducted research into atomic fission, but had not come close to producing an atomic bomb when the war ended.

When France fell to the Germans in June 1940, President Roosevelt began preparing for America's eventual entry into the war. To compensate for the country's technological backwardness, he appointed that month the National Defense Research Committee, headed by Dr. Vannevar Bush of the Carnegie Institution. A year later, Roosevelt reorganized the program and appointed Bush the head of the Office of Scientific Research and Development (OSRD). Assigned the responsibility of mobilizing the nation's scientists to prepare for the war, the OSRD performed brilliantly. During the war, the OSRD developed such weaponry as the proximity fuse, a radio-controlled fuse that detonated bombs when they were near their target. The OSRD also developed fire bombs, DDT for use against the malaria-bearing mosquitoes in the Pacific campaign, blood transfusion techniques, and penicillin, the last two helping to save thousands of lives.

American scientists also did an extraordinary job of improvisation to meet the changing needs of the war. For example, to erase the Japanese edge in fighter planes, they developed a series of fast, efficient planes that easily overcame the Zeroes during the last two years of the war. To destroy German tanks, they invented the bazooka, a hand-held, tube-shaped rocket launcher. To face the problem of the great distance between Allied air bases and German and Japanese civilian targets, they produced the B-29 bomber, a plane with a very long range and one capable of flying at high altitudes over its targets. To meet the challenge of large-scale amphibious operations, they built LST and other types of landing craft that would convey troops from the large ships to the landing beaches.

The most significant product of Allied scientific efforts during the war was the atomic bomb. In January 1939, the renowned Danish physicist, Niels Bohr, announced that two German physicists had recently accomplished atomic fission with uranium. The implications to Allied nuclear physicists became immediately apparent. Now that atomic fission had been demonstrated in practice, a new kind of bomb, far more deadly and destructive than any previously produced, could be manufactured. If the Germans developed this bomb, they would possess the ultimate weapon of war. Two of the nation's leading scientists, Enrico Fermi and Albert Einstein, both refugees from fascist oppression, urged President Roosevelt to institute a program of research and development that would enable the Allies to produce the bomb before the Germans. Roosevelt approved the idea and authorized funding for it. By the summer of 1941, American physicists had laid the foundations for turning the concept into reality. Dr. Ernest Lawrence of the University of California used a cyclotron to transform the readily available isotope of Uranium, U-238, into the much rarer Plutonium, which could easily be converted into the U-235 needed for the proposed bomb.

The scientists had demonstrated the feasibility of building the bomb, and President Roosevelt authorized a "crash" program to complete the task. Under the direction of Dr. Arthur H. Compton, a team of physicists produced the first controlled atomic chain reaction at the University of Chicago on December 2, 1942. In May 1943, a top-secret program, known as the Manhattan Project, was begun. Under the overall direction of General Leslie R. Groves, teams of mathematicians, chemists, and physicists worked at Oak Ridge, Tennessee and Los Alamos, New Mexico. The teams included scientists from other countries, among whom was the British physicist, Dr. Klaus Fuchs, who betrayed many of the atomic secrets to the Soviet government. By the beginning of 1945, the Los Alamos team, led by Dr. J. Robert Oppenheimer, completed its theoretical and experimental preparation. In early July, the final assembly of the bomb was started, and on July 16, 1945, near the air base at Alamagordo, New Mexico, the world's first atomic bomb was detonated. Justifiably proud of their scientific accomplishment, the men who observed the explosion nonetheless realized that they had created a weapon of awesome potential, and that the future of the world would forever be changed.

Suggested Readings

Scholarly studies of the period from 1920 to 1945 are many and varied. What follows is a selected list of some of the most important of those studies. In addition to the monographs listed below, the student should consult the extensive bibliographies contained in many of them, as well as the numerous scholarly journals covering the era.

General Histories

A standard history of twentieth century America is Arthur S. Link and William B. Catton, American Epoch: *A History of the United States Since 1900,* vol. I, 1900–1945, 5th Edition (1980). Other excellent histories of twentieth century America include: Frank Freidel and Alan Brinkley, *America in the Twentieth Century,* 5th Edition (1982); David W. Noble, David A. Horowitz, and Peter N. Carroll, *Twentieth Century Limited: A History of Recent America* (1980); and David A. Shannon, *Between the Wars: America, 1919–1941* (1979).

Politics of the 1920s

There are several excellent studies of the politics of the 1920s: John D. Hicks, *Republican Ascendancy: 1921–1933* (1960); William E. Leuchtenburg, *The Perils of Prosperity: 1914–1932* (1958); Paul A. Carter, *The Twenties in America* (1975); and Paul A. Carter, *Another Part of the Twenties* (1977). Harding is the subject of considerable controversy. On the favorable side is Andrew Sinclair, *The Available Man* (1975). A much more critical view is Francis Russell, *The Shadow of*

Blooming Grove (1968). Two balanced accounts are Robert K. Murray, *The Harding Era: Warren G. Harding and his Administration* (1969); and Eugene P. Trani and David L. Wilson, *The Presidency of Warren G. Harding* (1977). Two good accounts of internal Harding policies are Robert K. Murray, *The Politics of Normalcy: Government Theory and Practice in the Harding-Coolidge Era* (1973); and Burl Noggle, *Teapot Dome* (1962). For a lively, critical view of Coolidge, see William A. White, *A Puritan in Babylon* (1938). A more sympathetic view is that of David R. McCoy, *Calvin Coolidge: The Quiet President* (1967).

Other studies of the politics of the twenties include: David Burner, *The Politics of Provincialism* (1967), an account of the Democratic Party; Richard O'Connor, *The First Hurrah: A Biography of Alfred E. Smith* (1970); and LeRoy Ashby, *The Spearless Leader: Senator Borah and the Progressive Movement in the 1920s* (1972).

American Life in the 1920s

A good introduction to the twenties is Burl Noggle, *Into the Twenties: The United States From Armistice to Normalcy* (1974). Two lively accounts of American life in the twenties are Leuchtenburg, *The Perils of Prosperity* (1958); and Frederick Lewis Allen, *Only Yesterday* (1931). Excellent studies of specific aspects of American life in the twenties include: David M. Chalmers, *Hooded Americanism: The History of the Ku Klux Klan,* revised edition (1981); Ray Ginger, *Six Days or Forever? Tennessee v. John Thomas Scopes* (1958); James H.Timberlake, *Prohibition and the Progressive Movement* (1963); Norman F. Furniss, *The Fundamentalist Controversy: 1918–1931* (1954); Paula Fass, *The Damned and the Beautiful: American Youth in the 1920's* (1977); Lary May, *Screening Out the Past: The Birth of Mass Culture and the Motion Picture Industry* (1980); Robert Sklar, *Movie-Made America* (1975); Andrew Sinclair, *Era of Excess: A Social History of the Prohibition Movement* (1962); Norman H. Clark, *Deliver Us From Evil* (1976); Humbert S. Nelli, *The Business of Crime* (1976); David M. Kennedy, *Over Here: The First World War and American Society* (1980); Robert Creamer, *Babe: The Legend Comes to Life* (1977).

Hoover and the Great Depression

Herbert Hoover is treated with undisguised hostility in Arthur M. Schlesinger, Jr., *The Crisis of the Old Order: 1919-1933* (1957). A more balanced biography is Joan Hoff Wilson, *Herbert Hoover: Forgotten Progressive* (1975). Also valuable is David Burner, *Herbert Hoover: A Public Life* (1979). A good description of Hoover's political abilities may be found in Jordan A. Schwarz, *The Interregnum of Despair: Hoover, Congress, and the Depression* (1970). Two other accounts of Hoover are Albert U. Romasco, *The Poverty of Abundance: Hoover, the Nation, the Depression* (1965); and Gene Smith, *The Shattered Dream: Herbert Hoover and the Great Depression* (1970). Other aspects of the politics of the Hoover era may be found in Edmund A. Moore, *A Catholic Runs for President: The Campaign of 1928* (1956); and Allan J. Lichtman, *Prejudice and the Old Politics: The Presidential Election of 1928* (1979).

The economics of the 1920s are treated in James W. Prothro, *The Dollar Decade: Business Ideas in the 1920's* (1954); Preston J. Hubbard, *Origins of the TVA: The Muscle Shoals Controversy* (1961); Gilbert C. Fite, *George N. Peek and the Fight for Farm Parity* (1954); John Kenneth Galbraith, *The Great Crash* (1955); Milton Friedman and Anna L. Schwartz, *A Monetary History of the United States* (1963); Peter Temin, *Did Monetary Factors Cause the Great Depression?* (1976).

The impact of the depression is covered in Frederick Lewis Allen, *Since Yesterday* (1940); Dixon Wecter, *The Age of the Great Depression* (1948); Bernard Sternsher, ed., *Hitting Home: The Great Depression in Town and Country* (1970); Roger Daniels, *The Bonus March: An Episode of the Great Depression* (1971).

The New Deal

The best studies include: Arthur M. Schlesinger, Jr., *The Age of Roosevelt*, 3 vols. (1957–1960); William E. Leuchtenburg, *Franklin D. Roosevelt and the New Deal* (1963), a brilliantly written, balanced account; James MacGregor Burns, *Roosevelt: The Lion and the Fox* (1956); Frank Friedel, *Franklin D. Roosevelt*, 4 vols. (1952–1973); Harvard Sitkoff, ed., *Fifty Years Later: The New Deal Evaluated* (1984).

Biographies of other leading figures include: T. Harry Williams, *Huey Long* (1969); Alan Brinkley, *Voices of Protest* (1982); Michael E. Parrish, *Felix Frankfurter* (1982); Jordan A. Schwarz, *The Speculator* (1981); Joseph P. Lash, *Eleanor and Franklin* (1971), a lively account; Charles J. Tull, *Father Coughlin and the New Deal* (1965); Frederick H. and Edward L. Schapsmeier, *Henry A. Wallace of Iowa: The Agrarian Years, 1910–1940* (1968).

Among the best studies covering different aspects of the New Deal are John M. Allswang, *The New Deal and American Politics: A Study in Political Change* (1978); Richard Polenberg, *Reorganizing Roosevelt's Government: The Controversy Over Executive Reorganization, 1936–1939* (1966); Edgar E. Robinson, *The Roosevelt Leadership* (1955), a valuable critique; Michael E. Parrish, *Securities Regulation and the New Deal* (1970); Ellis W. Hawley, *The New Deal and the Problem of Monopoly: A Study in Economic Ambivalence* (1966), is the best account of the NRA; Michael J. McDonald and John Muldowny, *TVA and the Dispossessed: The Resettlement of Population in the Norris Dam Area* (1982), is a valuable critique; Francis Fox Piven and Richard A. Cloward, *Regulating the Poor: The Functions of Public Welfare* (1972); John A. Salmond, *The Civilian Conservation Corps, 1933–1942: A New Deal Case Study* (1967); Theron and Robert W. Frase, *Launching Social Security: A Capture-and-Record Account* (1971); Jane DeHart Matthews, *The Federal Theatre, 1935–1939: Plays, Relief, and Politics* (1967); Irving Bernstein, *Turbulent Years* (1970), discusses organized labor; James Patterson, *The New Deal and the States* (1969); Donald Worster, *Dust Bowl: The Southern Plains in the 1930's* (1979) Joseph Huthmacher, *Senator Robert F. Wagner and the Rise of Urban Liberalism* (1968); and Robert A. Caro, *The Years of Lyndon Johnson*, vol. I (1982), give excellent accounts of internal politics within the Roosevelt administration; Van L. Perkins, *Crisis in Agriculture: The Agricultural Adjustment Act and the New Deal* (1969); David E. Conrad, *Forgotten Farmers: The Story of Sharecroppers in the New Deal* (1965); Otis L. Graham, Jr., *Toward a Planned Society: From Roosevelt to Nixon* (1976).

The New Deal and the American people have attracted increasing scholarly attention. Some of the best studies include: Lois Scharf, *To Work and to Wed: Female Employment, Feminism, and the Great Depression* (1980); Graham D. Taylor, *The New Deal and American Indian Tribalism* (1980); Harvard Sitkoff, *A New Deal for Blacks* (1978); John B. Kirby, *Black Americans in the Roosevelt Era: Liberalism and Race* (1982); Richard H. Pells, *Radical Visions and American Dreams: Culture and Social Thought in the Depression Years* (1973); Studs Terkel, *Hard Times* (1970); Ann Banks, *First-Person America* (1980); Sidney Baldwin, *Poverty and Politics: The Rise and Decline of the Farm Security Administration* (1968), an excellent study.

Foreign Policy

Surveys of twentieth century foreign policy with full coverage of the 1920–1945 period include: Robert D. Schulzinger, *American Diplomacy in the Twentieth Century* (1984); Richard W. Leopold, *The Growth of American Foreign Policy* (1962); Thomas G. Paterson, J. Larry Clifford, and Kenneth J. Hagan, *American Foreign Policy: A History* (1983); Foster Rhea Dulles, *America's Rise to World Power: 1898–1954* (1955); George F. Kennan, *American Diplomacy: 1900–1950* (1951).

The foreign policy issues of the 1920s are covered in L. Ethan Ellis, *Republican Foreign Policy: 1921–1933* (1968); Selig Adler, *The Uncertain Giant* (1965); Merlo J. Pusey, *Charles Evans Hughes*, 2 vols. (1951); L. Ethan Ellis, *Frank B. Kellogg and American Foreign Relations: 1925-1929* (1961); Elting Morison, *Turmoil and Tradition: A Study of the Life and Times of Henry L. Stimson* (1960); Thomas H. Buckley, *The United States and the Washington Conference* (1970); Peter G. Filene, *Americans and the Soviet Experiment: 1917–1933* (1967); Carl P. Parrini, *Heir to Empire: United States Economic Diplomacy, 1916–1923* (1969); Joan Hoff Wilson, *American Business and Foreign Policy* (1971); Robert H. Ferrell, *American Diplomacy in the Great Depression* (1957).

The diplomacy of the 1930s is treated in Edgar B. Nixon, ed., *Franklin D. Roosevelt and Foreign Affairs*, 3 vols. (1969); Robert Dallek, *Franklin D. Roosevelt and American Foreign Policy: 1932–1945* (1979); Armin Rappaport, *Henry L. Stimson and Japan: 1931–33* (1963); Lloyd C. Gardner, *Economic Aspects of New Deal Diplomacy* (1964); Richard N. Kottman, *Reciprocity and the North Atlantic*

Triangle: 1932–1938 (1968); Bryce Wood, *The Making of the Good Neighbor Policy* (1961); Arnold A. Offner, *American Appeasement: United States Foreign Policy and Germany, 1933–1938* (1969); Selig Adler, *The Isolationist Impulse* (1959); John K. Nelson, *The Peace Prophets: American Pacifist Thought, 1919–1941* (1967).

The background to American participation in World War II is extensively covered. The most important works include William L. Langer and S. E. Gleason, *The Challenge to Isolation* (1952) and *The Undeclared War* (1953); J. E. Wiltz, *From Isolation to War: 1931–1941* (1968); Robert A. Divine, *The Illusion of Neutrality* (1962), and *The Reluctant Belligerent* (1965); James MacGregor Burns, *Roosevelt: The Soldier of Freedom* (1970), a profound work; Warren F. Kimball, *The Most Unsordid Act: Lend-Lease, 1939–1941* (1969).

Among the works treating the Pearl Harbor controversy are: John Toland, *The Rising Sun: The Decline and Fall of the Japanese Empire, 1936–1945* (1970), an excellent work, and *Infamy* (1982), a prejudiced one. Herbert Feis, *The Road to Pearl Harbor* (1970); and Samuel Eliot Morison, *The Rising Sun in the Pacific* (1948), take the pro-Roosevelt side. Charles A. Beard, *President Roosevelt and the Coming of the War, 1941* (1948); and Charles C. Tansill, *Back Door to War: The Roosevelt Foreign Policy, 1933–1941* (1952), take the anti-Roosevelt side. The best and most balanced accounts of Pearl Harbor may be found in George M. Waller, ed., *Pearl Harbor: Roosevelt and the Coming of the War* (1976); and Gordon W. Prange, *At Dawn We Slept: The Untold Story of Pearl Harbor* (1981).

World War II

The military fighting of the war is covered in Martha Hoyle, *A World in Flames: The History of World War II* (1970); A. Russell Buchanan, *The United States and World War II*, 2 vols. (1964); Charles B. MacDonald, *The Mighty Endeavor: American Armed Forces in the European Theater in World War II* (1969); Samuel Eliot Morison, *History of United States Naval Operations in World War II*, 15 vols. (1947–1962); Kent Roberts Greenfield, *American Strategy in World War II: A Reconsideration* (1963); William Manchester, *Goodbye, Darkness* (1980), and *American Caesar: Douglas MacArthur, 1880–1964* (1973), both brilliantly written and provocative; Stephen E. Ambrose, *The Supreme Commander: The War Years of General Dwight D. Eisenhower* (1970).

The diplomacy of the war is covered in Robert A. Divine, *Roosevelt and World War II* (1969); Gaddis Smith, *American Diplomacy During the Second World War* (1965); Christopher Thorne, *Allies of a Kind: The United States, Britain, and the War Against Japan* (1978); Paul A. Varg, *The Closing of the Door: Sino-American Relations, 1936-1946* (1973); Barbara Tuchman, *Stilwell and the American Experience in China* (1975); Mark A. Stoler, *The Politics of the Second Front: American Military Planning and Diplomacy in Coalition Warfare, 1941-1943* (1977); Herbert Feis, *Churchill, Roosevelt, Stalin* (1967), *Between War and Peace:*

The Potsdam Conference (1960), and *The Atomic Bomb and the End of World War II* (1966); John L. Gaddis, *The United States and the Origins of the Cold War: 1941–1947* (1972); Gabriel Kolko, *The Politics of War: The World and United States Foreign Policy: 1943–1945* (1968), a highly provocative work. The home front during the Second World War is covered in John M. Blum, *V Was for Victory: Politics and American Culture During World War II* (1976); Geoffrey Perrett, *Days of Sadness, Years of Triumph: The American People, 1939–1945* (1973); Alan S. Milward, *War, Economy and Society: 1939–1945* (1977); Richard Polenberg, *War and Society: The United States, 1941–1945* (1972); Richard R. Lingeman, *Don't You Know There's A War On? The American Home Front, 1941–1945* (1970); Roger Daniels, *Concentration Camps U.S.A.: Japanese Americans and World War II* (1971); Allan M. Winkler, *The Politics of Propaganda: The Office of War Information, 1942–1945* (1978).

Miscellaneous Works

The following works treat various aspects of American history between 1920 and 1945 and did not fall into the preceding categories: W. Elliot Brownlee, *Dynamics of Ascent: A History of the American Economy* (1979); Morrell Head, *The Social Responsibilities of Business: Company and Community, 1900–1960* (1970); Alfred D. Chandler, *The Visible Hand: The Managerial Revolution in American Business* (1977); Daniel T. Rodgers, *The Work Ethic in Industrial America: 1850–1920* (1978); Irving Bernstein, *The Lean Years: A History of the American Worker, 1920–1933* (1960); Daniel J. Boorstin, *The Americans: The Democratic Experience* (1973), a fascinating study; Richard Weiss, *The American Myth of Success: From Horatio Alger to Norman Vincent Peale* (1969); Charles N. Glaab and Theodore Brown, *A History of Urban America* (1976); Zane L. Miller, *The Urbanization of Modern America* (1973); Fred M. and Grace Hechinger, *Growing Up in America* (1975); Laurence R. Vessey, *The Emergence of the American University* (1965); Sydney E. Ahlstrom, *A Religious History of the American People* (1972); Nathan L. Huggins, *Harlem Renaissance* (1972); Dan Carter, *Scottsboro: A Tragedy of the American South* (1969); Gerald Fetner, *Ordered Liberty: Legal Reform in the Twentieth Century* (1983); Mary P. Ryan, *Womanhood in America: From Colonial Times to the Present* (1979); Joseph H. Udelson, *The Great Television Race: A History of the Television Industry, 1925–1941* (1982); David Halberstam, *The Powers That Be* (1976); Bruce Allen Murphy, *The Brandeis/Frankfurter Connection: The Secret Political Activities of Two Supreme Court Justices* (1982); Trevor I. Williams, *A Short History of Twentieth Century Technology* (1982); Charles W. Johnson and Charles O. Jackson, *City Behind a Fence: Oak Ridge, Tennessee, 1942–1946* (1981); Zane L. Miller, *Suburb: Neighborhood and Community in Forest Park, Ohio, 1935–1976* (1981); William H. Harris, *The Harder We Run: Black Workers Since the Civil War* (1982); Foster Rhea Dulles and Melvyn Dubofsky, *Labor in America* (1984).

Appendix

Presidential Election Results

Year	Candidate	Popular Vote	Electoral Vote
1920	Warren Harding (Rep.)	16,143,407	404
	James Cox (Dem.)	9,130,328	127
	Eugene V. Debs (Soc.)	919,799	
1924	Calvin Coolidge (Rep.)	15,718,211	382
	John W. Davis (Dem.)	8,385,283	136
	Robert La Follette (Prog.)	4,831,289	13
1928	Herbert Hoover (Rep.)	21,391,993	444
	Alfred E. Smith (Dem.)	15,016,169	87
1932	Franklin D. Roosevelt (Dem.)	22,809,638	472
	Herbert Hoover (Rep.)	15,758,901	59
	Norman Thomas (Soc.)	881,951	
1936	Franklin D. Roosevelt (Dem.)	27,752,869	523
	Alfred Landon (Rep.)	16,674,665	8
	William Lemke (Union)	882,479	
1940	Franklin D. Roosevelt (Dem.)	27,307,819	449
	Wendell Wilkie (Rep.)	22,304,755	82
1944	Franklin D. Roosevelt (Dem.)	25,606,585	432
	Thomas E. Dewey (Rep.)	22,014,745	99

Party Control in Congress

Year	Party	House of Representatives	Senate
1921–22	Rep.	301	59
	Dem.	131	37
1923–24	Rep.	225	51
	Dem.	205	43
1925–26	Rep.	247	56
	Dem.	183	39
1927–28	Rep.	237	49
	Dem.	195	46
1929–30	Rep.	267	56
	Dem.	167	39
1931–32	Dem.	220	47
	Rep.	214	48
1933–34	Dem.	310	60
	Rep.	117	35
1935–36	Dem.	319	69
	Rep.	103	25
1937–38	Dem.	331	76
	Rep.	89	16
1939–40	Dem.	261	69
	Rep.	164	23
1941–42	Dem.	268	66
	Rep.	162	28
1943–44	Dem.	218	58
	Rep.	208	37
1945–46	Dem.	243	57
	Rep.	190	38

During some of these years, third parties held a small number of seats.

Index

A Farewell to Arms, 47
Absalom! Absalom!, 112
Abt, John, 84, 120
Acheson, Dean, 120
Addams, Jane, 103
Adkins vs. *Children's Hospital,* 14
Africa, 112, 144, 150–51
Agrarians, 112
Agricultural Marketing Act, 1929, 64–65
Agriculture
  general trends, 1, 10, 32, 55, 57,
    110–11, 165, 182
  and Great Depression, 61–62, 64–65
  New Deal and, 75–77, 79, 82–86, 91,
    93, 99–106
Agricultural Adjustment Acts (AAA), 1933,
  1936, 75–76, 82–86, 100–101
Air conditioning, 123
Air power, 144, 149–54, 161–62, 184–85
Alamagordo, New Mexico, 185
A.L.A. Schechter vs. *U.S.,* 99
Alaska, 6
Aleutian Islands, 150
Allen, Gracie, 116
Allied Reparations Commission, 24
Allies
  in World War I, 2, 23–25, 29
  in World War II, 143–44, 150–59, 162
American Civil Liberties Union (ACLU),
  45

American Federation of Labor (AFL), 22,
  96–98, 171
American Liberty League, 88
American Metal Co., 6
American people
  social trends, 31–34, 51, 54–56,
    58–62, 108–11, 164–66, 172–82
  cultural trends, 34–50, 111–22
American Telephone & Telegraph Co.
  (AT&T), 13
Amherst College, 8
Amite, La., 42
"Amos 'n Andy," 116
Anacostia Flats, Md., 70
An American Dilemma, 176
An American Tragedy, 48
Anderson, Maxwell, 49
Andrews Sisters, 117
Anti-Evolution Crusade, 44–45
Anti-Inflation Act, 1943, 182
Anti-Saloon League, 42
Antwerp, Belgium, 154
Arabian American Oil Co. (ARAMCO), 23
Argentia, Newfoundland, 136
Arkansas, 45, 110
Armstrong, Louis, 49–50
Army. *See also* World War II
  in 1930s, 70–71, 135, 143–44
  in World War II, 149–62, 166–68,
    176–79

Arnhem, Belgium, 154
Arnold, Hap, 153
Arnold, Thurman, 84
Arrowsmith, 47
Art, 93
Artillery, 183–84
Asia, 17–22, 29, 38, 125–26, 136–55, 159, 160–63
Astaire, Fred, 115
Atlanta, 33
Atlantic Charter, 136, 156, 174
Atlantic Coast, 150
Atomic bomb, 144, 155, 160–62, 184–85
Augusta, 136
Austin, Gene, 50, 117
Australia, 143, 151
Austria, 66
Automobiles
    production of, 12–13, 165, 169, 170
    social influence of, 33–34, 175

B-29 bomber, 155, 184
Babbitt, 47
"Baby Boom," 109
Bailey vs. *Drexel Furniture Co.*, 14
Baltic Sea, 133
Bankhead, John, 75
Bankhead-Jones Farm Tenancy Act, 1937, 75
Banks, 57, 67, 75–76
Barker, Arizona Clark "Ma," 119
Barrow, Clyde, 119
Baruch, Bernard M., 169
Barzun, Jacques, 122
Baseball, 117
Bataan, 149
Batista, Fulgencio, 127
Battles, 149–55
Bazooka, 184
Beard, Charles A., 146
Belgium, 21, 154
Benét, Stephen Vincent, 113
Bergman, Ingrid, 115
Berlin, Germany, 154, 162
Berlin, Irving, 50
Bernays, Edward, 12
Bible, 42–45
Bilbo, Theodore G., 176
Birmingham, Ala., 7
Birthrate, 32, 109
Black, Hugo L., 78, 100
"Black Monday," 99–100

Blacks. *See also* Race
    discrimination against, 1, 7, 41–42, 76, 85, 104–106, 111, 164–65, 174–76
Blackstone Hotel, 3
"Black Tuesday," 57
Blood transfusions, 184
Blooming Grove, Ohio, 4
Bogart, Humphrey, 115
Bohr, Niehls, 184
Bombing. *See also* World War II
    138, 141–44, 149–55, 160–62, 183–85
Bootlegging, 43–44, 119
Borah, William E., 103
Borneo, 149
Boston, 9
"Boston Blackie," 116
Boston police strike, 9
Boulder Dam Project Act, 1928, 15
Briand, Aristide, 26
Briggs, Ralph T., 148
Brotherhood of Pullman Porters, 175
Brown, Prentiss M., 181–82
Brussels, Belgium, 154
Bryan, William Jennings, 18, 44–45, 137
Buck, Pearl S., 117, 138
Budget, Bureau of, 7
Buenos Aires, Argentina, 128
Bulge, Battle of the, 154
Burma, 149
Burner, David, 53
Burns, George, 116
Burns, James MacGregor, 102, 146, 158
Burns, John A., 148
Bush, Vannevar, 183
Butler, Rhett, 113, 115
Byrnes, James F., 159, 170

Cabell, James Branch, 49
Cabinet officers, 5, 6–9, 19–30, 75, 80, 83–84, 94, 127, 134, 137–41, 146–48, 157
California, 22, 41, 97, 108, 110, 176–79
Calles, Elias, 28
Capone, Alphonse "Scarface Al," 44
Carnegie, Andrew, 13
Caroline Islands, 18, 150
Casablanca, 115
Cather, Willa, 113
Caucausus Mountains, 150
Central America, 26–28, 127–28
Chamoro, Emiliano, 27
Charles II, 117
"Charlie Chan," 116

Cheever, John, 93
Chevrolet, 33
Chiang Kai-shek, 137, 139, 147, 163
Chicago, 3, 43, 44, 49, 58, 83, 111, 184
Child Labor, 14, 83, 100–101
China, 18, 20–21, 137–42, 146–47, 163
Churchill, Winston, 135–36, 143, 155–59, 162
Chrysler Corp., 13, 98
Chuikov, Vassily, 151
Civilian Conservation Corps (CCC), 1933, 79, 86
Civil Liberties, 7, 36, 39–43, 85, 104–106, 174–79
Civil Works Administration (CWA), 1933, 80–81, 86
Clayton Act, 1914, 14
Clements, Robert, 90
Clowen, Richard, 103
Coal Industry, 14, 55
Cohan, George M., 8
Collective Bargaining, 13–14, 78, 96–98, 171–72. See also Labor Unions
Collier's, 116
Colorado River, 15, 67
Commager, Henry Steele, 7
Comic strips, 116–17
Commodity Credit Corporation, 1933, 76, 86
Compton, Arthur H., 184
Computers, 123–24
Congress, 5–7, 10–11, 15–16, 19, 22–23, 38, 64–67, 72, 74, 78–79, 91, 94, 97, 99–101, 131–35, 160, 168, 172, 176
Congress of Industrial Organizations (CIO), 98, 171
Conkin, Paul, 103
Connelly, Marc, 113
Conventions, nominating
    Democratic, 2, 15–16, 53, 70–72, 98, 134, 159
    Republican, 2–4, 16, 52, 98, 134, 159
Convoys, 152
Coolidge, Calvin, 63
    background, 8–11
    nomination of, 4, 15–16
    domestic policy, 8–14
    foreign policy, 22, 25, 27, 29
    mentioned, 52, 56, 63
Cooper, Gary, 115
Coronet, 116
Corregidor, 149
Correll, Charles, 116

Coughlin, Rev. Charles, 88–90, 175
Coupons, ration, 180–82
"Court packing," 100
Cox, James M., 3
Crawford, Joan, 115
Crime, 43–44, 119–20
Crimea, USSR, 150, 158
Crosby, Bing, 117
Cryptology, 20
Culberson, Charles, 41
Cultural trends, 31–51, 108–25
Cyclotron, 184

D-Day, 153–54
DDT, 183
Daladier, Edouard, 130
Darrow, Clarence, 45, 82
Darwin, Charles, 44–45
Daugherty, Harry M., 4–7
Davis, Bette, 114
Davis, John W., 16
Davis, Stuart, 93
Dawes, Charles G., 24–25
Dawes Plan, 24–25
Death Comes for the Archbishop, 49
Death in the Afternoon, 112
Debs, Eugene V., 7
Democratic Party, 1–4, 15–16, 53, 70–72, 90, 98–99, 134, 159. See also Conventions, Nominating; Politics
Denmark, 133
Desire Under the Elms, 49
Des Moines, Iowa, 97
"Destroyer Deal," 133–34
Detroit, 33, 59, 88, 111, 175–76
Dewey, John, 46, 122
Dewey, Thomas E., 119, 134, 159–60
DeWitt, John L., 177
Diaz, Adolfo, 27
Dillinger, John, 119
Dimaggio, Joe, 117
Diplomacy, 17–31, 125–43, 144–48, 154–58
Disarmament, 19–21
Disease, 2, 153, 184
Dnieper River, 154
Doheny, Edward L., 6
"Dollar Diplomacy," 23
Dominican Republic, 128
Dorsey, Jimmy, 117
Dorsey, Tommy, 117
Dos Passos, John, 39, 48, 113

Douglas Aircraft Co., 183
Douglas, William O., 100
Dreiser, Theodore, 48
Dresden, Germany, 162
Dutch East Indies, 150

Economic sanctions, 129, 137–39
Economy, 1, 7–14, 51, 54–69, 74–85,
  90–98, 101–107, 168–74, 179–82. *See
  also* Industry; Labor; Great Depression;
  Employment
Economy Act, 1933, 74
Eddy, Nelson, 115
Eden, Anthony, 157
Education, 44–46, 121–22
Egypt, 151
Einstein, Albert, 44, 184
Eisenhower, Dwight D., 151, 153–56,
  162, 167
El Alamein, Battle of, 151
Elbe River, 162
Eliot, T. S., 49
Ellender, Allen J., 176
Ellington, Duke, 117
Ellis, Ethan, 29
Elmer Gantry, 47
Embargo, 129, 131–32, 137
Emergency Banking Act, 1933, 74, 86
Emergency Price Control Act, 1942, 182
Emergency Relief Appropriation Act,
  1935, 92
Employment
  trends, 2, 11–14, 55–59, 63–67, 69–70,
    78–81, 85, 91–94, 165–66
  government policies toward, 7, 91–94,
    96–98, 104, 170–75
England, *see* Great Britain
Estonia, 157
Ethiopia, 128–29
Europe, U.S. relations with, 18–21,
  23–26, 29–30, 66, 126, 129–36, 144,
  155–59, 162–63
Executive Order No. 9066, 177

Fair Employment Practices Commission
  (FEPC), 175–76
Fair Labor Standards Act, 1938, 101
Fall, Albert B., 6
Farley, James A., 71
Farmers, *see* Agriculture
Farm Security Administration, 101
Farrell, James T., 113
Faulkner, William, 112

Federal Art Project, 93
Federal Bureau of Investigation (FBI), 119
Federal Emergency Relief Administration
  (FERA), 1933, 79
Federal Farm Board, 65
Federal Highway Act, 34
Federal Housing Authority (FHA), 1933,
  81, 86
Federal Reserve Board, 60, 63, 67, 74, 81
Federal Theater, 93
Feis, Herbert, 145, 158
Feller, Bob, 117
Feminists, 36
Fermi, Enrico, 184
Ferrell, Robert W., 29
Fields, W. C., 115
Firebombing, 162
Fisher, Dorothy Canfield, 36
Fitzgerald, F. Scott, 47–48, 112
Five Power Naval Treaty, 1921, 20
Flappers, 37–38, 42
Flood control, 77
Floyd, Charles "Pretty Boy," 119
Flushing Meadows, N.Y., 124
Food Administration, 53
Food and Drug Administration, 103
Forbes, Charles R., 6
Ford, Henry, 12, 33
Fordney-McCumber Tariff, 1922, 10
Foreign policy, 17–31, 125–43, 144–48,
  154–58. *See also* Diplomacy
Forever Amber, 117
Formosa, 141, 147
Fortas, Abraham, 120
Fort Dix, N.J., 167
Fort Hood, Tex., 167
Fortune, 131
Fort Worth, Tex., 44
Forty-Second Parallel, The, 113
For Whom the Bell Tolls, 112
Four Power Treaty, 1922, 21
France, 19–21, 23–24, 26, 130, 133, 138,
  153–54, 158, 170
Franco, Francisco, 129
Franco-Prussian War, 24
Frankfurter, Felix, 39
Frank, Jerome, 84, 120
Freidel, Frank, 102
Fringe benefits, 13, 172
Frost, Robert, 49
Frozen food, 123
Fuchs, Klaus, 185
Fundamentalism, 31, 38–45

Gable, Clark, 115
Galbraith, John Kenneth, 63
"Gangbusters," 116
Garbo, Greta, 115
Garner, John Nance, 71–72
Gehrig, Henry "Lou," 117
General Motors, 13, 98
Germany, 23–25, 66, 125, 128–30,
    132–36, 143–44, 150–59, 161–62,
    183–84
Gershwin, George, 50
GI, 167
Gilbert Islands, 153
Gilded Age, 10
Gilman, Charlotte Perkins, 36
Glasgow, Ellen, 113
Glass-Steagall Act, 1932, 67
Gold Reserve Act, 1934, 81
Gold Standard, 66, 126
Gone With the Wind, 113, 115
Good Earth, The, 117
Goodman, Benny, 117
Good Neighbor Policy, 127–28
Gosden, Freeman, 116
Government Reorganization Act, 1939, 86
Graebner, Norman A., 145
Grand Design, The, 113
Grapes of Wrath, The, 113
Great Depression, 56–63, 111. See also
    New Deal
Great Gatsby, The, 48
Green Hills of Africa, The, 112
"Green Hornet, The," 116
Groton Academy, 72
Groves, Leslie R., 184
Grumman Aircraft Corp., 172
Guadalcanal, Battle of, 151
Guam, 149

Hanihara Letter, 22
Hanihara, Masanao, 22
Harding, Warren G., 63
    background, 4–5
    election of, 2–4
    domestic policy, 5–7, 9–11, 14
    foreign policy, 19–21, 23–24, 26–27, 29
    scandals under, 5–7
    assessment of, 7–8
Harlem, N.Y., 49, 111, 176
Harlow, Jean, 115
Harriman, Averill, 158
Harris, Sir Arthur H., 153
Harvard University, 72

Hawaii, 141, 144, 148
Hawley-Smoot Tariff, 1930, 65
Hawthorne, Nathaniel, 47
Hauptmann, Bruno Richard, 119–20
Havana, Cuba, 127
Hays, John, 18
Hays, Will H., 3–4
Hearst, William Randolph, 116, 131
Hellman, Lillian, 113
Hemingway, Ernest, 47, 112
Herrin, Ill., 14
Highways, 33–34
Hiroshima, Japan, 155, 160–61
Hiss, Alger, 84, 120
Historians, interpretations of, 3–5, 7, 9,
    20, 63, 65, 85, 100, 102–107, 144–49,
    158
Historic Records Office, 93
Hitler, Adolf, 89, 112, 125, 128–30,
    132–36, 143
Holland, 133
Hollandia, New Guinea, 153
Hollywood, Calif., 114–15
Home Owners Loan Corporation (HOLC),
    1933, 86
Hong Kong, 149
Hoover, Herbert, 63, 137
    background, 53
    elections, 53, 70–72
    domestic policy, 64–68
    foreign policy, 24–25, 28
Hoover, J. Edgar, 119, 148
Hopewell, N.J., 120
Hopkins, Harry L., 79, 80–81, 92, 158
Hornbeck, Dr. Stanley, 138, 147
House Ways and Means Committee, 10
Houston, 33
Hughes, Charles Evans, 17, 19–22,
    24–28
Hughes-Obregon Agreement, 1923, 28
Hull, Cordell, 127–28, 138–42, 145–48,
    157
Hull House, 103
Hull Ultimatum, 141, 147
Hydroelectric power, 15, 76–77

Iceland, 135–36
Ickes, Harold L., 80
Idaho, 62
Illinois, 3, 14, 43, 44, 49, 58, 83, 111,
    184
I'll Take My Stand, 112
Immigration, 22, 38–39

Immigration and Naturalization Bureau, 38
Imperial Valley, 110
Income tax, 11, 168–69
Indian Reorganization Act, 1934, 81–82
Indians, 81–82
Indonesia, 162, 180
Industrial engineering, 12
Industry
  in 1920s, 11–14
  in 1930s, 54–58, 63, 67, 78, 82–83,
    96–98
  in World War II, 165, 169–74
Indochina, 139, 140, 141, 162
Inflation, 182
Insull, Samuel, 13
Intellectuals, 45–46, 120–21
Inter-American Conferences, 1933, 1936,
  127–28
International Health Organization, 26
International Labor Organization, 26
"Invasion From Mars," 116
Iowa, 62, 97
Isolationism, 17, 25, 29, 125, 130–33
Israel, 162
Issei, 177
Italians, 39, 42
Italy, 19–21, 89, 128–29, 153
It Can't Happen Here, 112
Iwo Jima, Battle of, 155, 160

Jack Armstrong: All-American Boy, 117
James, Harry, 117
James, Jesse, 119
Japan
  U.S. relations with, 17–22, 125–26,
    136–42, 143–48
  in World War II, 149–63, 165, 176–77,
    183–84
Japanese–American Commercial Treaty,
  1911, 138
Jazz, 49–50
Jefferson, Thomas, 8
Jeffers, Robinson, 49
Jews, 39, 41–42
Jitterbug, 117
"Joe Palooka," 117
Johnson, Hugh S., 78
J. P. Morgan & Co., 57
Justice Department, 6, 70

Kaltenborn, H. V., 116
Kearny, sinking of, 136

Kellogg-Briand Pact, 1928, 25–26
Kellogg, Frank B., 25–26
Kelly, George "Machine Gun," 119
Kentucky, 62, 110
Keynesian economics, 88, 104
Kidnapping, Lindbergh, 119–20
Knox, Frank L., 133
Knoxville, 77
Konoye, Fumimaro, 140
Kreditanstalt, 66
Ku Klux Klan, 32, 39–42
Kursk, Battle of, 151–52

Labor unions, 13–14, 96–98, 171–74, 175
Labor violence, 14, 91, 96–97
La Follette, Robert M., 3, 16
Laissez-Faire Economics, 1, 9–11, 63, 64,
  99
Landon, Alfred "Alf," 98–99
Lansing, Robert, 18
Latin America, 26–30, 127–28
Latvia, 157
Lawrence, Ernest, 184
League of Nations, 2–3, 25–26, 128–29,
  130, 137
Leigh, Vivien, 115
Lend-Lease, 135
Lenroot, Irvine L., 4
Lewis, John L, 14, 97–98, 171–72
Lewis, Sinclair, 47, 112
Leuchtenburg, William E., 7, 82, 85
Leyte Gulf, Battle of, 154–55
Lichtman, Allan J., 53
Life, 116
Light in August, 112
"L'il Abner," 117
Lippmann, Walter, 177
Literary Digest, 98
Lithuania, 157
Live Poultry Code, 100
Lodge, Henry Cabot, 3–4
Long, Huey P., 42, 72, 89–90
Longshoremen, 97
Look, 116
Look Homeward, Angel, 112
Los Angeles, 33
"Lost Generation," 47, 111
Louisiana, 42, 89–90
Louisiana Railroad Commission, 89
Louis, Joe, 118
Ludlow Amendment, 132
Ludlow, Louis, 132
Lynd, Robert and Helen, 33

MacArthur, Douglas, 70–71, 149, 153–55, 156
MacDonald, Jeanette, 115
MacLeish, Archibald, 113
Mafia, 44, 119
Maine, 99
Main Street, 47
Malayasia, 180
Malay Peninsula, 149
Manhattan Project, 154
Mao Tse-tung, 163
Mariana Islands, 154
Marion, Ohio, 4–5
Marion *Star,* 5
Marriage and divorce, 32, 37–38, 109
Marshall, George C., 135, 156, 160
Marshall Plan, 29
Massachusetts, 4, 8–9
Massachusetts General Court, 9
Matsuosa, Yosuke, 139
McAdoo, William G., 3, 71
McCumber, Porter J., 10
Melville, Herman, 47
Memphis, 49
Mencken, H. L., 8
Mendieta, Carlos, 127
Messerschmidt, 183
Mexico, 28, 127
Miami, 33
Middle East, 23, 162
Midway, Battle of, 150
Millay, Edna St. Vincent, 39, 113
Miller, Thomas W., 6
Minimum Wage, 14, 78, 100–101
Minnesota, 62
Mississippi, 61, 102
Mitchell, Margaret, 113
Mitsubishi, 183
Model T, 33
Moley, Raymond, 78, 126
Molotov, Vyacheslav, 157
Monetarist economic theory, 63, 103
Monroe Doctrine, Roosevelt Corollary to, 28
Montgomery, Bernard Law, 151, 154, 156
"Moral embargo," 129, 137–38
Morgenthau, Henry, 81
Morison, Samuel Eliot, 7, 29, 145
Morrow, Dwight, 28, 127
Mortgage foreclosures, 58, 61–62, 81
Mortimer, Mort, 5
Morton, "Jellyroll," 49
Moscow, 139, 157
Motion pictures, 113–16

Mountbatten, Louis, 156
Munich Conference, 1938, 130
Murray, Robert K., 7
Murrow, Edward R., 116
Muscle Shoals, Ala., 15
Music, 49–50, 117
Mussolini, Benito, 89, 128–29
"Mutt and Jeff," 117
Myrdal, Gunnar, 121, 176

Nagasaki, Japan, 155, 160
Nagumo, Chuichi, 141, 144, 150
Nanking, China, 138
National Association for the Advancement of Colored People (NAACP), 111, 175
National Defense Council, 170
National Defense Research Committee, 133, 183
National Guard, 8, 41
National Industrial Recovery Act (NRA), 1933, 78–80, 82–83, 86
National Labor Relations (Wagner) Act, 1935, 86, 97
National Origins Act, 1924, 38–39
National Socialist Workers' Democratic (Nazi) Party, 128
National Youth Administration (NYA), 1935, 93
Native Son, 113
Nativism, 22, 38–42
NATO, 29
Naval rivalry, 18–21
Nebraska, 15, 62
Nelson, Donald M., 170
Nelson, Edward "Baby Face," 119
Nelson, Ozzie and Harriet, 116
Netherlands, 21
Neutrality Acts, 1935, 1936, 1937, 132
Nevada, 132
New Deal
  programs, 74–84, 86, 90–101
  impact of, 76–80, 92–98
  assessment of, 84–86, 102–107
New Guinea, 150, 153
New Hampshire, 49
New Mexico, 184
New Orleans, 43, 49, 89
Newsweek, 116
New York, 3, 42, 53, 57, 58, 59, 70, 72, 73, 75, 92, 99, 111, 119, 120, 124, 176
New York Stock Exchange, 55–57, 63
New York Times, 117
Nicaragua, 27–28

Niebuhr, Reinhold, 121
Nimitz, Chester A., 143, 150, 153
Nine Power Treaty, 1922, 21
Nineteenth Amendment, 36
Nisei, 176–78
Norris, George W., 15, 103
Norris, J. Frank, 44, 175
North Africa, 150
North Carolina, 53
Northhampton, Mass., 8
Norway, 133
Number One, 113
Nye Committee, 131
Nye, Gerald P., 131–32

Oak Ridge, Tenn., 184
Obregón, Alvaro, 28
Office of Economic Stabilization, 170
Office of Price Administration and Civilian Supply (OPA), 170, 182
Office of Production Management (OPM), 170
Office of Scientific Research and Development (OSRD), 183
Office of War Mobilization, 170
Of Time and the River, 112
O'Hara, Scarlett, 112, 115
Ohio, 3, 4, 5
"Okies," 113
Okinawa, Battle of, 155, 161
Oklahoma, 41, 62, 108, 110, 113
Oliver, Joe "King," 50
O'Neill, Eugene, 48–49, 113
Open Door Policy, 18, 21, 138, 147
Oppenheimer, J. Robert, 184
Oregon, 41
Organized Crime, 44, 119
Origin of Species, 44
Owens, Jesse, 118
Owsley, Frank, Sr., 112

Pacific Ocean, 21, 141, 143, 144, 150, 153
Pact of Paris, 1928, 25–26
Paducah, Ken., 77
Page, Walter Hines, 38
Palmer, A. Mitchell, 2, 3
Panay, sinking of, 138
Pan-American Conference, 1928, 28
Paradise Valley, 111, 175
Parker, Bonnie, 119
Parker, John M., 42
Paris Peace Conference, 1919, 18
Paris Island, S.C., 167

Patton, George S., 154
Pearl Harbor, 137, 141, 143–49, 176, 179, 183
Peek, George, 84
Pennsylvania, 42, 59
Perkins, Frances, 94
Perkins, Van L., 76
Permanent Court of International Justice (World Court), 25
Pittman, Key, 132
Pivens, Francis Fox, 103
Platt Amendment, 1901, 127
Plutonium, 184
Plymouth, Ver., 8
Poland, 133, 157–58
Political Parties. See Democratic and Republican Party.
Pollock, Jackson, 93
Poll Tax, 176
Popular Front, 129
Population Trends, 32–33, 109–11
Porter, Katharine Anne, 113
Portugal, 21
Prange, Gordon W., 146
Presidential Elections
  1920, 2–4
  1924, 15–16
  1928, 52–53
  1932, 70–72, 90
  1936, 98–99
  1940, 34
  1944, 159–60
Presidents, see individual listings
Prices, 59–61, 182
Productivity, 9–13, 54–64, 78–79, 165, 169–71
Progressive Education, 46, 122
Progressivism, 15, 103, 106
Prohibition, 42–44
Proximity fuse, 183
Public Relations, 12
Public Works Adminstration (PWA), 1933, 80, 86
Public Works Projects, 67, 79–81, 86, 89, 91–93

Quantico, Va., 167
"Quarantine the aggressors" speech, 129
Quonset huts, 167

Race, 1, 41–42, 76, 104–106, 111, 164–65, 174–76. See also Blacks
Radio, 116

Radio Corporation of America (RCA), 56
Randolph, A. Philip, 175
Raskob, John J., 88
Rationing, 179–82
Reader's Digest, 116
Reagan, Ronald W., 11, 102
Red Army, 150–52, 154–55
Relativism, 45–46
Religion, 38–45, 121
Reparations, 23–25, 126, 128
Republican Party, 1, 3–4, 9–11, 16, 17,
  52–53, 66, 70–72, 98–99, 101, 134,
  159. *See also* Conventions, nominating
Resettlement Administration, 86, 101, 106
Resistance fighters, 154
Reuben James, Sinking of, 136
Revenue Acts, 1921, 1924, 1926, 1942, 11,
  168
"Rhapsody in Blue," 50
Rhine River, 155
Rice, Elmer, 49
Roberts, Kenneth, 38
Robe, The, 117
Rockefeller, John D., 13
Rockets, 183
Rogers, Ginger, 115
Rogers, Will, 8
Rommel, Erwin, 150
Roosevelt, Eleanor, 176
Roosevelt, Franklin D.
  background, 72–73
  elections, 3, 70–72, 90, 98–99, 134,
    159–60
  personality, 72–73, 80–81, 84, 102–103
  political ability, 70–72, 74–75, 84,
    103–104
  domestic policy, 74–86, 90–107, 164–85
  foreign policy, 125–48
Roosevelt, Theodore, 3, 18, 22, 28, 63, 73,
  127, 130
Royal Air Force, 153
Rumanian Army, 151
Rural Electrification Administration (REA),
  1935, 93
Russell, Francis, 39
Ruth, George "Babe," 47

Sacco, Nicola, 39
Safford, Lawrence, 148
Saipan, 154
San Diego, 167
Sandburg, Carl, 113
San Francisco, 6, 43, 97

Sanger, Margaret, 36
San Martin, Ramon, 127
Saturday Evening Post, 38, 116
Scaduto, Anthony, 120
Scandals, 5–7
Schlesinger, Arthur M., Jr., 7, 63, 72, 100,
  102
Schwartz, Anna, 103
Science, 122–24, 182–85
Scopes trial, 44–45
Scopes, John T., 44–45
Sears, Roebuck, 170
Securities and Exchange Act (SEC), 1934,
  86
See Here, Private Hargrove, 117
Selassie, Hailie, 128
Selective Service Acts, 1940, 1941, 1942,
  135, 166
Senate, *see* Congress
Senate Finance Committee, 10
Senate Foreign Relations Committee, 132
Shanghai, China, 138
Shantung Province, China, 21
Sharecroppers, 55, 76, 106, 110–11
Share Our Wealth, 90
Sherwood, Robert, 113
Shirer, William L., 116
Shivers, Robert L., 148
Shroeder, Paul W., 146
Sicily, 153
Simmons, William J., 41
Sinclair, Andrew, 7
Sinclair, Harry, 6
Singapore, 149
Sixty-Second Army (USSR), 151
Smith-Connally Act, 1943, 172
Smith, Gerald L. K., 175
Smith, Jesse, 6
"Smoke-Filled Room," 3–4
Social Security, 93–95
Social Security Act, 1935, 94
Social Gospel, 121
Social Trends, *see* American People
Soldiers, 166–68
Solomon Islands, 151
Something About Eve, 49
Southeast Asia, 139, 149–50, 162
South Braintree, Mass., 39
South Carolina, 53
Soviet Union, 137, 147, 151–53, 154,
  156–59, 162–63
Spanish Civil War, 129
"Spanish Flu," 2

Sports, 117
Stalingrad, Battle of, 151
Stalin, Josef, 143, 156–59
Standard Oil Co., 13
Steel, 8, 56, 58, 98, 137, 139
Steinbeck, John, 113
Stephenson, David, 41
Stettinius, Edward R., Jr., 169
Stimson Doctrine, 137–38
Stimson, Henry L., 28–29, 133, 137–38
Stocks, 7, 51, 55–57, 63
Stone Mountain, Ga., 41
Strange Interlude, 49
Studs Lonigan, 113
Suez Canal, 150
Sun Also Rises, The, 112
Supplies and Allocations Board, 170
Supreme Court, 14, 99–100
Sutter, Jacob, 110
"Swing," 117
Synthetics, 123

Taft, Robert A., 134
Tammany Hall, 53, 73
Tansill, Charles C., 146, 158
Tariffs, 10–11, 65
"Tarzan," 117
Taxes
  Reductions in, 11
  Increases in, 168
Taylor, Frederick, 12
Taylor, Robert, 115
Taylor, Telford, 120
Teacher in America, 122
Teamsters Union, 97
Teapot Dome, Wyo., 6
Teheran Conference, 157
Temple, Shirley, 115
Tenant Farmers, 55, 62, 76, 106, 110–11
Tender Is the Night, 112
Tennessee, 44–45, 76–77, 184
Tennessee River, 76–77
Tennessee Valley Authority (TVA), 1933, 76–77
Texas, 41, 44, 53, 110
Textile Industry, 14, 55, 98
Third Parties, 16
This Side of Paradise, 48
Thompson, James C., 147
"Three Little Fishes," 117
Three Soldiers, 48
Tiger Tank, 152
Time, 116

Tinian, 154
Tojo, Hideki, 140
Tokyo, 162
Toland, John, 146
Toledo, Ohio, 58
Townsend, Francis, 90
Traffic Congestion, 34
Treasury Department, 9–11
Truman, Harry S, 111, 155, 159, 160–62
Truth-In-Securities Act, 1933, 86
Tugwell, Rexford G., 78
Tulagi, 150
Tunisia, 151
"Tutti-Frutti," 117
Twenty-First Amendment, 44

Underwood-Simmons Tariff, 1913, 10
Unemployment, 7, 55, 57–62, 79–80, 91, 92–93, 94-95, 104, 171
Union Theological Seminary, 121
United Nations, 158–59
University of California, 184
University of Chicago, 184
University of Tennessee, 44
Uranium (U-238), 184

Vallee, Rudy, 117
Vandenburg, Arthur H., 134
Vanderbilt, Cornelius, 13
Vermont, 8, 99
Veterans Bonus March, 58, 70
Veterans Bureau, 5–6
Vichy France, 139
"Victory Tax," 168
Virginia, 53
Volga River, 150
Volstead Act, 1920, 43
Von Braun, Werner, 183
Von Paulus, Frederick, 151

Wages, 13–14, 54–55, 57, 60, 83, 165–66, 171–72, 182
Wainwright, Jonathan, 149
Wake Island, 149
Wallace, Henry A., 75, 83–84, 134, 159
Wall Street Crash, 56–57
War Industries Board, 169
War Labor Board, 171
War Manpower Commission, 171
Warm Springs, Ga., 160
War Production Board, 179
Warren, Earl, 179
Washington Arms Conference, 19–21

Wasteland, The, 49
Water Power Act, 1920, 15
Web and the Rock, The, 112
Wehrmacht, 167
Welles, Sumner, 27
West, Mae, 115
West-Running Brook, 49
White House, 9, 90, 106
Whiteman, Paul, 50
Wilder, Thornton, 113
Williams, William Appleman, 29
Wilson, Woodrow, 1–4, 8, 27, 63, 127, 169
Windsor, Kathleen, 117
Winnfield, La., 89
Wolfe, Thomas, 48, 112
Women, 35–38, 172–74
Women's Christian Temperance Union, 42
Works Progress Administration (WPA), 1935, 86, 87–88, 92–93, 106
World Court, 25, 130, 131
World Economic Conference, 126
World War I, 6, 17–20, 23–24, 38, 43, 47, 51, 53, 70, 128, 129, 130, 131, 133, 166, 169

World War II, 57, 76, 93, 104, 108, 111, 116, 122, 123
causes, 128–49
diplomacy, 155–59
battles, 149–55
home front, 164–85
legacy, 160–63
World War Foreign Debt Commission, 23
Wyoming, 6

Yalta Conference, 158–59
"Yankee Doodle Dandy," 8
Yardley, Herbert O., 20
Young Manhood of Studs Lonigan, The, 113
Young, Owen D., 24
Young Plan, 24–25

Zero Fighter Plane, 183
Zhukov, Georgi, 155

The Challenging of America: 1920–1945 was copyedited by Harlan Davidson, Jr. Production editor was B. W. Barrett. The cover was designed by Roger Eggers. The text was proofread by Harlan Davidson, Jr., and Muriel Jensen. The book was typeset by PageTypes and printed and bound by Edwards Brothers, Inc.